THE BODY IN H

The Body in Health and Social Care

Julia Twigg

First published 2006 by
PALGRAVE MACMILLAN
Houndmills, Basingstoke, Hampshire RG21 6XS and
175 Fifth Avenue, New York, N.Y. 10010
Companies and representatives throughout the world

PALGRAVE MACMILLAN is the global academic imprint of the Palgrave Macmillan division of St. Martin's Press, LLC and of Palgrave Macmillan Ltd. Macmillan® is a registered trademark in the United States, United Kingdom and other countries. Palgrave is a registered trademark in the European Union and other countries.

ISBN-13: 978–0–333–77619–3 hardback
ISBN-10: 0–333–77619–4 hardback
ISBN-13: 978–0–333–77620–9 paperback
ISBN-10: 0–333–77620–8 paperback

This book is printed on paper suitable for recycling and made from fully managed and sustained forest sources.

A catalogue record for this book is available from the British Library.

A catalog record for this book is available from the Library of Congress.

10   9   8   7   6   5   4   3   2   1
15   14   13   12   11   10   09   08   07   06

Printed in China

Contents

Acknowledgements   vii

1 Introduction: The Body in Health and Social Care   1
   The field of health and social care   1
   New writing on the body   3
   The limitations of cultural analyses   8
   Downplaying the bodily   9
   Conclusion   12

2 Debates About the Body   13
   The sources of the debate   13
   Feminist influences   14
   Foucault and poststructuralism   20
   The body, consumption and identity   22
   Real bodies: Towards a more concrete embodiment   24
   Dimensions of difference   26
   Conclusion   38

3 The Body and Ageing   40
   The neglect of the body in ageing studies   40
   Aged by culture   42
   Ageism and the body   44
   Ageing in consumer culture   46
   Limitations of culturalist approaches   48
   The challenge of the Fourth Age   50
   Conclusion   52

4 Disability and the Body   55
   Revising the social model: Refocussing on the body 56
   Representing disability: Visual culture   58
   Disability, eugenics and the new genetics   61
   Disability and sexuality   64
   Gender and disability   67
   Conclusion   70

5   **The Body in Medicine and Health Care**   71
    The medical construction of the body: The dominate
        paradigm   72
    Dissection and the use of body parts   73
    Organ donation and transplants   78
    The patient's experience of embodiment   83
    Bodywork in health care   85
    Embodied practitioners   89
    The body in alternative medicine   92
    Conclusion   97

6   **Diet, Health and the Body: Obesity and Eating Disorders**   99
    Eating disorders   100
    The rise of obesity   107
    The politics of ingestion   114
    Conclusion   118

7   **Home Care: The Body in Domestic Time and Space**   119
    The absent body of social care   119
    Personal care   122
    Spatio-temporal ordering: The body in domestic time
        and space   124
    Spatio-temporal re-ordering   127
    Conclusion   131

8   **The Bodywork of Care**   133
    Bodywork as an occupational category   133
    The bodywork of care   136
    Carework and women's employment   142
    Gender and bodywork   148
    Conclusion   151

9   **The Body in Public Space: Breastfeeding and Toilets**   153
    Public space   153
    Public toilets   156
    Public breastfeeding   162
    Conclusion   169

10 **Conclusion**   170

References   174

Index   195

Acknowledgements

I would like to thank, for their help and support, friends and colleagues who have kindly read and discussed sections of this book, in particular Andy Alaszewski, Helen Charnley, Jan Pahl, Avner Offer and Azrini Wahidin. I am also grateful for comments from the two anonymous readers of the manuscript. Most of all, however, I would like to thank my partner Martin Peach for the support and help he has given me over many years.

Chapter 1

Introduction: The Body in Health and Social Care

The body is central to both health and social care, but this fact has not always been reflected in the literature that analyses the area. Health and social care are increasingly constituted as a unified field, encompassing policies and interventions across the health and social care boundary. But the analytic traditions used to explore this territory have until recently remained narrow. The cultural turn that has been so marked across the humanities and social sciences has been slow to make an impact in this area. In particular the topic of the body has yet to achieve the prominence that it has elsewhere, with the result that, what is mainstream in sociology and cultural studies has remained marginal in social and public policy. The purpose of this book is to redress this imbalance, and to suggest some of the ways in which the subject of the body, and new cultural analyses within which its analysis is embedded, have much to contribute to the area of health and social care.

The field of health and social care

In recent years, health and social care have increasingly been presented as a unified field. The ways in which its constituent elements are constructed are, however, different, and these differences have consequences for how the body is perceived in each. At the simplest level, the body is central to health care. But its very centrality means that it is sometimes, paradoxically, overlooked – so completely does it occupy the field of vision. Furthermore, it is a particular version of the body that dominates – the body as constituted in medicine: that is, the object body of science, observable, neutral, reductive, stripped of meaning, a collection of functioning systems and cells. This account provides the scientific underpinning of the medical project, the master narrative of the activity; and we will explore its historical emergence in subsequent chapters.

There are, however, other versions of the body current in health care. Nursing, for example, contains elements of a rival account, one that puts greater emphasis on embodiment and subjectivity. This is, however, only weakly articulated within the institution of the hospital, the key site of the

1

medical enterprise, where the discourses of nursing, particularly in its more holistic versions, lack power, and where the dominance of the medical paradigm relegates them to a subordinate status. The bio-medical model of the body is also at odds with what patients feel about their bodies. Part of the experience of entering the health care system as a patient is one in which the body becomes alien from the self, an object of observation and intervention by others. We will explore this more fully in later chapters, and simply note here the disjunction between the patient's own experience of embodiment and the dominant medical paradigm. These tensions are also carried forward into alternative versions of health care for, as we shall see, part of the appeal of alternative medicine lies in its capacity to respond to the experiential feelings of patients and to their own sense of embodiment. Lastly, the significance of the body in medicine is not confined to patients, but extends to the bodies of health care practitioners also, who are themselves embodied subjects. In Chapter 5 we will explore how the culture of health care constitutes the bodies of practitioners in ways that reflect ideas of gender, hierarchy and status, so that the values and meanings of the health care system are borne in the bodies of workers themselves.

There is thus no single body in health care, but a plurality of bodies, and recent work within the sociology of health and illness has begun to explore this diversity. Medicine has long been the focus of sociological and anthropological study. As a result there is a highly developed literature, both theoretical and empirical, analysing the area, in which the topic of the body is well represented. What perhaps has been lacking is an elaboration of these analyses in a policy context. As we shall see, however, thinking about the body and how it is constituted within health care brings considerable benefits, allowing us to address important tensions within provision. We will explore these more fully in later chapters.

When we turn to social care, however, we find a very different picture. Social care has never received the same attention from sociology that health has. As a result it has remained relatively underdeveloped and untheorised, largely presented in terms of discourses generated within the field. The principle academic disciplines analysing the area have been social policy and social work. Social policy inevitably takes a policy-oriented approach in which social care is one of a series of governmental, or quasi-governmental, activities and in which the dominant modes of analysis are institutional and rationalistic; and within this tradition, the new cultural analyses have made relatively little headway. The body is not seen as a particularly relevant subject; indeed social care is itself largely conceived as non-bodily in nature. This is certainly how social work has traditionally defined the remit of its interventions, particularly in relation to medicine. In Chapter 7 we will explore more fully the reasons that underlie this – mistaken – presentation of social care as non-bodily, simply noting the ways in which the body remains a largely unexplored dimension in this area.

New writing on the body

The new focus on the body that has emerged across the social sciences and humanities reflects a plurality of theoretical and empirical approaches; and in Chapter 2 we will explore the principle sources of this complex and diverse literature. As we shall see much of this work has its roots in postmodern and poststructuralist theorising and what can broadly be characterised as the Cultural Turn. Postmodernism is now somewhat on the wane intellectually, appearing to be something of a rag-bag theoretically – a set of ideas that in the 1980s and 1990s had coherence, but that has increasingly unravelled into its separate strands. In its heyday it encompassed theories about late capitalism; the compression of time and space; the shift from production to consumption in the constitution of identity; the role of the media in modern culture and the dominance of the visual and the virtual. It asserted the end of Enlightenment values and the repudiation of the possibility of the Grand Narratives, and with that the fragmentation of analysis into relativism, particularity and difference, in which no secure account could be given, a tendency reinforced by the emphasis on discourse and discursive production. Postmodernism has always contained a dual focus, presenting both a theory of knowledge and language, and an account of society and culture under presumed conditions of postmodernity. Within this, post-structuralism, which largely addresses the former, was initially treated as part of the mix, but is now increasingly acknowledged as presenting a distinctive strand of theorising, and one that has, in general, proved more enduring.

This intellectual inheritance presents both advantages and disadvantages for the analysis of policy-related areas such as health and social care, and in the sections that follow I will suggest some of the benefits such theorising brings to the field, as well as some of its limitations. What are the benefits?

First, poststructuralism has re-conceptualised power in ways that are significant for health and social care, reconfiguring its operation at the level of the body and the front line of service delivery. The work of Foucault is particularly significant here (Rabinow 1984, Williams and Bendelow 1998, S. Watson 2000). For Foucault, power operates at a capillary level, located in a web of cultural processes. It is all-pervasive and anonymous. In this it differs from the dominant accounts of political theory that present it as possessed and exercised by distinctive individuals or groups. Here power has no definable centre, so its sites are diverse and scattered, and this helps to refocus analysis away from the classic arenas of the State or overt political conflict towards the micro-politics of daily life and of the body.

For Foucault, power and knowledge are intertwined. Expert bodies of knowledge constitute, order and control fields by means of their discourses and related practices, so that the act of definition and classification is itself an act of power. This is a central perception for the analysis of health and social care, where groups of professionals – doctors, nurses, public health planners, social workers, dieticians – exercise authority through systems of power/knowledge and through their capacity to order and discipline the bodies of clients and patients. Indeed the history of the welfare state in the twentieth century, Dean (2000) suggests, can be seen as a process of perpetual refinement and extension of the disciplinary gaze of experts, so that the modern state rests not on the exercise of overt, violent power over the citizens' bodies, but on disciplinary techniques whereby individual bodies are ordered and controlled.

Professional bodies and social welfare agencies like to present their work in terms of expert, knowledge-driven progress that draws on universalistic and Enlightenment values. But Foucault's account reverses these claims, presenting the histories of penal policy or sexuality not in terms of the growth of humanitarian values and the demise of repression but of new forms of disciplinary power in which the discourses of experts increasingly regulate the intimate behaviour of individuals. This capacity to unmask the claims of experts helps question the humanitarian account of welfare services and the Enlightenment narrative of social progress on which it rests. As Penna and O'Brien (1996) note, modern welfare institutions operate according to logics that are often at extreme variance with the vision embedded in normative policy analysis. Questioning the nature of professional power helps us to analyse this more clearly.

The second major gain from poststructuralist theorising comes from its emphasis on discourse and the discursive production of subjects. Health and social care is to significant degree constituted within the discourses of social policy. Poststructuralist analysis exposes the assumptions that underlie this account, allowing us to look at the ways in which welfare subjects are themselves constituted (Carter 1998, Lewis *et al.* 2000, Lewis 2000, S. Watson 2000). Foucauldian-influenced work on the body also enables us to explore the ways in which welfare subjects are embodied, and the consequences of this for how classic subjects such as 'need' are constructed. Policy-related analyses have traditionally regarded the body as fixed, as solid, pre-social and as a generator of needs, rather than something on to which needs are inscribed. But as Watson argues, poststructuralist approaches start from the other end, asking instead which ideas of power, control and normalisation are involved in producing concepts like need (S. Watson 2000). From this perspective, social policy is a classic normalising discipline, and one that is implicated in many of the processes that Foucault studies. Indeed the key institutions on which he focuses – the clinic, the asylum and the prison – are all instruments of social policy. Social policy has traditionally been actively engaged in constituting welfare subjects like the 'single parent', the 'battered wife' and the 'girl in moral danger' in ways that parallel those of Foucault's classic nineteenth-century subjects (S. Watson 2000). It has long been involved in the constitution of mass populations, through surveys, statistics and investigations, establishing norms and deviations from them. Poststructuralism allows us to deconstruct these categories, exploring the normalising processes and legitimations that underpin them, and thus to mount a more sophisticated challenge to dominant policy paradigms and the ways in which they constitute the world.

The new cultural approaches also expose ways in which relations of domination and subordination, and privilege and inequality are located as much in cultural processes as in structural relations (Gibbins 1998, Clarke 1999, Lewis *et al.* 2000). In Chapters 3 and 4, we will explore the cultural constitution of old age and disability and the ways in which these discourses are presented as rooted in the body so that features of the body come to define and limit the experiences of individuals. We will note similar points in relation to sexuality in Chapter 2. For these groups, cultural exclusion based on aspects of identity and difference can be as significant as more straightforward economic exclusion (Penna and O'Brien 1996).

These approaches have also encouraged a new focus on identity as a key dimension in academic analysis. Postmodernists argue that there has been a fundamental change in the nature of social identity, resulting from a series of social and cultural shifts: the emergence of mass consumer culture; the post-industrial, information-driven economy; the re-structuring of production and employment under the impact of globalisation; the mediaisation of culture whereby the media and advertising take over aspects of socialisation previously performed by the family or social class. The self has become disembedded from traditional social structures and roles, with the result that identity has become both more fluid and more significant in the negotiation of daily life, something to be created and fashioned. The self becomes, in Gidden's (1991) words, a project to be worked on. Identity and lifestyle replace the earlier emphasis on class in defining who and what people are. This fluidity extends to some degree also to sexuality and – to a lesser extent – gender and 'race'. What this means for the policy arena is that there is no longer a single, stable 'we' that is the source and focus of policy making. Of course, there never was, but to large extent policy, particularly in relation to the issues of the welfare state, was predicated on a set of universalist assumptions about citizenship (F. Williams 1989, Lister 1997, 2001). The new focus on diversity disrupts these, presenting a more fluid, contradictory, and adversarial account. The plurality of narratives that postmodernism endorses also points up to the existence of different histories, different accounts, and ones – as we shall see in relation to gay and black narratives – rooted in the politics of self-identity.

The emphasis on culture also opens up the territory of the Visual. The visual realm in postmodernity has assumed a new prominence, largely through the impact of the media and associated consumer culture. This underpins a range of issues in relation to health and social care. We will see its impact particularly clearly in relation to the new perfectionism of the body and the associated rise of eating disorders. It is relevant also to issues concerning disability, as we shall see when we explore arguments concerning the scopic regime of modernity and its role in the construction of disability. Disabled people are oppressed not just by societal assumptions about physical capabilities like walking or hearing, but also by ideas about bodily appearance and its meanings. This is relevant also to age and the judgements that are made about it. The shift towards the visual also underpins the emerging politics of appearance in relation to, for example, obesity. In a visual culture that promotes perfect bodies, fatness has become a derogation, a sign of moral failure, a basis for social exclusion in relation to not only forms of employment – many organisations will not employ obese people – but also the culture of public esteem. Obesity is increasingly associated in the public mind, and in the statistics, with low social class, and is stigmatised. In a similar way, teeth have also become exemplars of social position. As expensive orthodontic interventions are increasingly popular among the middle class, perfect teeth have become the new norm. This has occurred in conjunction with the effective collapse of publicly funded dentistry in the UK, and the return of the kind of visibly damaged teeth among the poor that the NHS and the welfare state came to eliminate. Both these examples point to the role of symbolic and cultural dimensions in stratification and exclusion.

Work relating to the body is also associated with the wider revival of interest in space and time within sociology (Adam 1995, Urry 1996); and there have been parallel developments within geography, particularly in association with phenomenological and feminist influences (McDowell 1983, 1997, Rose 1993, Greed 1994, Sibley 1995, Kearns and Gesler 1998, Teather 1999, Longhurst 2001, Valentine 2001, Eade and Mele 2002). The body is now recognised both as an aspect of spatial relations and as a means through which space is apprehended (Lefebvre 1991, Rodaway 1994). The body, space and time are fundamental categories of being, ordering social relations; and we will see some of the interlinkages between these in the chapters on social care and public space. Social care is all about the spatial and temporal ordering of care, and its interaction with the management of the body. Bodily activities, like washing, dressing, sleeping, eating and excreting, mark out the temporal ordering of the day; and they largely take place in the symbolically ordered space of home. Home is quintessentially a private space; and it draws meaning from the contrast with the public. The public/private divide has been one of the key organising principles of Western social relations since the Enlightenment, and it plays a central part in many of the debates concerning space and the body. In Chapter 9, we will pursue these issues further, exploring the ways in which public space is constituted, and the significance of this for the management of the body.

The new emphasis on the body has also brought to the fore debates around emotion and well-being. Though the subjects of 'emotion' and the 'body' are not the same, they are linked; and the intellectual influences that have produced the new concern with the body – in particular the desire to redress the over-rationalistic account prevailing in the social sciences – have also made emotion visible academically (Williams and Bendelow 1998). This applies not just to personal matters, but to institutions also. Until recently, the dominant sociological account of organisations, particularly that influenced by the Weberian tradition, ignored emotion, regarding it as peripheral, a disruptive intrusion into the work setting. Emotion sat uneasily with the bureaucratic values of impartiality, efficiency and predict-ability. But as Fineman (1993) and others argue, emotions are central to organisations because they are fundamental to all social order, constitutive of the day-to-day realities of our lives. These insights have relevance across a range of settings. As we shall see in Chapter 7, emotion is a key element in the work of many of those employed in health and social care; and we will explore this in particular in relation to debates around emotional labour and its role in carework. Here emotion is not just an additional feature of the work, but is at the core of the exchange, a central part of the thing – care – being produced.

Emotional labour is also a dimension in social work, though one that is often consciously limited and controlled. Gunaratnam and Lewis (2001) draw attention to what they see as the

> fundamental contradiction of emotionality in the provision of social welfare...[A] significant part of the discursive formation of welfare services is that they have been constituted as sites that deal with, and also intervene in, matters of the emotional lives of service users – often in highly intimate and 'private' areas. Yet, 'bureaucratic professional' imperatives...are based on an ambivalent and uneven privileging of rationality over emotion. (p. 135)

Hoggett (2000) makes a similar point about the welfare system in general, pointing to the ways in which the institutions of social welfare act to repress and contain emotion, eroding rather than increasing well-being. Hospitals, for example, are places of raw feeling – fear, disgust, humiliation and abandonment – and these feelings are experienced in the body. They are, however, closely contained. Nursing is organised around the denial of the emotional experiences of both patients and nurses. It operates as a social defence system, using rules and regulations, uniforms, formal bodily stance, Taylorised task performance, and a culture of professional detachment and depersonalisation as a shield against naked emotion, anxiety and pain. For Hoggett (2000), the institutions of welfare are organised systems of defence against anxiety and ontological threat. Part of the purpose of the welfare services is precisely to separate society from pain, to keep it out of sight, locked in asylums, back bedrooms and residential homes.

The limitations of cultural analyses

I now want to turn briefly to some of the reasons why – despite their attractions – these new theoretical approaches have made limited headway in the policy-related arena of health and social care. A major part of the problem lies in their roots in postmodern and poststructuralist theory. From the perspective of policy makers, the radical epistemology of post-structuralism poses considerable problems. Poststructuralism presents the world as constituted in and through discourse, so that our knowledge of it is limited to a knowledge of the discourses that constitute it – our capacity to grasp it permanently deferred behind grids of meaning (Shilling 1993). But this acts to undermine the possibility of direct knowledge of the world. The tendency is reinforced by the influence of literary theory. Much work on the body emerged in the humanities and in the cross-over territory of Cultural Studies. Such approaches encourage us to see social phenomena as if they were texts, open to rival and sometimes counter readings, but without any clear sense of how such interpretations might be judged against or disciplined by empirical evidence. These impulses act to undercut empirically based research, undermining the claims of social science to be able to engage directly and authoritatively with the social world, and with that the rationale for much social science work in the policy arena. As Sophie Watson (2000) argues, postmodernism threatens to substitute an impotent theoretical critique for a social one.

In addition, the denial of the possibility of grand narratives, which was characteristic of postmodernism and was itself a response to the death of Marxism both as a political theory and as a unifying intellectual response within the academy, means that such traditions cannot engage with what is effectively the current Grand Theory – that of neo-liberalism. Neo-liberalism is now the dominant and overriding force constituting the social world – certainly the parts of the world that relate to policy concerns – and it provides the key theorising within it. But postmodernism, as Taylor-Gooby (1994) notes, has proved weak in the face of this social reality, whatever it may like to believe concerning its intellectual capacity to undermine it.

Not all the social sciences have succumbed to these influences. Economics has proved notably impervious to postmodernism – as it had done to earlier critiques from sociology and social theory. Though there has been some loosening up of the orthodoxies of economics with the presence of feminist economics and other non-standard approaches, these remain marginal to the main enterprise. Economics is the most socially powerful of all the social sciences. In the wider world it is accepted as providing not just the key facts of a situation, but also the key tools in its analysis. This is particularly true within the world of policy making. Here postmodernist theorising cuts no ice at all. Governments and policy makers have little interest in discourse or representation. They want to engage with 'reality' – even though we may accept that that reality is not as straightforward as they might like to think.

The denigration of empirical evidence within some postmodern writing has also proved harmful. The policy world is still constituted – officially at least – by the Enlightenment values of rationality, truth and progress. Postmodernism in substituting a lexicon of desire, caprice, ephemerality and irony cuts itself off from serious consideration, contributing to the feeling that this is an essentially teasing, self-regarding literature that has little to say of relevance on serious matters. This sense was reinforced by the emphasis in early work on the body on fashionable, media-focussed topics. Transsexuality, body building, Internet sex, the semiotics of the suspender belt – all in fact raise interesting theoretical questions, but they also contribute to a sense that this is work that is marginal to the concerns of public policy.

Downplaying the bodily

I now, finally, want to turn to a rather different set of reasons for the relative neglect of the body within these policy-related fields. This arises not from the limitations of postmodern theorising, but from the wider cultural estimation of the bodily within the Western tradition. This affects the degree to which policy makers, planners, government agencies – and indeed academics – are willing to engage directly with the body as a subject of discussion and analysis.

There is a long history in the West, rooted in Neo-Platonic influences and their transmission through Christianity, whereby the body is denigrated, presented as lesser in contrast to the mind or spirit. In this tradition, the body represents the dross, the gross materiality of existence, that ties the spirit down; and the goal of spiritual as well as intellectual cultivation in the West has traditionally been presented in terms of transcending the limitations of the bodily. This has implications, as we shall see in the next chapter, for the way in which academic knowledge has itself been constructed. This is of course not the only way in which the body has been understood historically, and there have always been counter-tendencies, some of which have celebrated the carnevalesque and the Dionysian. But it has been a powerful strand in Western thinking, and one that still influences current judgements.

The suppression of the bodily finds its expression in social behaviour. Mary Douglas (1966, 1970) has analysed the ways in which the body is downplayed in formal social situations, so that the more formal the circumstances, the less the body is present. Areas of life that have a strongly bodily character tend to be downplayed or erased in formal social settings. Elias (1978) has presented a historical account of these processes, in which the transition to modernity is accompanied by a gradual imposition of constraint over the body and its natural functions. Through the analysis of early modern conduct books and advice on correct behaviour, Elias traced the ways in which a range of bodily behaviours that were once common-place become increasingly frowned upon and condemned; and he does this across a range of bodily behaviours in relation, for example, to eating, sleeping, sexuality and excretion, as well as in the parallel expression of emotion. This imposition of restraint is accompanied by a growing individ-ualisation of the self and the body, as bodily functions are gradually moved behind the screens of domestic life, confined to separate, specialised and private spaces. Elias argues that in the modern period, self-restraint becomes internalised, to the extent that overt rules and sanctions become less significant; the seemingly more relaxed bodily regime of the twentieth century was thus only possible by virtue of an internalised bedrock of restraint. His work can, however, be criticised for not doing justice to the changes that have occurred, and are occurring. There are signs of growing bodily disinhibition, most obviously in relation to sexuality, but also eating, with the return of eating with the hands through the growth of fast foods, snacks and the fragmentation of table manners, or excreting, with the increase of urinating in the streets, particularly by young men. Both of these have implications for the discussions in Chapters 8 and 9 on diet and the body in public space. The pattern is, thus, more complex – more histori-cally and socially specific – than his account would suggest. It is still useful, however, as part of the broad background to the ways in which the bodily has been downplayed, and partially erased, in modern social discourses.

These general tendencies contribute to the way in which the world of policy making and its language is constituted. This is a disembodied world *par excellence*, where problems and issues are presented in abstract, neutral language. It is a cool, dry, controlled world: the very reverse of Rabalasian. The body – its problems and pleasures – does not sit easily in this setting; and work that tries to address these issues face-on can seem crude, disjunctive and at odds with the overall tone of policy decorum. And yet, as we shall see in relation to health and social care, bodily issues are of central importance to many of these areas of policy making.

Similar problems can arise in academic work. Longhurst (2001) recounts the unease she felt as a graduate student in proposing a study of the body and its boundaries. To suggest it

> meant breaking social (and academic protocols). I did not feel as though I could use words such as 'ejaculate' and 'lactate' during my first meeting with the geography chairperson. In 1991 (and perhaps still today) there was a limited discursive space to discuss bodies, especially their weighty, sexed/gendered and messy materiality in respectable places such as staff offices at the university. (p. 3)

I have also felt something of this in trying to describe the realities of carework in ways that are acceptable in formal writing: Can I talk about 'shit'? Will the word leap distractingly from the page? And yet being able to talk directly about what the work of care really involves is central to our capacity to grasp the issues in this area. There is, however, a second reason why the body is avoided in accounts of these sectors, and this concerns the potentially demeaning character of such discourse. To refer directly to the bodies of individuals is to lessen and reduce them. Polite, or formal, speech avoids direct comment on physical attributes, reserving that for gossip or malicious asides. Characterising people in terms of the bodily is a feature of subordinated social groups; and it is part of the ways in which they are objectified, presented as Other. There is, for example, a long history in racism that focusses demeaningly on the bodies of racialised groups; and we will explore this more in the next chapter. Women have similarly been subject to crude bodily emphases, presented in terms of their bodies, or of specifically sexualised parts of them. Focussing on the body can thus be a process that operates to lessen people, undercutting their status, subverting their subjectivity in potentially humiliating ways. And it is for these reasons that social care has tended to fight shy of the body. The bodies of individuals, or clients, are not emphasised in these fields, indeed good practice consciously attempts to counteract such processes of objectification. In relation to disability or old age – as we shall see – this means focussing, not on bodily matters, but on other aspects: on people as feeling individuals, rather than failing bodies. But this can have consequences that are limiting for the ways in which old age and disability are analysed.

It is this element of denigration and objectification that also underlies the unease some have felt in applying strongly Foucauldian approaches to social care. Foucault is all about bodies. Indeed part of the *frisson* of his analysis lies in the way that he focusses so overtly and heavily on bodies. But in doing this, his analysis threatens to activate the processes of objectification and denigration referred to above. As I have argued elsewhere

(Twigg 2000b) there is a sadistic quality to Foucault's analysis that has played no small part in his academic appeal. His work encourages us into a relationship of domination with our research materials, in which they too are ordered, controlled and disciplined – their independent subjectivity undermined as they are reduced to the level of bodies. A Foucauldian approach can thus reduplicate the processes it analyses, becoming complicit in the very relations it seeks to expose, or at least analyse.

Conclusion

As will have become clear, my views on the literature on the body, and in particular the postmodern/poststructuralist element in it, contain some reservations. There are problems in applying these approaches to policy-related areas, and some of the reasons for the slow take-up or neglect have been well based, particularly the concerns about the shifting, fluid nature of these analyses, their retreat from empirical evidence and the amorality and lack of engagement that can seem to characterise some of them, at least. But at the same time, these literatures and approaches have brought considerable benefits in the form of new theories, insights and perspectives that allow us to question and disturb the assumptions on which policy-related work is based, proposing new subjects for enquiry, as well as new perspectives on established subjects. Foucault in particular, for all his faults, has opened our eyes to processes and relationships of central importance to health and social care.

Chapter 2

Debates About the Body

Over the past two decades, the body has become the focus of vigorous debate across the social sciences and humanities. In this chapter, I will review some of the central themes in this literature, concentrating on three areas: feminist writings; the influence of poststructuralism particularly the work of Foucault; and debates concerning the body in consumer culture. Early work on the body was often highly theoretical, and at times the body seemed, paradoxically, to disappear in a cloud of language. More recently there has been a welcome revival of empirically grounded work that focusses on real bodies and real embodiment, and in the main part of the book, I will draw on this. Though gender has been a major concern in this literature, other dimensions of difference are also significant; and in the second part of this chapter, I will explore these cross-cutting dimensions, focussing in particular on class, 'race' and sexuality. Age and disability are dealt with in separate chapters.

The sources of the debate

The current focus on the body resulted from the confluence of a number of intellectual influences. The first was a growing dissatisfaction with the rather thin, rationalistic account that had dominated the social sciences from their origins in the eighteenth century (Turner 1991). As part of the Enlightenment project, this had privileged what Nietzsche characterised as the Appollonian virtues of the rational, controlled and abstract over the Dionysian ones of the emotional, uncontrolled and concrete. The body belonged to the latter, and was relegated to a subordinated, and as we shall see gendered, status, something largely passed over in analysis. The 'crisis' in Enlightenment thinking, however, has led to a radical reassessment of this rationality, which now seems inadequate as an account of human nature and society (Bauman 1993). Theorists have looked for a deeper, fuller and also darker account than that provided by the Enlightenment project – at least as characterised by postmodern writers, for that tradition is more complex than they allow. Indeed not all theorising in the past excluded the body, and Turner has outlined an oppositional intellectual tradition that has its origins in Nietzsche, in which the body is more fully acknowledged.

Presented as the seat of desire, irrationality and pleasure, it represents a source of opposition to the dominance of instrumental rationality (Turner 1991). The pedigree is complex, encompassing a range of often divergent thinkers, from Schopenhauer to Marcuse and Foucault. All are united, however, in a critique of the narrow rationality that has dominated mainstream social science.

Neglect of the body also arose from sociology's concern to establish its intellectual territory. As Turner argued, sociology in its origins, as part of an attempt to throw off the spectre of biological reductionism, engaged in a distancing exercise in which the conceptual realm of the social was established and secured by means of excluding the biological, and handing that over to science. The price of this disciplinary definition, however, was the exclusion of the body from sociological analysis (Turner 1984, 1991). This has implications, as we shall see, for the conceptualisation not only of medicine but also of disability and old age.

From the 1980s, however, this tradition of neglect began to be reversed: Bryan Turner's *The Body and Society* of 1984 was groundbreaking here. Since then, there has been an upsurge of work on the body that extends far beyond the disciplinary boundaries of the social sciences. In the sections that follow, we will explore the main sources of this theorising.

Feminist influences

From the start, feminism had been concerned with questions of the body. Many of the campaigns of the women's movement of the 1970s centred around bodily issues: for example, the rights of women to control their own bodies, especially in relation to contraception and abortion; or the desire to regain control over natural processes like childbirth; or the right to enter the public sphere and public space on equal and secure terms through campaigns like reclaiming the night; or attempts to ensure women's bodily integrity and safety in campaigns against domestic violence and rape (Lovenduski and Randall 1993). Many of these campaigns drew on classical liberal theory and its conception of the rights of the individual to bodily integrity and possession, but they developed beyond that to explore the ways in which women's bodies were enmeshed in relations of power and domination, in which the oppression of women by men was often exercised at the bodily level, whether overly or in more subtle ways. Pateman (1989) and others stripped the gender neutrality from political theory to show how control over and access to the bodies of women was at the heart of the sexual contract that underlay the social contract of traditional political theory. The body, far from being beneath politics, was at its centre.

Feminists were thus early in recognising that the body was a crucial topic, and one that had been excluded from academic analyses. Part of the feminist project has been to widen the scope of what is recognised as important and studiable within the academy, destabilising its implicitly masculinist bias. In this way, feminism has opened up a new range of subjects, many of which relate to the body, so that areas of life previously excluded or passed over, such as emotion, sexual experience, maternity, beauty, food, fashion – the list is endless – are now fruitful subjects for academic analysis.

There is a long cultural tradition, looking back to Plato and the Greeks, that presents the body as in opposition to the mind or soul. Here the body is seen as reason's underside, its negative inverted double (Longhurst 2001). This division is carried through into a series of binary oppositions in which the mind is associated with the positive terms of reason, subject, consciousness, activity, man; and the body with the negative ones of passion, object, the unconscious, passivity, woman. This binary scheme is capable of almost limitless extension across a range of cultural and social spheres: light/dark, nature/culture, hard/soft, head/heart, cure/care, public/private; and we will explore some of the ways in which these resonate through health and social care in subsequent chapters. The point to note, however, is that the division is gendered; and that women are persistently located on the unmarked, devalued side. This imposes a distorting form of asymmetry that not only lessens and denigrates women, but it also evacuates the subject of 'woman' of any meaning in her own right. Here 'women' as a concept is defined by lack of male attributes and exists only to point up the nature of 'man'. As Brook (1999) argues, this system of binary Twos disguises what is in reality a monolithic masculine One.

The imbalance is carried across into questions of knowledge. Social science has traditionally rested on a masculinist vision that privileges the viewpoint and experiences of men, presenting what is partial and particular as if it were universal and transcendent. Within this Cartesian Enlightenment tradition, the mind is regarded as separate from and untainted by the body. The bearer of knowledge is presented as disembodied, rising above corporeal particularity into a realm of pure reason. This disembodied knower is implicitly male. Though both men and women have and are bodies, men are traditionally considered to be able to seek and speak universal knowledge, unencumbered by the limitations of the material body (Rose 1993, Shilling 1993, Longhurst 2001). They are presented as capable of transcendence, able to treat their bodies as containers of pure consciousness. Women by contrast are traditionally presented as bound up in the desires of their fleshly, natural bodies, prey to the shifting tides of emotion, located in time and space and corporeal in a way that men are not. This lesser and bodily bound status is extended to other subordinated groups: the working class, servants, children, the poor, blacks, slaves, all of whom are traditionally deemed more deeply enmeshed in their bodies, and lacking the capacity for fully rational thought. For white bourgeoisie men, such groups represent the Other, against which their reason is contrasted and their experiences validated.

For these reasons, destabilising binary thinking has been one of the central aims of feminist thinking. Among the most prominent examples of this is the public/private divide (Pateman 1989, Walby 1990, Lister 1997). We will explore the significance of this more fully in Chapters 7 and 9, when we look at issues in relation to home and public space, but will note here its historical emergence in the early modern period, when the development of the concept of civil society within political theory acted to construct its contrast – the domestic sphere – as an area of privacy and non-intervention (Pateman 1989). The family and women were constituted as a natural and private realm. This binary division was reinforced in the nineteenth century with the development of the doctrine of separate spheres (Davidoff and Hall 1987, Hall 1992). The ideology was given bodily expression in the shift in the understanding of sexual difference, from what Laqueur (1990) identifies as a two-gender, one-sex model – in which women represented lesser, inverted versions of men – to the two-sex model – in which women and their bodies were presented as radically different and opposite to men.

Since then feminism has been concerned to deconstruct and destabilise the public/private division, showing how the two are interrelated and mutually dependent. Men's advantaged position in the public realm is made possible by the servicing work of women in the private. A significant part of this relates to bodily needs of various sorts, again reinforcing the idea that the body is something that is associated with women or the private world of home, whose mundanity men are able to transcend as they move between the two spheres. Subverting the public/private divide has thus been important not only in arguments for the inclusion of women as equals in the public sphere, but for the expansion of protective scrutiny and legislation into the private. Feminist writers in their analyses of domestic violence or child sex abuse have exposed how the private realm of the family is constituted around relations of patriarchal power, in which the bodies of women and of children can sometimes be subjected to violence and abuse (Mullender and Morley 1994, Mullender 1996, Hague and Malos 1998, Hanmer and Itzen 2000, Mooney 2000, Pahl *et al.* 2004).

Feminists have also been interested in the ways in which gender operates directly on the body, building up bodies that are recognisably masculine and feminine. Young's (1990) article 'Throwing like a girl' was a classic expression of this, in which she explored the ways in which women learn to lack physical confidence. 'Feminine' movements are marked by hesitancy and caution, by reactive rather than proactive engagement with things, by using only parts of the body rather than its full force. This creates an experience of the world in which women occupy space cautiously, and in which they experience their bodies as closed-in, disconnected from the wider spatial field. Men, by contrast, learn to throw in a way that expresses a direct connectedness between their bodies and the wider world, which they view as constituted by their intentions. Men live their bodies in an open way, moving out to master the world. These differences are written into the body in such a way as they act upon and reinforce the individual's daily experience of self and of body, contributing to the difficulties women face in attempting to access images of power and authority, particularly in the public sphere. McDowell (1997) has analysed this in relation to women in corporate banking and the City, where men's constructed embodiment reinforces their dominant position, just as women's undermines theirs, making it hard for them to exert authority or succeed in the context of heavily sexualised culture of work.

Feminists have also drawn on the work of Foucault to explore the ways in which women's bodies have been made subject to discipline and power, though in doing so they have shifted the focus away from formal institutions like prisons that are the centre of his analyses, towards more personal and individual arenas in which women's bodies are made subject to control and discipline, often under the male gaze. These approaches, as we shall see in Chapter 7, are particularly relevant to the analysis of eating disorders and dieting, which represent major 'technologies of the self' in modern society.

The feminist literature on the body thus picks up many of the ambivalences that women and wider culture feel about their bodies. Aspects of this have been explored through Kristeva's concept of abjection (Oliver 1993). The abject is that which is expelled, rejected and presented as Other; and it implies a dissolution of boundaries, in this case the boundaries of the body. Drawing on Mary Douglas (1966) and on psychoanalytic ideas, she presents abjection as an indeterminate, liminal state, often seen as threatening or polluting, regarded with revulsion and sometimes horror. These ideas reverberate through popular accounts of women's bodies which are often presented as leaky, swampy, messy, particularly in relation to menstruation, pregnancy and lactation, when the boundaries of the body are breached or indeterminate. This is in contrast to men's bodies, which are presented as hard, clearly defined, contained (Newman 1997). The quality of the abject helps to maintain the devalued character of women's bodies. Longhurst (2001) argues that it also contributes to the selective character of academic work on the embodiment. She suggests that there is a tendency, even in work overtly about the body, to edit out what is dirty, or inappropriate, or 'unacademic'. As we noted in Chapter 1, writing on the body is still sometimes constrained in how it presents its subject and in what topics it is willing to look at; and Longhurst in her own work on pregnancy, breastfeeding, toilets, bathrooms and excretion cites them as examples of areas of life that have been passed over in the mainstream literature. She argues that this evasion derives from the continuation of the masculinist vision that privileges certain forms of being, and regards aspects of, particularly female, embodiment with unease and even distaste.

This partial presentation of the body is also reflected in certain postmodern writing, with its media-driven emphasis on beautiful, young and fashionable bodies and neglect of less glamorous topics like sickness and old age. These are, however, an important part of bodily experience and we will explore elements of them in the chapters on disability and old age. In Chapter 7 we will also address the aspects of the body as it relates to work, in particular the category of bodywork, exploring its evaded, hidden character, as well as its association with women. Some of the meaning of these aspects lies in questions of abjection, and the cultural association of women with bodies that leak and flow. We will pick up these themes again in the final chapter when we look at the body in space, exploring issues in relation to lactation and excretion in public spaces.

The body is also implicated in key debates around equality and difference. Liberal feminists of the Second Wave sometimes advocated a form of androgyny that erased bodily differences between men and women. Emphasising the bodily was associated with attempts to legitimate the exclusion of women, providing reasons 'why women could not do things', or were 'less suited' to others. From this perspective bodily difference was a somewhat ambivalent subject. But the idea of a single androgynous, equal body can be problematic for women, failing to reflect key aspects of their experiences, endorsing a model of humanity that is implicitly male (Shilling 1993, Tseelon 1995). This is particularly so in relation to reproduction and its consequences. The liberal, androgynous model thus frees women to compete with men, but on terms that are far from equal. Lister (1997, 2001) in her analyses of citizenship has explored the tensions between difference and equality strategies across a range of public issues, and we will reflect on these tensions in the chapter on the body in public space.

Some feminist thinkers, such as Cixous and Irigaray, rather than seeking to erase bodily difference have emphasised it, aiming to revalue women's physical and biological roles, placing them at the heart of their experience, and overturning the negative or limited interpretation assigned to them (Whitford 1991, Sellers 1994, Bray 2004). Such ideas have long been a strand in radical feminism, and they are prominent also in eco-feminism (Daly 1979, Warren 1994). In some writers this has led to the assertion of the existence of distinctly female ways of thinking, creating and being that are intimately bound up with women's physicality; and Irigaray makes the link between women and the watery virtues of fluidity, flux and inconstancy. She thus embraces aspects of binary thinking, though in ways that reverse its traditional valuations. Others have valourised motherhood, asserting the possibility of a gynocentric vision that is fundamentally different from the patriarchal perceptions of men (Rich 1986).

Judith Butler (1993) approaches the question of the body and its status from a different direction, one that draws on Foucault and poststructuralism to present a radical critique of the constitution of sex, and in doing so she destabilises the division of sex and gender that was one of the key conceptual developments of 1970s feminism. She rejects the formula that biology underlies sex, and that gender is inscribed on naturally sexed bodies, arguing that sex is itself constituted by gender, so that our understanding of sex is determined by our understanding of gender. Gender for her is performative, not so much in the sense that Goffman suggested in his dramaturgical analysis, but in the way that, drawing on linguistic theory, speech acts are performative, creating what they declare; and by this means 'repeated stylisations of the body,...congeal over time to produce the appearance of substance' (Butler 1990, 33). Daily unconscious acts of citation through repetition produce the body as either male or female, so that the process of 'doing gender' creates the appearance of being a particular gender. The gender order, she argues, rests on the ideology of compulsory heterosexuality which, far from being natural, is coercive, produced by disciplinary practices; and Butler draws attention to phenomena-like drag that parody and disrupt this normality, exposing the possibility of discrepancy between the sexed body, the gendered performance and the sexuality of the individual. Butler's work has also been used to destabilise and question the category 'woman', and with that the earlier feminist political project that rested on the assertion of commonality and sisterhood.

Work on the gendered body was initially mostly concerned with women's bodies, reflecting the wider pattern whereby masculinity was taken as the unexamined norm against which women's difference was made visible and studiable (J. Watson 2000, Sheldon 2002). This has the effect of both privileging and yet erasing masculinity. When work did begin to emerge that looked specifically at men's bodies, it tended to focus on the hyper-masculine areas of sport, war, violence. This produced an account of male embodiment that was all about muscles, strength and aggression, which implicitly idealised a certain sort of male body and masculinity. It presented what Morgan (1993) termed an 'overphallused' picture of men. In itself this reflected, as Connell (1995, 2000) argues, the values of the form of masculinity hegemonic on Western society, one centred around physical toughness, authority, paid work and heterosexuality. This emphasises bodily strength and power, so that even in modern Western society where physical prowess is not of central importance in determining the social status of men, its expression is still linked to dominance; and powerful men use their physicality to buttress their position in the work place and wider society, not only against women but also against other, lesser, men. More recently work on masculinity and the body has attempted to get behind this dominant imagery to explore more plural accounts of men's embodiment across a wider range of experiences, including those of illness and old age (Pringle 1995, Sabo and Gordon 1995, Newman 1997, J. Watson 2000, Sheldon 2002).

Foucault and poststructuralism

Foucault is one of the key theorists in the emergence of the sociology of the body. In a series of works he explored the ways in which power and knowledge operate at the level of the body: in relation to madness and psychiatry in *Madness and Civilisation* (1971); health and medicine in *The Birth of the Clinic* (1973); penology, crime and deviance in *Discipline and Punish* (1977); and sexuality in the three volumes of *The History of Sexuality* (1979, 1987, 1988). Together these present a radical historicisation of knowledge, that draws on Nietzsche's earlier analysis of the relations between truth, knowledge and power. For Foucault the body is not constant, but an entity saturated with historically specific meanings. Power is key in this, and we have touched on features of this in Chapter 1. For Foucault power is continuous and anonymous; and he uses his famous image of the panopticon to express the quality whereby surveillance is all pervasive and perpetual – all are caught in the machine, both watcher and watched.

Central to his work is the concern to present a history of the different modes whereby human beings are made subjects. He identifies three as key. The first is dividing practices. These are social and institutional practices that separate, categorise, define and thus create distinctive, usually stigmatised, social groupings: the mad, poor, delinquent, sick and old. These are managed, cared for and disciplined in distinct institutions: the asylum, the poor house, prison, hospital and old people's home. Dividing practices serve to spatialise power by ordering different sorts of people or experiences in specific spaces. Thus the nineteenth-century asylum is divided up into sections or wards that order the population according to sex, social rank, category of illness and degree of behavioural abnormality (Markus 1993). By means of such processes, populations can be subdivided, and individuals objectified and classified. Thus the general poor of the nineteenth century were re-ordered into distinctive sub-classes – the vagabond, the delinquent, the sick, the demented, the aged – and ordered accordingly. Such categories still have force, and divisions such as 'deserving' and 'undeserving' poor still resonate through modern social policy.

The second mode of subjectification is classificatory practices. These order and define subjects, designating both the persons or things to be known, and the individuals who have the authority to know and speak about them.

What is normal and what is deviant is the product of discourses that define and determine these terms. It is by such processes of division that subjects are created and objectified. The social sciences as they emerged in the nineteenth century are closely associated with these processes; as are the professions with their systematic bodies of knowledge which were also developed and codified in the nineteenth and twentieth centuries.

For Foucault, subjectivity is constituted not primarily at the level of the individual but at the level of the body and the population; and the body lies at the heart of the strategic configuration of power-knowledge. For Foucault the body is not natural, but is the product of the discourses within which it is constituted. The techniques of bio-power analyse, control, regulate and define the body, its disciplinary gaze construing the body as an object of knowledge. For example, penal practices aim to control and reform the character of the delinquent by disciplining his body. In the prison the body's intimate needs – food, light, space, privacy and sex – become the materials on which the regime of schedule, curfews, timetables, micropunishments are enacted (Katz 1996). These techniques can be found across a range of institutions that developed in the nineteenth century to deal with populations and individuals – schools, armies, hospitals and factories – and they form the key institutions of carceral society. Thus from the organisation to architectural space to the temporal ordering of the institution, the body has been surrounded and invested with technologies of power which serve to analyse, monitor and fabricate it in ways that render it docile and useful (Foucault 1977).

Classificatory practices also operate at the level of populations. Foucault explored the ways in which social surveys, demographic data, official statistics all served to order, measure, monitor and classify the population. The rise of statistics was particularly important in the development of technologies of normalisation because they allowed the establishment of norms and averages, and with them deviance. The nineteenth century saw the elaboration of social categories of anomaly: the pervert, the delinquent and the mentally defective. Statistical techniques also allowed for the standardisation and prediction of risk. They enabled public bodies to monitor and trace the development of diseases, the patterns of population growth and the health of the nation. Public health was thus able to re-draw the city as a sociological territory, subject to surveillance and control. These developments made possible, for the first time, knowledge about and control over the most minute aspects of behaviour in the name of the population's welfare, leading to the growth of public health as a regulatory regime of central importance in the twentieth century (Armstrong 1983).

For Foucault, disciplinary practices have not ceased to be significant with the rise of seemingly more humanitarian approaches in the twentieth century. Progressive and enlightened responses are just as much expressions of power as overtly repressive ones. Here the disciplinary forces are not external and physical, but internal, embodied in systems of thought and the discourses and practices that support them. Among these can be forms of self-discipline.

This brings us to Foucault's third mode of subjectification, which concerns the technologies of the self. These are active forms of self-formation in which individuals apply disciplinary techniques to themselves. The extension of confession from its original religious context into wider secular forms of self-reflection and therapy provides one example; the control of the body through regimes of diet and exercise is another. Often, these processes of reflection, self-understanding and development are mediated by a specialist – a priest, a therapist or a personal trainer. Technologies of the self exist slightly apart from the earlier two modes, and they developed later in Foucault's thought, partly in response to criticism concerning the lack of agency in his work. These technologies allowed him to develop a critical ontology of the self that could provide a basis for establishing a standpoint of resistance to normalising power (Williams and Bendelow 1998). It allowed him to develop concepts of autonomy, reflexivity and critique that might overcome what were seen as the negative implications of his earlier work on disciplinary power.

Foucault's work has been subject to many criticisms. From the perspective of historians, his evidential base is weak and his argument sometimes dishonest (Hamilton 1996). His emphasis on disciplinarity, though enlightening, can seem partial – limited in its focus. The radical character of his epistemology, as we noted in Chapter 1, seems to deny the possibility of knowing the world, and with that of acting effectively in it. His critique of universalism and of Enlightenment values undercuts notions of justice, truth and equality that are central to the policy debate (S. Watson 2000). His account of subjectivity lacks agency, though he attempted to meet this criticism in later work. His concept of power, although of central importance for many of the areas discussed in this book, remains unsatisfactory precisely for its neutral, anonymous qualities. His account of resistance leaves its basis untheorised. Despite these criticisms, however, he remains of central importance to many of the areas discussed in this book, and we will explore the impact of his ideas in subsequent chapters.

The body, consumption and identity

The third broad area where work on the body has assumed new significance is in relation to consumer society and arguments, sometimes reflecting the influence of postmodernism, concerning the constitution of modern selfhood and the role of consumption in this. The emergence of mass consumption in the twentieth century, it is argued, has re-oriented society away from the old virtues of frugality, hard work, thrift and restraint towards the new ones of conspicuous display and consumption (Featherstone 1991, Giddens 1991, Jagger 2000). As structural factors rooted in production such as class become less influential, consumption has come to play an increasingly important role in identity. Indeed, identity, it is argued, has itself become more fluid and open, less embedded in social structure and more the product of choice and self-creation, and with that more fragile and unstable. Individuals seek means to externalise and fix it; and possessions and consumption offer one way. Cultural goods thus become an important part of how individuals mark out and distinguish themselves from others, as exemplified in the modern power of brands and designer labels.

The body is a central site for these processes. Much modern consumption focusses directly on the body, in the form of fashion, beauty, food, leisure and health products. In some postmodern accounts, the body itself becomes a lifestyle accessory, something to be fashioned, controlled and presented as the exemplar of the self. Consumer culture is notoriously preoccupied with perfect bodies, spread through glamourised representations of advertising and the increasing dominance of the visual image in culture. A mass of body products, cosmetics, clothes, dietary aids, body maintenance activities, products, publications and so on are promoted through these means. But the new body emphasis also contains strongly ascetic strands, that suggest anxiety and unease as much as the pursuit of pleasure. Body techniques require denial, control, the assertion of dominance over the body in pursuit of the slim, toned physique that modern culture demands. These are panopticon technologies in which the body is monitored and controlled as part of Foucault's disciplinary practices. The rewards of such ascetic bodywork, as Featherstone (1991) and Turner (1991) argue, are no longer religious – as it was in the past with techniques of fasting and self-denial – but strongly material in the form of a more attractive, more marketeable self. Fitness and slimness are associated with attractiveness, prudence, prescience and other virtues of self-control and success. Even health promotion, despite its official focus, is heavily embued with the values of consumer culture, the idealisation of youth and the body beautiful. Such body techniques often operate on the borders of the new spirituality that has to significant degree displaced religion. The erosion of public forms of belief and practice consequent on the fragmentation and privatisation of society (Berger 1969) has resulted in people seeking alternative sources of personal meaning; and the body and bodily techniques of a spiritual or quasi-spiritual kind have become an important element in this, underwriting a range of phenomena from meditation, yoga, new age therapies, modern spa and beauty culture.

Feminism has traditionally been critical of the impact of bodily perfectionism on women. During the 1970s, feminists focussing on the sexual objectification of women tended to adopt a puritanical approach to issues like clothes and make-up, rejecting them as oppressive. But as Elizabeth Wilson (1985) argued, all cultures shape and present the body in distinctive ways; and fashion, clothes and display are inescapable aspects of living. Since then feminists of the 'third wave' influenced by postmodernism have re-evaluated aspects of consumption and have been more willing to give recognition to them as sources of pleasure, recovering the sense that women actively make their own bodies, and that this self-fashioning can be a source of engagement and enjoyment. For many women, fashion is an expression of aesthetic pleasure, a form of self-expression and empowerment (Entwhistle 2000, Guy *et al.* 2001, Holland 2004). We will return to this in Chapter 3, when we explore the paradoxes and dilemmas around the presentation of the self in ageing.

Lastly Shilling (1993) argues that our increasing capacity to control the body has contributed to a crisis in its meaning. New reproductive techniques, organ transplants, high-tech interventions, cosmetic surgery and so on destabilise our sense of what is natural for the body. At the same time, virtual reality raises questions about its existence and its links to identity. Media culture has explored these anxieties through the popular genre of Horror (Williams and Bendelow 1998), or the current preoccupation in high art with the body and its disintegration, again something we will pick up in Chapter 5 in relation to debates around body parts.

Real bodies: Towards a more concrete embodiment

Early literature on the body was often marked by an oddly disembodied character. Though ostensibly concerned to reassert the reality and significance of the corporeal life, at times it seemed to lose sight of it. This partly arose from the status of theorising within sociology, where as Scott and Morgan (1993) comment, theory and theorising occupy a privileged position. This is the High Game of the subject, undertaken by the Grand Masters of the discipline – their use of gendered terminology is intentional. The result was an account that while critiquing mainstream sociology for its failure to encompass the bodily, managed to reduplicate this disembodied character within its own analysis. Nettleton and Watson (1998) identify this as the problem of 'theoreticism', where attention is limited to theory which is not grounded in the empirical domain.

The sense of the body as absent was also encouraged by the postmodern emphasis on discourse. This produced a picture of the body as evanescent, a floating presence and a cobweb of signs, in which there was little sense of real bodies that lived real, corporeal lives. Indeed the radical epistemology that underlay many postmodern accounts denied the possibility that we could know the body except through the discourses that constituted it, and in doing so seemed to erase the body itself. But as Williams (2001) points out, these assumptions conflate two levels of analysis, confusing epistemological and ontological claims, mixing up what we know and how we know it with what there is to know.

One of the most significant sources of challenge to the radical social constructionism of postmodernism has come from work in the areas of pain, illness, ageing and death. These are contexts in which the independent, physiological significance of the body is undeniable. People suffer and die; and these brute facts intrude into the solipsism of postmodern thinking. Such realities also impinge upon the status of knowledge. As Williams (2001) argues, though postmodernists may choose to regard medicine as a modernist discourse, one of a series of optional accounts in a plural world, when the chips are down,

> when we are ill, when the uncertainties or contingencies of our mortal bodies and their fleshly demise are all too apparent, recourse to medicine may seem an eminently preferable option to the relativising spirit and deconstructionist desires of postmodernism. (p. 150)

In reality, postmodernism is an attractive option only for the healthy, an intellectual luxury that only the young and fit can entertain, at least in its most radical form. In this context Critical Realism has presented an increasingly influential formulation, one that allows the body to be brought back in, but without recourse to biological reductionism (Williams 1999). It makes possible the recognition that we have fleshly, sensate bodies that can be described in biological terms, while at the same time recognising that these bodies are not simply given but also interpreted, mediated and in part constituted in social and cultural meanings, allowing us to see how the body can be both a generator and a receptor of meanings. These developments have occurred in conjunction with a revival of interest in the work of Merleau-Ponty (1962). His phenomenological analysis is increasingly seen as offering both a way through the problems of mind/body dualism, and a means of refocussing sociological analysis back directly on embodiment. In line with this, though not necessarily sharing the same theoretical position, there has been a welcome growth of empirical work that has explored embodiment across a range of social situations and cultures, and in the chapters that follow I will draw on this work. Some collections reflecting this include Nettleton and Watson (1998), Davis (1997), Backett-Milburn and McKie (2001) and Evans and Lee (2002).

I now want to turn to the ways in which the body intersects with key dimensions of difference, in particular with gender, 'race', class, disability, age and sexuality.

Dimensions of difference

Difference emerged as an important theoretical debate in feminism in the 1970s and 1980s. Initially it addressed the differences between men and women, exploring the tensions between liberal feminist strategies that emphasised the essential sameness and equality of men and women, and approaches that recognised significant differences in relation to key aspects of women's lives or natures, usually in relation to reproduction. We have already noted how the latter view gave rise to different interpretations of the meaning of bodily experiences and their social and cultural significance. But from the late 1970s, feminism was increasingly criticised by black and lesbian feminists for its universalising, homogenising and 'white' assumptions about women (Maynard 1994). The debate on difference shifted to be about the differences between women; and 'difference' is now deployed to express diversity. At times it is used to subvert, destabilise and even deny the category of 'woman'. This has been reinforced by the new fluidity in regard to subjectivity that denies the single subject position of Enlightenment thought, and emphasises a plurality of identities and selves that are not fixed but are constituted socially and linguistically through competing discourses.

The emphasis on difference was also the result of a shift away from the earlier Marxian focus on class as the key social division, as claims were increasingly made for gender and 'race', and for a greater emphasis on the symbolic and cultural dimensions of stratification. These intellectual shifts were themselves the product of social change, as the impact of globalisation and the fragmentation of the labour market has helped to shift class from its previously dominant position, making it possible to reflect on other sources of social division. Analysts like Anthias (2001) while welcoming these developments remain wary of the tendency of postmodernism, with its emphasis on fragmentation and diversity, to endorse a wider dismantling of 'the social' view of society, as composed of systems and practices that cohere around stable sets of defining elements. She argues for the need to acknowledge both material and symbolic facets of stratification. This is a view shared by Maynard (1994) in her critique of difference, where she points to the dangers of loss of capacity to analyse situations in terms of inequality and power.

Shifts in the political realm have also been influential, with the rise in the 1970s and 1980s of New Social Movements that pushed for the recognition of oppressed social groups – black and ethnic minorities, women, the disabled, gays – and for their civil rights. These pressures have destabilised the nature of public discourse and the assumptions of unity that it previously rested upon, showing them to be partial and particular. Increasingly the State and the political realm is challenged to reflect these differences in its practices, resulting in growing prominence in public life of the anti-discrimination, equal opportunities agenda. The codification of anti-discrimination legislation has also encouraged the dimensions of difference to be seen as forming a unity, and one to be conceptualised in terms of discrimination and exclusion.

Age, in this context, has not achieved the same recognition as the other classic areas of gender, 'race' and class. It still languishes in the territory of the assumed and commonsensical; much as gender did before the feminism of the second wave. It can be argued, however, that age and age ordering are at least as powerful in determining the experiences of individuals as other categories of difference. Anthias (2001) is inclined to exclude age, on the grounds that it encompasses everyone, and is better seen as a factor constituting position in the life course than a social division in itself. But this is to fail to recognise how stratification by age is not a neutral matter, a simple unfolding of changing social roles. Like other social divisions she analyses, it 'involves attributions of capacities and human value and the existence of differential treatment on this basis, including systematic social processes of inferiorisation, hierarchicalisation and unequal resource allocation' (Anthias 2001, p. 843).

The list discussed here is not exhaustive, and claims can be made for other categories of difference – notably religion, but also other social divisions. There is indeed a widely noted tendency for the list itself to proliferate, at times in a somewhat mechanical fashion, as new groups make claims for recognition and acknowledgement. Part of the problem comes from the complex and varying ways in which the categorisations are themselves constructed and deployed within both academic and wider discourse. There is a tension between constructions rooted in discrimination and exclusion, linked to claims in relation to civil rights, equality and citizenship, often the product of conscious mobilisation of identity, and ones based in the academic analysis of social relations of power in which the dimensions of differences represent significant social divisions structuring social relations, cultural expressions and life chances. The ways in which these categories operate and their significance also varies over time and space, between different societies and different historical periods. Fiona Williams (1995) and others suggest that for twentieth-century industrial societies, class, gender and race are the most salient, but that other categories will be significant in other circumstances. Nor are all the categories of equal relevance to all aspects of a given society: sexuality, for example, may be central to certain debates but not others. The categories are, moreover, mutually constitutive, their effects interrelated and multifaceted.

This brings me to the ways in which discussions of difference are increasingly dominated by the debate around intersectionality – the recognition that forms of difference do not simply operate in an additive way, nor necessarily in the same way, but intersect in distinct and particular ways.

Theorising thus needs to be historicised and contextualised in ways that reflect this (Brewer 1993). As yet the debate is most developed in relation to 'race' and gender, though also to some degree, class. Less attention has been paid to other categories, and the ways that these too intersect. Early attempts to address the 'race' critique within feminist analysis rested on an additive approach in which 'race' was added to gender in a way that implied that 'race' increased the degree of inequality and oppression experienced by black women, and that oppression could somehow be compared, even quantified. But race does not make the degree of women's subordination greater; it qualitatively changes its nature (hooks 1984, 1994, Brewer 1993, Maynard 1994). We need to get away from the idea of double or triple marginalisation, with its implications of league tables of oppression, and recognise how the dimensions are interlocking, so that they result in a complex experience of simultaneous, rather than separate, oppressions. hooks's (1984, 1994) work has been particularly influential here. She argues that 'race', gender and class are mutually constituted forms of oppression that together influence the degree to which male domination and privilege can be asserted. Racism and sexism are interlocking systems that uphold and sustain one another; we need to analyse them together, and not as discrete systems of power. These issues have emerged particularly strongly in relation to debates around the family and domestic labour. White feminists had focussed on the family as a key site of the oppression of women. But as black feminists point out, the family was for many women of colour a site of resistance and solidarity in the context of a surrounding white, and often racist, society (hooks 1984). Different family forms in black communities have also meant that the family may not play such a central role in women's subordination. Glenn (1996) and Macdonald and Sirianni (1996), for example, in their account of the re-emergence of paid domestic labour also explore the ways in which gender, 'race' and class interact. Domestic labour particularly in the US, and also in parts of the UK and Europe, is a racialised sector, with work differentially performed by women of colour. Macdonald and Sirianni (1996) argue that white, middle-class women are subordinated to their husbands, and are expected to perform domestic labour for them. Rather than challenging this relationship, they choose to resolve the tension by transferring the burden of work over to black and working-class women. In this way race, gender and class are interlocking systems that draw meaning and power from each other.

The body and difference

The body contributes to the nature of difference, but it does so in complex ways. New theorising has alerted us to the ways in which the body is socially and culturally constructed, inscribed with meanings that locate it within wider systems of ideas and practice. But the relationship between these inscriptions and the body that underlies, receives or expresses them remains contentious. There is a tension, as we noted earlier, between exponents of radical social constructionism and those who are willing to accord some independent reality to the body. These debates are made more complex by the differential way in which the body operates within each of the categories of difference. In the case of class, for example, this operates both at the level of symbolic and expressive practices in the form of bodily gestures and manners inscribing the body and at the more directly physiological level in relation to the building up of differential musculature, height, health status and so on. Class thus operates to create classed bodies in both direct and symbolic ways. In the case of 'race', however, the relationship is slightly different, in that race draws on the prior existence of physical difference, though is not based in it. What is significant in relation to 'race' is the way in which continuous physical differences are turned into social categories. In this way racialised bodies are inscribed with cultural meanings. In relation to gender, there is a tendency to accept that biology has a greater part to play, particularly in relation to reproduction, though its exact role remains contentious; and we have already noted debates between feminists who accord some significance to bodily difference and indeed at times celebrate it, and those who view with suspicion all physiologically based assertions of difference. In relation to ageing, the role of biology is often presented as overwhelming, determining and defining the nature of old age. But, as we shall see, this is increasingly challenged by critics who stress the role of culture in the constitution of old age and old bodies. Parallel debates occur within the disability movement in relation to the significance of impairment. Sexuality presents yet another set of relations between the body and social meanings. The relationship between the body and the dimensions of difference is thus complex and variable. It is important to note, however, how all these categories are constructed against a prescribed norm: that of a white, middle-class man of middle years, able-bodied and heterosexual. It is this dominant subject that constructs other subjects as lesser and Other, and presents their views, or interests, as partial and specific.

Two of the dimensions of difference – age and disability – have their own chapters, and in these we will explore the ways in which we are aged by culture, or made disabled by it. We will look at the heavy emphasis on the body that is characteristic of the cultural presentation of these groups, and the ways in which this is used to undermine their status and restrict their lives. A range of, largely negative, meanings are read onto the aged or disabled body, which is then treated as the source of these meanings. But we will also explore the limits of social constructionism, and the ways in which the fields of ageing and disability present challenges to the more radical versions of this.

We have already referred to the large literature that has emerged around gender and the body; and in the chapters that follow we will explore this further. For example, in the chapter on dieting, we will look at the significance for women of the increasing emphasis on bodily perfectionism that is characteristic of the media-laden consumer society, exploring the rise of eating disorders. The growing use of cosmetic surgery to achieve an idealised gendered body provides another example of the ways in which gender is inscribed on the body, in this case literally with the knife. Gender is also of central significance in health care; and this applies not just to the bodies of patients but also of staff. It is most clear in relation to nursing where the gendered body of the nurse underwrites the construction of nursing as a female occupation, but it is relevant to medicine also. Medical practitioners are also embodied and gendered subjects, and we will explore the significance for this for the differential status accorded to different medical specialisms. Much social care is in fact body care and this effects how the sector is constructed. Bodywork is differentially performed by women, and that gendered character is central to both its organisation and evaluation. The very term 'care' is heavy with gendered connotations, and this again affects how the whole sector is seen – as lesser, as female, as unmarked compared with medicine. Gender is also of central significance in the experiences of old age, and in the chapter on old age (Chapter 3) we will explore the differential impact on men and women of the cultural evaluation of bodily ageing. Lastly gender is also a central theme in the chapter on the body and space, where we will explore the implicit gendering of public space and the implications of this for women who enter such spaces.

In this section I will briefly review issues in relation to class, 'race' and sexuality, since these do not have specific chapters, and comments in relation to them might otherwise be scattered.

Social class

Social class impacts directly and profoundly on bodies. We can see this at a number of levels, the most obvious of which relates to differential morbidity and mortality. The association between social class and health outcome is one of the most persistent in social science and has generated a large and complex literature in the attempt to explain its nature (Blaxter 1990, Delamothe 1991, Townsend *et al.* 1992, Marmot and Shipley 1996, Wilkinson 1992, 1996, Shaw *et al.* 1999, Deaton 2003). Some analysts have tried to look behind the category of 'class' to unpick discrete causative influences, for example, lifestyle factors; the role of low income; differential exposure to danger or environmental damage; psychological influences such as stress or level of esteem; social support; the persistence of earlier causal factors from childhood and before. Others have questioned the conceptualisation in terms of class, preferring other forms of social differentiation such as inequality. There are also suggestions that class may operate differentially through the life course, for example, leading in old age to what has been termed the 'erasure of the social', in which class categorisation comes to have less explanatory power the older the individual gets (Gilleard and Higgs 2000). The role of class is also evidenced in the long-established relationship between social class and height, something that persists today despite improvement in living conditions (Harris 1994). More recently new forms of bodily differentiation have arisen, as we shall see in Chapter 6, with the growing links between obesity and low social class. Similar associations, as we have noted, have emerged – or re-emerged – in relation to teeth.

Social class also inscribes the body in more symbolic and expressive ways. From the work of Mauss and his techniques of the body (1973) to Goffman (1968, 1969) and Douglas (1970) we have been made aware of the ways in which individuals deploy their bodies to express social categorisation, through gestures, bodily stance, hairstyles and clothes, enabling us to 'read' the bodies of others in class terms. The work of Bourdieu has been particularly influential here. Bourdieu (1984) suggests that bodies bear the impact of social class in three main ways. The first relates to social location, in the sense of class-based material circumstances that contexualise individuals' daily lives and contribute to the development of their bodies (Shilling 1993, p. 129). The second factor is habitus, in the sense of socially constituted system of cognitive and motivating structures that provide them with predisposed and class-related ways of behaving and relating. These become located within the body, affecting every aspect of human embodiment (Shilling 1993, p. 129). Habitus is evident in the automatic gestures, or in techniques of the body such as eating, blowing the nose and talking, all of which display and signal the class location of the individual. Lastly bodies are also formed through taste, the processes whereby individuals appropriate choices and preferences that are themselves rooted in material constraints. Taste is thus class culture turned into nature, in that it is embodied. These patterns of taste are how social classes display their cultural capital, and place themselves within the hierarchy of social distinction, and they operate not only at the symbolic or expressive levels, but act directly to build up different forms of bodies. Bourdieu (1984), for example, suggests that the working class traditionally values bodily strength and robustness, and this results in a culture that favours rich, heavy meals, in contrast to the bourgeoisie who pursue slim, chic bodies and refined delicate food, using food choices as a means of displaying discrimination and distinction. Though Bourdieu's work was based in France in the 1970s, as we shall see in Chapter 8, it does have some resonance today. Weight does correlate with social class, and there continue to be significant differences between the classes in terms of food choices (Fine *et al.* 1996, Warde 1997, Crotty 1999). The links between class and the body are thus complex, a mix of the material and the symbolic in which bodies are both formed by, and expressive of, social class.

'Race'

The body is the central site for the processes of racialisation whereby bodily difference is inscribed with social meaning. Social and cultural categories are mapped on to what are continuous bodily differences, so that in relation to skin colour, terms like 'black' and 'white' come to function, not as descriptions of physical difference, but as racialised forms of identity (Mason 2000, Ahmed 2002). Some critics, following Miles, have attacked the continuing use of the term 'race', arguing that it legitimates the views of those who seek to suggest that there are real, biological differences between races (Solomos and Back 1996, Mason 2000). A number of analysts prefer 'ethnicity', as it is less rooted in biological essentialism, more plural and fluid in nature, and more open to self-ascription. Such approaches can, however, support a naïve multiculturalism, especially when allied to postmodern ideas about choice and self-identity. Ethnic identities are not always negotiable, nor are different identities negotiable to the same degree (Song 2003). Like other difference-based discourse, such approaches present the danger of fragmenting into pluralism, where endless differences are described and noted, but their 'real' effects, both material and representational, downplayed and lost. It can also lead to a failure to acknowledge the profound ways in which racism operates as a form of Othering, which objectifies, essentialises and subordinates particular social groups (Maynard 1994). It is thus important to retain a concept of difference that recognises its location within hierarchical relations. Ahmed (2002), while accepting that 'race' as bodily difference is a consequence, rather than the origin, of ethnicity (reversing the commonly held cultural idea that 'race' is an intrinsic property of bodies that comes before ethnicity), argues for the need to retain a concept of 'race'. Substituting ethnicity, she argues, erases too much of the history of the racialisation of bodies.

Ahmed argues that the constitution of 'race' in the nineteenth century presents a similar process to that analysed by Foucault in relation to sex and sexuality. There was a parallel desire to know the 'truths' about the bodies of Others; and this resulted in elaborate taxonomies of race and races, in which the bodies of lower, colonised groups were ordered, characterised and pathologised (sometimes literally, in accounts that stressed their greater vulnerability to disease or their poorer position in the Darwinian competition). The bodies of these Others thus became the means whereby scientists could mark out the difference and superiority of the white man. Rather than finding racial difference, they constituted it, and in this process defined what was normal, ideal and 'white'. In this, whiteness (that the term is still widely used is itself significant) was associated with purity, cleanliness, advancement and reason, and Blackness with dirt, disease, primitiveness and the bodily. Such discursive formations acted to legitimate the colonial project (McClintock 1995, Collingham 2001). Knowledge about these new racialised subjects was collected into an imperial archive, consisting of descriptions, photographs, artefacts, bodily measurements, and at times even flesh and bones. Until recently the bodies of 'primitifs' were displayed in Western museums and ethnographic collections. Bones and tissue samples are still held in anthropological and medical archives; and recently they have become the focus of dispute, as descendants of colonised people have made claims for their return. There are parallels here, as we shall see, with other debates concerning the retention of body parts that we will explore in Chapter 5.

The most notorious example of such appropriation was that of Sarah Bartmann, the 'Hottentot Venus' (Fausto-Sterling 2000) whose body was displayed and, after her death in 1816, publicly dissected and embalmed. As late as the 1980s her skeleton and a cast of her body were on show at the Museum of Natural History in Paris (Fausto-Sterling 2000). Bartmann's body was the subject of a particularly prurient and sexualising discourse focussed on her genitals and buttocks. hooks (1992) in her essay 'Selling hot pussy' relates this to a long subsequent history from Josephine Baker to Tina Turner in which women of colour are presented in popular entertainment as primitive and sexual. These processes of racialisation, in which the bodies of Others are demeaned, apply to other groups also. Gilman (1991) has explored this in relation to anti-Semitism and the 'Jew's body'. The bodies of Irish people in the nineteenth century were similarly racialised in cartoons, given a simian appearance (Curtis 1997). Racism is very bodily in its preoccupations and operation. The processes of racialisation intersect with gender. Bartmann was particularly the focus of interest for comparative anatomists because she was both a 'primitive' and a woman. Nature, as Jordanova (1989) argues in her account of the pictorial representation of doctors and anatomists in the nineteenth century, was presented as a female, as a territory to be unveiled and explored by male doctors and scientists, just as they dissected and laid bare female bodies (at least in pictorial accounts of the processes). That Bartmann was female was important, Fausto-Sterling (2000) argues because it presented the double trope as a person of colour and thus a primitive, and as a female and thus linked to nature. We cannot isolate the production of racialised bodies from the gendering and sexualising of them. Race and gender here interact and reconfigure each other in complex and particular ways. We can see this, for example, in the creation of distinctive subjects, such as that of the black Mammy in nineteenth-century America, or the welfare mother in the twentieth (Jewell 1993). In these, assumptions about race and gender intersect in particular and distinctive ways (Willis and Williams 2002). In relation to masculinity, race has a different set of meanings, as evidenced in the constitution of young black men within discourses about crime and violence, in which their bodies are presented as threatening and primitive.

These processes are not just about the constitution of bodies, but also of emotions. Ahmad, drawing on Merleau-Ponty and phenomenological approaches, points to the ways in which racialisation is something that is experienced and felt, involving the body in its sensual and emotional registers. Gunaratnam and Lewis (2001) in a perceptive article, explore the complex ways in which race is 'felt' and experienced directly in the body. They explore the deep emotionality of racialising practices and discourses, showing how 'anger and fear are absolutely and corrosively intertwined with racism' (p. 133). They use these insights to explore the unconscious aspects of racial dynamics in the setting of social care; and in doing so they foreground the ways in which we are both embodied and psychic subjects. They also suggest some of the ways in which subordinated groups are presented as more emotional than dominant ones, and how this acts both to lessen them, and to confine them to poorly regarded areas of emotional labour. We will return to this in Chapter 7 in relation to carework.

'Race' is of central significance to many of the areas discussed in this book. It is commonly used as a variable in the analysis of health status and outcomes, though some of this literature, particularly in relation to categories of illnesses and diseases, has been criticised for an essentialising approach and for a tendency to treat 'whiteness' as the unexamined body norm (Ahmad 1993, Kelleher and Hillier 1996). 'Race' remains, however, significant in relation to morbidity and mortality, though its operation intersects with other structural factors such as class. The ethnic patterning of ill health in Britain is complex (Nazroo 2001), and is affected by a variety of influences, social and cultural, most of which lie outside the health and social care system. The system itself does, however, reflect systematic racial biases in relation to, for example, differential access to high quality services, or culturally insensitive services, or stereotypical and racist assumptions and behaviour by health care staff (Ahmad and Atkin 1996). The differential treatment that black and ethnic minority people receive within the psychiatric services is particularly well attested (Fernando 2002). Once again this interacts with gender, and it is young black men who are so negatively constituted within psychiatric discourse.

Employment within health care is also racialised, with doctors of colour, along with women, commonly found in less favoured medical specialisms such as psychiatry and geriatrics. Nursing also displays a racialised pattern of employment, with black nurses clustered in the lower levels and in less technically advanced sectors (Mama 1992, Ward 1993 in Ahmad and Atkin 1996). Nursing in Britain also bears the marks of an earlier racialisation in the form of a cohort of older Irish nurses (Kelleher and Hillier 1996). Neo-marxist critics argue that the welfare state plays a key part in the production of race, class and gender divisions, and that it relies on such divisions to help exert downward pressure on the costs of welfare provision. It is certainly the case that black women, particularly of African-Caribbean background, have a long history of employment in the state sector in Britain, particularly in lower levels of the welfare services, not only in nursing but also catering, cleaning and ancillary work, so that they find themselves differentially employed in sectors involving physically heavy, often dirty, work (Mama 1992). In Chapter 7 we will explore some of the implications of this for the analysis of carework, particular the body-based aspect. Within social services, black and ethnic minority clients also find themselves overrepresented in the punitive and controlling areas like child protection and juvenile criminal justice, and underrepresented in the parts of the welfare system that are about distributing benign goods like meals or access to day centres and talking treatments (Dominelli 1989, Ahmad and Atkin 1996, Law 1996). This pattern is repeated in relation to staff, where black workers are also differentially located in lower levels and in the more punitive sectors.

Sexuality

Sexuality is intimately connected with the body. It is through bodies that sexuality is expressed, and sexual acts are quintessentially bodily in character. Indeed there is a sense in which all bodily experiences have a sexual aspect to them, in some degree at least. The link between the body and particular expressions of sexuality is, however, complex and contented. Running through the field of lesbian and gay studies there remains a tension between a predominant social constructionist view of sexuality and the body rooted particularly in postmodernism, and essentialist views that see sexuality as more clearly rooted in the body and individual desire (Plummer 1992, Segal 1997, Saraga 1998). The latter remains a powerful basis for claims to equal treatment; and the postmodern presentation of sexuality has been criticised by some gays and lesbians as denying the reality of gay and lesbian sexual desire, and the very real negative consequences of being gay or lesbian in heterosexual society.

Though homosexual acts have been known for centuries, it is clear that modern homosexual experience is historically distinct, emerging in the nineteenth century when the category of the homosexual was established as part of a wider codification of sexual behaviour and desire (Weeks 1985, Plummer 1992). The key theorist here is Foucault, and his *History of Sexuality* was a major landmark in establishing the new understandings of the fluid and different ways in which same-sex relations have been constituted historically (Foucault 1979, 1987, 1988, Plummer 1992). Sexuality for Foucault is never natural but the product of constellations of power/knowledge. Sexual 'drives', 'preferences' or identities are regulatory fictions, and his work traces the emergence in the nineteenth century of regulatory regimes that order, codify and constitute different forms of sexuality, focussing in particular on the creation of 'the homosexual' as a distinctive category of sexual being. The codification of perverse sexualities acts to define in opposition the nature of normality, entrenching the binary division of heterosexuality/homosexuality that still in large part organises sexuality today. It is, however, an asymmetrical division in which heterosexuality is assumed. It remains simply an aspect of the life of an individual, while homosexuality is deemed to characterise and define the person and his/her life.

The emergence of Queer theory took forward these Foucauldian insights, but allied to the deliberately provocative language of Queer Politics. Queer theory aims to subvert and 'queer' natural sexuality, disturbing hegemonic assumptions about heterosexuality and its links to gender identities. It has been particularly influential in the humanities (Butler 1990, Sedgwick 1990). Heterosexuality not only acts to regulate deviant sexuality, but is also a key institution in the constitution of gender relations; and Butler argues that it is compulsory and naturalised heterosexuality that requires and regulates gender as a binary relation. Heterosexuality is thus not just a sexual practice, but an institution of patriarchal power (Rich 1986). This has important implications for the ways in which gender and sexuality intersect, for heterosexuality is constitutive of both sexual and gender relations. Men use heterosexual privilege against both women and other men, in relation to whom the imputation of gayness acts as an ordering and controlling mechanism (Connell 1995). These complex intersections of gender and sexuality also mean that the meanings and social consequences of being a lesbian women and a gay man are different.

Most of the work that recognises sexuality as a significant social division focusses on homosexuality. To this degree the category of 'sexuality' within public discourse has largely come to imply homosexuality; and most of the literature on the subject is concerned with gay and lesbian experiences. Heterosexuality itself remains undertheorised, rather in the way that masculinity was in the earlier stages of gender studies. More recently, however, work has begun to address this lack, though much of it remains rooted in a gay and lesbian critique (D. Richardson 1996).

Though sexuality is often treated as an area of private life in modern society, public policy plays an important part in its definition and constitution, containing as it does a network of assumptions that implicitly privilege heterosexual relations, acknowledging, supporting and underwriting them, while ignoring, silencing, and to some extent penalising, other sexualities (Richardson 1992, Carabine 1996, 1998). For example, the law has been highly influential in the past in constituting the nature of homosexuality through the definition of deviant and punishable sexual practices. Public policy also operates more indirectly as a regulatory regime through assumptions that reflect, but also amplify, normative ideas about the family and gender relations. At the core of the post-war welfare state has been a set of assumptions about the family, motherhood, women and sexuality (Wilson 1977, Barrett and McIntosh 1982, Carabine 1998). Though there has been some shift towards the recognition of other family forms, the heterosexual family, as currently constituted, retains its dominant position within political discourse. Public policy thus acts to define and reaffirm heterosexuality as the norm, but in doing so, Carabine (1998) argues, also presents opportunities for resistance and sites of contestation, places where the current 'truths' of sexuality can be questioned and the rival discourses of equality and sexual citizenship articulated (Carabine 1998, Donovan *et al.* 1999). The recent growth of legal recognition of homosexual couples across Western societies is an example of this.

Sexuality resonates through many of the subject areas of this book. It is most clearly present in health care. Since the nineteenth century and earlier, doctors and medicine have been closely involved in defining and constituting what is sexual normative, in terms of frequency, patterns, positions, desires and behaviours. Doctors were intimately connected with the discovery, codification and definition of deviant sexualities, and their discourses have played a key role in the constitution of perverse sexuality. Though medicine and psychiatry have retreated from these nineteenth-century roles, they still offer one of the most important sources of discourse regulating sexuality today.

Within the provision of health care, sexuality tends to be a hidden dimension. Heterosexuality is assumed (Wilton 2000). This has implications not just in the more obvious areas of access to fertility treatments, where lesbians may find themselves excluded, or assumptions concerning sexual or reproductive health where heterosexual intercourse may be assumed, but also for a network of assumptions concerning lifestyle and family relations. Gay partners, for example, have only recently in Britain been accepted as next of kin. In the past they have often been excluded from consultations about treatment; and the bodies of partners have not been discharged to them for burial. Similar issues arise in relation to social services where heterosexuality has until recently been the assumed norm, though the spread of anti-discriminatory practice has begun to erode this (Wilton 2000). Gay people in contacting social services are often circumspect in revealing their orientation, partly from a general wariness in exposing personal life to public scrutiny, and also from a concern that homosexuality may be treated as a form of psychological deviance, or at least lesserness, in the eyes of therapeutic, social work culture. Gay people may fear being subsumed under their sexuality, their lives presented in terms of it. Lesbian women in particular have had reason to be wary of this in relation to child custody. Issues of sexuality also resonate through carework particularly in relation to its more intimate bodily forms as we shall see in Chapter 10, where we explore questions of same- and cross-gender tending.

Lastly sexuality – in conjunction with gender – is also relevant to questions of public space and assumptions about the kinds of bodies that are permitted openly to occupy this space. As we shall see in Chapter 9, public space is to important degree constituted around masculinity, and women who enter it do so on terms that require them to behave in ways that do not contest or disrupt this. But in a similar way, public space is heterosexual, as gays and lesbians discover if they attempt to express their sexuality openly in public (Valentine 1996). Gay people can only perform their sexuality in specifically gay spaces, which are typically relegated to the margins (Duncan 1996). The regulatory regime of heterosex is enforced at a number of levels: through public order acts and regulations over behaviour; by verbal aggression and violence against people who behave in a gay way or appear to present a gay identity; or more subtlety through the stares and whispers of the heterosexual gaze. Confronting and contending the production of public space has thus been an important part of Queer politics (Carter 1992, Smith 1992, Valentine 1996).

Conclusion

The body is no longer the unexamined field it was 20 years ago. Rather it has become the focus of a mass of writing, theorising and exploration. Much of this has been rooted in postmodern/poststructuralist perspectives, concerned to show the ways in which the body exists in and through culture, the product of signs and meanings, of discourses and practices. These vary historically and cross-culturally, so there is no single, essential body, but a plurality of bodies, reflecting the shifting configurations of social meanings and material forces that shape the production and reproduction of bodies in different and distinct settings. Among these configurations the dimensions of difference – gender, 'race', class, age, disability and sexuality – are particularly significant. How they operate on the body and how their discourses interact with and constitute bodies, however, varies between the different dimensions and across different historical and cultural settings. In the chapters that follow, we explore the significance of this new writing on the body for understanding the territory of health and social care.

Chapter 3

The Body and Ageing

It may seem strange to start the main part of a book with a chapter on old age. Typically, ageing comes late on, forming the final chapter. Partly this mirrors the progress of the life course, but it also reflects the marginal status of old age, something to be covered quickly at the end. I have chosen, however, to start with ageing because it encapsulates many key themes of this book. Older people, after all, represent the majority client group for health and social care. The bulk of health and social care interventions, and certainly expenditure, in advanced societies are focussed those of late middle age onwards, though this reality is sometimes obscured in order to protect the social and political status of the institution in the context of a wider societal ageism.

Ageing is also central because it enables us to explore the ways in which culture interacts with the bodily. Of all the dimensions of difference, age is the one that seems most deeply embedded in physiology. This is certainly how it is regarded within the popular account of age, which focusses heavily on the bodily signs of age. Indeed to a large extent the popular understanding of age is constructed in terms of such bodily markers. Bio-medical understandings, with their emphasis on the processes of senescence and their account of decline and loss of function, reinforce these perceptions. And yet, as we shall see, culturally based critics have begun to challenge this, suggesting ways in which the aged body is socially and culturally constructed, showing how cultural categories are naturalised in bodies, so that we are as much aged by culture as by physiology. Finally ageing also alerts us to some of the limitations of social constructionism. Bodies themselves age and die, and these brute facts intrude on our discussions, as they do on life. We will address this in particular at the end of the chapter when we turn to the question of the Fourth Age.

The neglect of the body in ageing studies

Ageing studies have not until recently addressed the question of the body. Partly, this was from a desire to get away from the overly medical account of ageing that dominates both professional and popular accounts. Social gerontology in recent years has been strongly influenced by the Political

Economy approach that rightly argues how the lives and experiences of older people are not so much determined by biology, as by social processes and divisions, particularly those of class and gender (Estes 1979, Phillipson and Walker 1986, Estes and Binney 1989, Arber and Ginn 1991, 1995, Phillipson 1998). The approach aims to separate the subject of ageing from the processes of ill health and physical decline that are commonly thought to define it. From this perspective, the body is an uneasy topic, something that should not be stressed; and attempts to focus attention on it can appear a retrograde step.

Resistance to the topic has also come from a feeling that to focus on the bodies of older people is in some sense to demean and reduce them. We noted in Chapter 1 how reference to the bodily in Western culture has the capacity to reduce and objectify, and how these processes are often used in relation to disparaged groups to undermine their status. Older people already suffer from cultural disparagement, and this often centres on their bodies. As a result, social gerontology has tended to avoid the subject of the body as part of its attempt to support good practice and positive images of ageing.

This situation has, however, begun to change, partly under the influence of the new cultural approaches. The intellectual shift away from an emphasis on structure, exemplified by the Political Economy approach, and towards agency, has also encouraged the development of more reflexive accounts that focus on the formation and maintenance of identity, including identity in old age. These have brought questions of the body and its relationship to the self into analytic focus. The changing agenda of feminism has also been influential. Feminism, which was one of the key sources of new writing on the body, was itself initially guilty of a form of ageism in its neglect of the lives and bodies of older women (Ginn and Arber 1995). Increasingly, however, feminist writers have begun to extend the perception of the Personal as Political to the later stages of life, and this has given rise to an engaged body of work addressing the gendered politics of the body in later years. The shift towards a consumer-oriented society and the extension of this to middle and later years has also brought questions of the body and its meaning into prominence in relation to old age. As we shall see, consumer culture is much preoccupied with age resistance, and products and practices focussed around the body play a prominent part in this. Lastly, there has been a growing awareness within sociology of the significance more generally of age and age ordering in the constitution of social relations (Irwin 1999, Hockey and James 2003, Vincent 2003). With the displacement of the centrality of 'class', other dimensions of difference like gender, 'race' and with them age have assumed a new importance in sociological analysis. Just as studies of gender and sexuality have examined the ways in which sex/ gender systems operate in different societies, so age studies are increasingly exploring the ways in which age differences are located in discursive formations, social practices and material conditions (Woodward 1999). The body is prominent in many of these.

Aged by culture

New writing around the body and age emerged particularly strongly within the humanities, influenced by postmodern and poststructuralist perspectives (Cole 1992, Featherstone and Wernick 1995, Katz 1996, Gubrium and Holstein 1999, Tulle-Winton 1999, Walker 1999, Woodward 1999, Andersson 2002). Such cultural approaches have aimed to replace essentialising discourses in relation to the body by ones that recognise its nature as a social text, something that is both formed and given meaning within culture. The ageing body is thus not natural, not pre-discursive, but fashioned by and within culture. Foremost among these cultural critics is Margaret Gullette (1997), and in her classic account *Declining to Decline*, she argues that though we think we are aged by our bodies, in fact we are aged by culture. Culture is saturated with ideas of age and ageing, with the result that people internalise a mass of beliefs and feelings about midlife and beyond. Dominant culture teaches us to feel bad about ageing and to start this early. The system that maintains the decline meanings of midlife depends on an enormous range of subtle and blatant coercive discourses. We inhale this atmosphere daily: doses of its toxicity waft from cartoons, billboards, birthday cards, coffee mugs, newspaper articles, fiction, poetry (Gullette 1997, p. 5). Youth in this ideology is the period of fun, energy, sexuality, intensity and hope, holding all the cultural goods. In the soliloquy of age anxiety, we debate with ourselves the point at which we too have to move on to the new and unhappy aged class, reading our bodies for signs of decay that point to this transition.

Declining to Decline is a passionate book that uses the language of struggle, as its subtitle *Cultural Combat and the Politics of Midlife* suggests. Gullette believes that we are precociously and cruelly aged by culture, and that our response should be one of resistance. This does not mean that she denies the physical realities of ageing, but she argues we have been taught to read these in a narrow and particular way that is erosive of the self, so that the narrative of decline has replaced all other sources of interpretation and meaning. Woodward (1991) similarly locates the issue in culture. For her, our cultural categories here are essentially reducible into two: youth and age, hierarchically arranged. We are judged not by how old we are, but by how young we are not. The old, from the perspective of dominant culture, represent a disruption of the visual field (Furman 1999). Like the disabled or abnormal, they come to be presented as the Other, evaluated as 'less than...', so that ageing becomes a version of Goffman's 'spoilt identity'.

Identity is also at the heart of Featherstone and Hepworth's (1991) account of the Mask of Ageing, in which they characterise ageing in terms of the growing tension between external appearance and internal identity. They recount the commonly expressed feeling of disjunction between the ageing face in the mirror and the sense of self as persistently young. The self becomes a prisoner of the ageing body which is no longer able to express its identity behind this culturally imposed mask.

The negative meanings of bodily ageing are often thought to impact particularly strongly on women, and feminists have been prominent in the new writing on age (Sontag 1979, Greer 1991, Woodward 1991, 1999, Friedan 1993, Gullette 1997, Bartky 1999, Walker 1999, Twigg 2003). Much of the power of this literature comes from the fact that it is grounded in the voices of those who are themselves subject to age oppression, or see themselves as becoming increasingly so. To this extent feminist gerontology can be located within the wider set of emancipatory projects that aim to develop epistemologies in the social sciences that challenge dominant perceptions, by starting from the perspective of the lives of the marginal-ised and oppressed, in this case, the old (Laws 1995). Sontag (1979) argues that women are subject to a double standard in ageing that undermines the traditional source of their power. Women are traditionally evaluated in terms of their looks, their status residing not just in beauty but also in youth. Ageing thus represents a diminution of status. Power for men, by contrast, resides in money, status and social dominance; and for them the early signs of ageing, like grey hair, are read as marks of authority and maturity. Some women report becoming socially invisible after the meno-pause, no longer a focus of male attention (Greer 1991), sidelined in the power stakes and finding no reflection of their situations in the cultural imagery of advertising or the media. As Woodward (1999) comments, the older female body is both invisible – in that its is no longer seen – and hypervisible – in that it is all that is seen.

Feminists have long argued that women are subject throughout their lives to beauty ideals that erode their confidence, divert their energies and act to keep them subordinate to men (Wolf 1990). For Furman (1997, 1999), such processes continue to operate in old age, but in a new and more damaging way. Furman studied the attitudes of older women using a beauty shop in New Jersey. The majority of her respondents were active and vital, though in their late sixties and older. The disability they suffered from was a socially constructed one: the incapacity to look young and be considered attractive, and thus to be publicly 'visible' and valued. As women, they were not just subject to the male gaze, but to an additional and erosive force, that of the gaze of youth. The loss of the ability to meet the youthful beauty norm produced shame. Women feel pressure to look as young as possible and to hide the secret that they are old because that admission is devastating to social acceptability and self-esteem. Looking old transgresses contemporary ideals of feminine beauty. A woman who had let herself go was felt to have failed to maintain the disciplinary practices of femininity, transgressing central norms of the culture.

Ageism and the body

Ageism is a bodily form of oppression (Laws 1995). It operates on and through the body. Meanings of a largely negative character are read on to the aged body, which are then used to justify exclusionary practices, underwriting the presentation of the old as essentially different. Relatively minor physical differences become manifestations of fundamental Otherness, as old people are constructed as a category in themselves. Here age is different from other dimensions of difference. Unlike sexism or racism, those who practise ageism will someday themselves be old (Andrews 1999, Irwin 1999). They will join the group that at present they discriminate against. Denial as well as projection is thus fundamental to the way in which it works. At the heart of ageism is the fear not just of illness and decline, but also of death. Existential fears about death as Robert Butler, Norbert Elias and others have argued, act to reinforce the idea of older people as separate and Other (Bytheway 1995, Irwin 1999). Ageism and the practices that go with it are thus part of the way in which society deals with a reality that it is afraid of, and that it fundamentally has little to say about.

These elements of fear and denial are part of the reason why age has not become a focus for identity politics in the ways that some of the other dimensions of difference, such as gender and sexuality, have. There have been attempts to mobilise older people, for example, in the UK in the pensioner movement, or in grass-roots local groupings such as the Hen Co-Op (1993), but they have remained marginal and small scale. In the US there has been greater mobilisation with associations like the Gray Panthers, but in general age has not become the basis for a mass movement or achieved the status of lifestyle politics. The fundamental problem lies in the culture of age denial and its erosive impact on solidarity. This is particularly strong, Gilleard and Higgs (2000) argue, among older people with material and cultural capital, who are not attracted by appeals to aged status. Their aspiration is to stay 'young', and to hold on to their status within mainstream culture. By the stage when they have unequivocally moved into the category of the 'old', their capacity to challenge oppression and to mobilise opposition has been considerably reduced.

Ageism and denial also underwrite many of the negative ways in which older people are treated in the care system. It plays a profound part in the dynamics of abuse, which rest on a denial of connectedness with the abused other. At a lesser level it underlies the often puzzled responses of careworkers to the disjunction presented to them between the past lives and present bodies of their clients. Careworkers, for example, are often perturbed when presented with photographs of their clients in their earlier years. They find it difficult to link up the youthful picture in the photograph – the wartime RAF pilot, the beautiful bride – with the old person in front of them (Twigg 2000a). The body is key to this because it is there that the disjunction is experienced. It is the bodily appearance of the old person that places them into the category of the old. This is then reified, in such a way that the fact that these are people who were themselves once young is suppressed and denied, at least at the emotional level.

Ageism does not just operate at the level of cultural interpretation and representation, but can act directly on the bodies of older people, creating and building up distinctively aged bodies (Gilleard and Higgs 2000). The clearest examples of this are in relation to health care where ageist assumptions exclude older people from beneficial treatments, and endorse low expectations of functioning and well-being by treating them as a natural consequence of old age. Examples of this in the UK include: the failure to provide routine breast cancer screening for women over 65, though the incidence of such cases rises with age; the denial of dialysis to older patients, though they would continue to benefit from this; the failure to investigate cancers fully; and the limited use of beneficial surgery in relation to heart conditions. All in their way act on the bodies of older people, increasing their likelihood of illness and premature death (Gilleard and Higgs 2000). As significant as these denials of potentially life saving treatments is the failure to provide forms of rehabilitation that would improve functioning, or to address conditions like incontinence that are associated with old age but that suffer from low medical priority. Though in Britain the recent National Service Framework for Older People (Department of Health 2001) aims to root out such practices and assumptions, they are still pervasive in the care system. The bodies of older people are thus shaped to be more disabled and more dysfunctional than they need be, and this fact is obscured by the pervasive discourse of senescence that presents old age as a time of illness and physical failure, naturalising problems that could be alleviated.

Ageist culture also impacts on the bodies of older people in more subtle ways. Gilleard and Higgs (2000) argue that older people internalise negative messages about themselves and their bodies in such a way as to erode their confidence and self-esteem, and undermine bodily and mental performance. Failings or errors that in a younger person would be passed over without remark become signs of age and evidence of decline and, in their turn, a source of further loss of confidence. Ageist attitudes can also limit older people's access to health-promoting practices and sites. Many older people retreat from engagement with aspects of social life because they feel that they are no longer appropriate for someone who is not young. Older women in particular can feel self-conscious about taking exercise, or engaging in sport. Gyms and swimming pools are perceived as spaces that belong to the young; indeed the whole idea of sport and exercise is imbued with a youthful ethic that discourages participation by the old. Though health promotion strategies now do more to target those of middle years, relatively little is done to promote physical activity among older age groups.

Ageing in consumer culture

Negative attitudes to old age and bodily decline are not new, but what is new is their pervasive articulation within a consumer culture. We discussed earlier the significance of consumption for the experience of the body in high modernity and its role in the negotiation of contemporary identities. The key link here lies in the nature of consumer culture as quintessentially youth oriented. The bodily perfection it celebrates is that of youth, and this has profound consequences for how we experience ageing in post or high modernity. Resisting age is now an integral part of the Western lifestyle, and one that supports a massive consumer industry in terms of cosmetics, hair dyes, vitamin supplements, exercise regimes, advice books – all dedicated to keeping young. This culture of anti-ageing is not confined to those in middle or later years, but extends to younger age groups.

This perfectionism of the body finds one of its clearest expressions in the expanding industry of cosmetic surgery. Though most of the debate on this has centred around issues of breast augmentation or other proce-dures aimed at younger women (Davis 1995, Negrin 2002), a major part of cosmetic surgery is concerned with anti-ageing (BAAPS 2005). Leisure too has become increasingly implicated in age resistance, with a range of bodily practices – toning, jogging, exercising – each with its own commercial expression in the form of venues, clothes, equipment and publications. These technologies of the self are often promoted and experienced in terms of empowerment and of taking control of your life, the bodily expression of new beginnings and new engagement, but, as we shall see in Chapter 7 in relation to the culture of dieting, they also contain harsher and more puritanical strands. Consumer-oriented interven-tions are highly ambivalent here. Though they contain upbeat, optimistic messages about how to remain youthful in body and spirit, they also feed the fear of ageing, creating a surrounding culture of age denial. Consumer culture creates and amplifies the desires and fears that its goods claim to be able to satisfy or assuage; and this is as true of ageing as it is of other aspirations. The vast industry of age denial thus does not just reflect culture, but amplifies it.

Part of the reason for the increasing focus on bodily ageing comes from the rise of new technologies of surveillance. The contemporary body is subject to review to a degree that was not so in the past. The modern ubiquity of mirrors and the arrival in the twentieth century of the bathroom as a space where the whole body could be observed naked have allowed for new forms of reflexive self-scrutiny in which the body and its changes become the focus of acute attention. Photographs, as Sontag argues, rather than preserving a sense of identity act to undermine it. They testify to time's relentless melt, augmenting the sense of temporal dislocation (Hockey and James 2003).

We are increasingly surrounded by a visual culture that erases the old. There has, of course, always been something of this, and earlier pictorial culture was also biased towards youth and beauty. What has changed however is the massive increase in the level of visual representation. We are surrounded by images; they are presented to us from all sides by the media. But these rarely depict the old, indeed even for those in middle years the presentation is highly selective. Media culture is also preoccupied with the body, and images of naked or semi-naked bodies have become ubiquitous. But they are the bodies of advertising: selected, disciplined and airbrushed into perfection. Feminists like Susan Bordo (1993) and Naomi Wolf (1990) have critiqued this emphasis on unattainable perfection and its impact on the self-esteem and well-being of younger women in terms of the cultures of dieting and of the beauty myth, but these arguments extend to later years also. Older women do not find cultural endorsement in public images, indeed the depiction of old bodies has become something of a taboo, as Tulle-Winton (2000) shows in her discussion of the photographic images presented in Cumming's *Pretty Ribbons* (1996), which depicts a naked woman in her eighties in strong, hard light. In current culture these images are highly transgressive.

Changes in relation to the life course have impacted on the way we regard our bodies. The pathways to ageing are less clear. Established patterns of employment, education and family building have become disrupted, partly as a result of greater flexibility and choice in individuals' lives and also of unstable labour markets. These can unpredictably precipitate individuals back into earlier stages of life, presenting issues around the relationship between bodily age and appearance. The greater instability of marriage and personal relationships means that questions of sexual attractiveness and physical appearance remain significant into the middle years in a way that was less so in the past. People's aspirations in relation to sexuality are also higher, and increasingly extended into later years, as the debates around Viagra and HRT suggest (Mamo and Tishman 2001, Marshall and Katz 2003).

Though most of the commercial culture of anti-ageing is aimed at women, men do not escape its impact. Gullette (1997) suggests that gender hierarchies are breaking down here, and though men once had immunity from such forces as a group, under the impact of consumer culture, they are losing it. The growing commercial exploitation of men's bodies is reducing older men to the same status as older women, in this case their identities undermined by the equation of masculinity with youth, as older men find themselves in a commercial culture of masculinity that is increasingly body focussed.

The engagement of older people in consumer culture should not be seen in wholly negative terms. It is a product of their growing economic and cultural presence in society. Increasing numbers of older people have the means and aspirations to spend money on consumption, including consumption in relation to the body and the enhancement of appearance and well-being. Furthermore, those now in their fifties and early sixties are the generation that was socialised in emergent youth culture (Gilleard and Higgs 2000, Gilleard 2002), and they are unwilling to accept exclusion from the majority concerns of fashion, personal appearance and attractiveness. Cultural practices like dying hair, for example, which in previous generations were furtive activities, are reassessed and presented in terms of continuity with the wider culture in which 'colouring' hair is commonplace.

Furthermore, these developments occur within a newly defined social space: that of extended middle years. This new social space has been created out of economic and demographic changes of the post-war era. Growing numbers of people survive into retirement, including lengthy periods of retirement with good health. The spread of pension provision has meant that there are rising numbers in this cohort who are comfortably off and who can support a consumerist life style. There are also, of course, significant numbers who live in poverty, and the current anxieties about the future of pensions suggest that this group will in fact grow. However, the aspiration to this consumption-oriented lifestyle in retirement has become culturally entrenched, to the extent that it has begun to change people's ideas of the later years, or at least the earlier stages of these. Gilleard and Higgs (2000) argue that social gerontology and social policy have failed to recognise the significance of these shifts. By focussing on problematic old age and on issues of poverty and social exclusion, they have missed what is the reality of later years for many people: a period of enjoyment, leisure and new opportunities in which issues of identity and self-development can be pursued. This, they argue, is the new norm, and one that the new cultural analyses have allowed us to see.

Limitations of culturalist approaches

I have argued so far for the gains that come from the use of culturalist approaches to old age, and I want now to discuss briefly to some of their limitations. The first concerns the radical social constructionism that underlies some of these accounts and that questions the existence of any bodily substratum to human culture – or at least to our capacity to know it. But as we have seen, ageing forces us to engage with physiology, not least because of the ultimate undeniability of death. There is a limit to the plasticity of the body. It is one thing to talk about hair dyes and face lifts but, as we all know, such attempts to deny the effects of ageing ultimately fail; and Hockey and James (2003) note the 'hollow laughter' that greets some of the more extreme postmodern assertions of agency and choice in this area.

For Kontos (1999) the emphasis on discourse and culture and the rejection of physiology within these approaches, is unhelpful, perversely acting to breathe new life into the old dualism of mind and body. The account given in Featherstone and Hepworth's (1991) Mask of Ageing, she argues, only really works if we accept the dichotomy between what is shown and a reality that lies beneath. But to think in this way is to remain bound in the old Platonic Christian tradition that presented the body as form of imprisonment, with the spirit or soul representing the reality that it seeks to transcend (Öberg 1996). Here the self is regarded as radically separate from the body, something dissociated from its corporeality. But recent work on the body and embodiment has been concerned to destabilise this inheritance of Cartesian dualism, exploring instead the ways in which body and self are inextricably entwined. By regarding the body as wholly constituted in discourse and only knowable through it, such accounts foreclose on the understanding of how the body and self are formed and reformed in a dialectal relationship (Kontos 1999). Andrews (1999) similarly argues that the ideal of agelessness, though seductive, is ultimately a false one, requiring the person to deny who or what they are. Our bodies and ourselves both age; and that is a central part of our being. To assert agelessness is not to challenge ageism but to internalise it. Though superficially an assertion of worth, Andrews argues, it endorses these negative valuations. Such strategies are ultimately disempowering because they require you to deny who or what you are, so that the dignity of the self is replaced by a form of self-loathing.

The second criticism concerns the focus in much of this literature on identity and its fluid nature within high or postmodernity. Though the perceptions that underlie this analysis are important, the argument is often exaggerated. Consumption is an important source of modern identities, and advertising certainly plays up this feature, but it is not the only, or indeed the most important, source. Traditional social structures like family, gender, class remain powerful sources (Tomlinson 2003).

Postmodern accounts in terms of consumer culture also fail to engage with the degree to which material and structural factors shape, even determine, the lives of older people. In reality, the consumption-oriented model of later life is only available to certain groups. Many older people on limited incomes are excluded from this dream. Current projections in relation to the income of future cohorts of pensioners in the UK, moreover, suggests that this group is likely to grow, as larger proportions of older people are forced to live on means-tested, poverty-related benefits. People may also be forced in the future to work longer into old age in order to build up adequate pensions. For large sections of the population therefore, the new social space of the post-retirement Third Age may be about to disappear.

This brings me to the problem of the scope of what we are talking about when we refer to ageing and old age. It is clear that what cultural critics like Gullette (1997) and Gilleard and Higgs (2000) are really addressing is the phenomenon of late middle age. Part of the problem comes from the width of the categorisation. Later years in the modern West have traditionally been defined in terms of the period post-retirement, and categories like 'older people', 'pensioners', 'elders' are often used interchangeably. But this is to lump together a very disparate group. It was to meet this criticism that the distinction between the Third and Fourth Age was developed. Flexibly defined, the Third Age is marked, at one end by the transition into retirement, and the other by the arrival of major health problems; and it corresponds roughly to the period of mid-fifties–mid-seventies, though individuals will make the transition at different ages. Gilleard and Higgs (2000) are right to identify the significance of the new social space of the Third Age, and the need for an analysis of it that is not rooted in problematic ageing. But their approach is open to the common critique of the concept of the Third Age that it is able to construct an optimistic account of ageing only by virtue of projecting into a dark Fourth Age all the problems and difficulties.

The challenge of the Fourth Age

The distinction between the Third and Fourth Age is, properly speaking, qualitative not chronological; and the factor that overwhelmingly precipitates individuals from one to the other is health. It is thus the body and its state that is the crucial determinant. But the new literature on the body does not tackle this stage. It remains wedded to the Third Age, and when we turn to writing on the Fourth Age, we encounter a very different literature, in which the postmodern themes of identity, subjectivity, cultural construction evaporate, to be replaced by dependency, frailty, deficit and burden. This is a literature that is written from the outside. It is objectifying, distant, often couched in the language of professionals and policy makers. It adopts the perspective of experts and other agents of control. It is about Them, not Us. These are the old as constituted in social care.

The challenge for writing on the body, therefore, lies in trying to recover the subjective experiences of this stage of life too. I tried to do something of this in a study of bathing (Twigg 2000a), but the focus was limited. Addressing the bodily in deep old age is not easy. We noted earlier some of the cultural barriers to doing this. There is also the point that the coping strategies of old age depend, to considerable degree, on the denial of the body. As with pain, and certain forms of chronic illness, the optimum strategy for the individual may be to try to transcend and escape from the bodily, so that there are circumstances in which the Cartesian division of mind and body, or spirit and body, may be the most helpful approach.

But the Fourth Age is also marked by the fact that it lies next to death. Modern societies as Vincent (2003) notes are unique in the degree to which death is concentrated in old age and this profoundly affects how it is regarded. By and large, modern secular society is silent about death. As a result, it can find little to say about the stage that precedes it: old age. Death empties old age of meaning. This in turn affects how old age is treated in the academic and policy literature. It is hard to invest the body in old age with a stronger sense of subjectivity, when old age itself is avoided as a topic, seen as having no meaning, or at least no meaning other than decay, decline and final absence. Death presents particularly acute existential problems for modern society. The radical individualism that underpins modern culture means that death is an affront to meaning (Berger 1969). Under conditions of high- or postmodernity, the body, Giddens (1991) argues, assumes new importance as a focus of identity, but this makes its decline and death all the more problematic. Death increasingly takes place in a culture that is secular. Though the concept of secularisation is sociologically contended (Martin 1978, Wilson 1982, Davie 1994), it is clear that the beliefs and practices within which death was once embedded and which gave it meaning have been severely eroded.

The evacuation of meaning from old age needs also to be seen in the context of the rise of scientific medicine as the socially authoritative source of knowledge about old age. Cole (1992) and Katz (1996) have outlined the slow historical transition from existential to scientific modes of understanding of ageing; and they trace the shift from communal ideals of transcendence, rooted in religious systems and embodied in images such as the pilgrimage of life, or the ages of man, to scientific and individualistic ways of understanding it. In the early modern period, the human body and its ageing was understood as something that occurred within a wider cosmological system (Katz 1996). The life course was divided into stages, each with its appropriate activities and duties. Spiritual growth could occur independently of bodily decline, so that old age, though a time of body failure, could also be a period of spiritual opportunity (Katz 1996). The period before death was meaningful; indeed it represented a particularly significant stage in the pilgrimage of life. But from the eighteenth century onwards this account of the body and of age was increasingly replaced by a modern scientific one that focussed, not on the state of the person as a whole – their vitality, humoural balance, or character of life – but on a level below, on discrete systems of the body and on specific pathologies. The body came to be seen as an object for neutral scientific study. The aged body was increasingly conceptualised in terms of a series of inevitable degenerative processes. It was also increasingly conceptualised as dying. In the early modern period, death was a mysterious force ranging through the world, outside the boundaries of bodily life. It came upon you unexpectedly. But from the early nineteenth century, clinical research began to locate death within the body itself. Ageing came to be seen as a progressive disease caused by a multitude of physiological changes. The aged body, no matter how healthy or alive, was conceptualised in terms of the signs of senescence that distinguished it from the healthy bodies of the young. Old age was thus pathologised within medicine, and presented in terms of a narrative of decline and loss of function (Kalz 1996).

Cole (1992) argues that this shift in understanding has had serious consequences for how we see old age, leading to its cultural and symbolic impoverishment. All societies establish systems of meaning that help people orient themselves towards the intractable limits of human existence. In the past such systems were dominated by religion. Today they are dominated by science. The problem is that the meanings science can offer are limited. It can do little to address existential questions. Ageing has moved from being understood as a problem requiring moral and spiritual engagement to being one that is scientific in nature, requiring technical solutions. Some of the problems of old age can be alleviated in this way – and Cole is clear that they should be – but others, like physical decline and death, are by their nature intractable. Modern medicine has little to offer here, and yet its systems of thought are the ones that have come to dominate the field.

Modern medicine is also, to considerable degree, structured around the goal of preventing death. It is heavily biased towards cure, rather than just care. In this context, the concept of a 'good death' – and with that, the concept of a good old age – becomes increasingly difficult to establish (Vincent 2003). From the perspective of bio-med, everything ends in failure, and this has profound consequences for the field of health and social care.

Conclusion

I want to conclude by suggesting some of the ways in which new work on the body, which has largely arisen within sociology and the humanities, can bring insights to the more policy-oriented fields of health and social care. Old age within these areas has traditionally been constructed in an overly narrow way, focussing on frailty, dependence, burden and cost. But as we have seen, this is far from the whole truth about old age, which is a much more diverse and varying experience than this would suggest. Gilleard and Higgs (2000) question the primacy of the state and social policy in determining the narrative of old age, arguing for the need to look at the multiplicity of sources that provide the texts and practices shaping the lives of older people. Among these are ideas about consumption and the body. The traditional social welfare account of old age does not adequately reflect the lives and experiences of older people, particularly the relatively large numbers who are healthy, active and socially engaged. Widening the account of old age to encompass cultural analysis helps us to do this. Focussing on the body can also, ironically, help to disrupt the narrative of frailty and decline that is commonly presented as rooted in the body, showing how bodily experiences in ageing are both more diverse and more rooted in social and cultural constructions than this account would allow.

Questioning the narrative of old age also allow us to see the ways in which social and public policy is implicated in many of the processes that this literature seeks to analyse. Katz (1996), with his Foucauldian account of the modern constitution of old age, presents three institutions as central in its emergence: the alms house, the pension system and the population survey. Each in its different way acts to define, separate out and classify the aged as a social group; and each is an instrument of social policy. Destabilising the discourses of age, looking behind the ways in which they work, allows us to question the ways in which policy is itself constituted. Social policy in dealing with old age needs to understand the forces, social and cultural, that have defined this stage of life.

This brings me to the third area of relevance which concerns the focus on questions of identity and self that are at the centre of much of this writing. Public policy in relation to the old has traditionally been conceptualised in terms of accounts from the outside, in which the objects of policy are presented for analysis, their lives measured, evaluated and ordered in terms of the concerns of policy makers and other experts. Such accounts rarely address questions of identity or subjectivity. The new writing on ageing, however, focusses strongly on these aspects, and in so doing attempts to wrestle the account of age out of hands of experts, and to relocate it at the level of agency and self-identity. This has potentially important consequences for how public policy views this stage in life, for example underwriting a potential shift towards a much stronger user-focus. As we shall see in the next chapter there are parallels here with disability. Recovering the narrative of subjectivity in old age also presents challenges. We noted the lack of work that addresses the subjective experiences of growing old in the Fourth Age, and we need to extend the insights deriving from the experiences of the Third Age to later stages of life also.

The new focus on the body also allows us to see the ways in which ageism operates at a directly bodily level. Within the dominant Political Economy approach, the marginalisation of old people is primarily seen as the product of economic and material exclusion. But as we have seen, there is more to the issue than just poverty. The meanings of ageing and the ways in which the ageing body is constructed within culture are themselves significant in determining the circumstances and experiences of older people, being used to justify responses that underlie their marginalisation and exclusion. Many of the negative feelings that people have about ageing are projected on to old people themselves and in particularly on to their bodies. Ageism, like other forms of prejudice, is very bodily in its operation, focussing on the bodies of the excluded, in a demeaning and objectifying way. Older people enjoy a lesser form of citizenship, and this underwrites a variety of discriminatory practices within the service system. At one extreme, it endorses recurrent institutional abuse in the form of violence, cruelty, denigration and active neglect. In lesser form, it justifies poor facilities, casual responses, and a take-it-or-leave-it style of provision. The staff who care for and manage older clients are less likely to be qualified, and harder to recruit than those who deal with other client groups. The ethos of services for older people is less likely to be optimistic or client-centered than is the case where the clients are younger, and this clearly reflects ageist attitudes.

Lastly, themes around the body are relevant to arguments concerning the restructuring of the welfare state under late capitalism, in particular the shift away from collective, state-based solutions towards individualised, private ones. Under the impact of neo-liberalism, welfare in many Western countries is being increasingly reconstituted as a private responsibility, the outcome of individual agency and self-determination. This chimes well with the rhetoric of the Third Age, with its emphasis on personal responsibility, self-improvement and active choice. Consumer culture is strongly individualistic; it celebrates agency, encouraging people to see their bodies as the products of personal intervention and effort. This can bring benefits, encouraging people to take action in regard to their health, for example in relation to smoking, weight, exercise, but it also endorses a view of health and illness as the product of personal effort and virtue, rather than deeper structural determinants. In a subtle way, illness, together with poverty, depression and other social ills, comes to be seen as forms of individual failure, and with this commitment to their alleviation as a collective responsibility is undermined.

Chapter 4

Disability and the Body

The last three decades have witnessed a flowering of disability theory. Driven forward by disabled activists, this challenges not just the day-to-day oppressions that disabled people face, but the implicit theoretical structures that underlie them. The approach is particularly associated with the social model of disability, which provides a unifying and politically oriented account of the field. It rejects the dominant medical account with its emphasis on physical impairment and discourse of personal tragedy, and presents disability as arising instead from a disablist society that erects barriers, both physical and mental, to the inclusion of disabled people, confining them to segregated and stigmatised spaces and social conditions (UPIAS 1976, Oliver 1990, Morris 1992, 1993, Campbell and Oliver 1996). It is a civil-rights approach that presents disabled people as a politically oppressed minority on a parallel with other groups, and locates the problem in the social environment, not in the individual.

Within this paradigm, the topic of the body has been associated with a reactionary and oppressive discourse, one that demeans disabled people by focussing on the dysfunctional nature of their bodies and the individual problems these pose. As a result, there has been little engagement until recently with the sociology of the body. This contrasts with other identity-based movements like feminism and the gay movement, which have drawn heavily on such theorising. As we have seen, feminism in particular has been interested in renegotiating the boundaries of the biological and the social, deconstructing the earlier distinction between sex and gender, exploring how sexuality and the body are themselves socially constructed, the product of discourses and performative regimes. Queer theory has explored similar territory in relation to sexuality. Until recently, however, the disability movement has been keen to maintain a clear boundary between impairment, understood in terms of specific physiological dysfunction, and disability, understood as the impact of wider societal expectations, focussing only on the latter. In part this points to the different role of embodiment and the physical body in the constitution of different dimensions of difference, but it also reflects the degree to which a single theoretical model – that of the social model – has dominated thinking in the field.

Revising the social model: Refocussing on the body

More recently, however, the social model has been subject to challenge, and the role of the body and of impairment has been central in this. Critiques have been advanced from a number of directions. The first focusses on the nature and diversity of the disabled population. The social model reflects the experiences of the generation who pioneered the disability movement in the 1970s. Many were young, fit men, wheelchair users with spinal injuries caused by traffic accidents and, in the United States, by the Vietnam War, and this gave a particular character to their activism and theorising. But as Bury (1995, 1997), S.J. Williams (1996, 1999) and others point out, the majority of those with disabilities are in fact in late middle age or older, suffering from degenerative illnesses or other chronic conditions. These critics question the relevance of the social model's exclusive focus on disabling society, arguing that it presents a falsely unitary account of disability that fails to address the range of conditions and impairments. For example, problems with communication and language such as stroke or deafness are poorly caught by its theorising, as are mental or intellectual difficulties, whether arising from head injuries, severe mental health problems, learning disabilities or dementia. The social model assumes a certain type of independence, rationality and self-sufficiency – that is the basis of its advocacy and demands for autonomy – and people who need someone to speak for them cannot always command these qualities (Barnes and Mercer 2003). The nature of impairment is thus highly significant in the experience and meaning of disabilities, and cannot simply be treated as background to a wider societal exclusion.

The second critique relates to the undertheorising of impairment. The social model draws a sharp distinction between disability and impairment. But, as Hughes and Paterson (1997) argue, wresting disability from the conceptual clutches of medicine and presenting it as something socially created has had the negative consequence of driving impairment back into the theoretical shadows, leaving a large part of the experience of disabled people undescribed and untheorised.

This connects with the third area of criticism, which concerns the way that the social model fails to engage with the lived experiences of disabled people, particularly the lived experiences of the body. As Morris percipiently wrote in 1991: 'there is a tendency within the social model of disability to deny the experience of our own bodies' (p. 10). Pioneers of the social model like Finkelstein (1996) dislike any focus on the personal and experiential, seeing it as a return to the old case-file mentality, something that undermines political activism, through its emphasis on private areas of life, rather than the public domain of political struggle. There is a gendered dimension in this. As many commentators have noted, the disability movement in its early years was imbued with a masculinist ethos, and Morris and other feminists had to struggle to get their voices heard (Morris 1991, 1992, 1996). The exclusion of the personal was part of this. But as Carol Thomas (1999) argues, rejecting the personal is a poor strategy for an emancipatory movement like disability. She draws parallels with feminism, showing how it explored the ways in which personal life was labelled female and devalued, and thus excluded from malestream academic analysis, with the result that important areas of social life remained shrouded, hidden from enquiry. For Thomas, Finkelstein's approach reflects this sort of approach, offering a throwback to an earlier discredited model of politics, one that shies away from the personal, treating it as of no real political or intellectual interest.

Concern with the personal is important for disability because it lies at the heart of some of its most painful experiences, many of which relate directly to the body and the way it is perceived. The social model has in many ways rendered these subjects unspeakable, putting off-limits aspects of the social oppression of disabled people that are deeply felt, concerning issues such as sexuality, self-esteem, personal relationships. As Seymour (1998) comments, the hardest aspects of disability are often the most difficult to talk about, partly because they are so personally painful, and partly because they relate to areas of life that are traditionally treated as private. Some impairments are accompanied by pain or incontinence, and these bodily experiences affect the experience of disability profoundly. The social model with its focus on the surrounding social world seems to want to erase discussion of them. This is not to argue that incontinence or sexuality or issues around appearance and self-esteem are pre-social phenomena, or that the difficulties that disabled people face in these areas are the natural result of impairment. They need to be seen in the context of wider disablist culture and the discourses of disability that shape the experiences of disabled people in a profoundly negative way. But they remain of central significance to disabled people, and need to be discussed and theorised.

This brings me to the fourth area of critique, which concerns the general neglect of culture within the social model. Disabled people have to fight against not only social segregation and exclusion, but also the damaging discourses that construct them as Other, as deformed, as abject. The body is central in much of this. It is socio-cultural processes that sustain these negative stereotypes, meanings, images, that are in turn internalised by disabled people, impacting profoundly on their self-esteem. For these reasons the social model's concept of oppression needs to be extended to include what Thomas terms 'the socially engendered undermining of [disabled people's] psycho-emotional wellbeing' (1999, p. 60). Culture and the cultural interpretation of the body play a key role in this.

Representing disability: Visual culture

In response to these criticisms, disability theorists have recently turned their attention to the cultural realm and to the politics of representation, and in doing so they have broken through earlier taboos concerning the discussion of the impaired body, exploring the ways in which the constitution of the visual realm is central to the invalidation of disabled people and their bodies (Hevey 1992, Shakespeare 1994, Hughes and Paterson 1997, Hughes 1999, 2000, Paterson and Hughes 1999). For Hughes (1999) the key to this lies in what he terms the scopic regime of modernity. The social model was influenced by Marxism and the critique of capitalism, in which the oppression of disabled people was an outcome of structural determination. Hughes, drawing on poststructuralist and postmodernist influences, argues for the need to supplement this with a critique of modernity in which the oppression of disabled people is organically linked to the visual constitution of modernity, so that the invalidation and disfigurement of impaired bodies is not simply an economic or social response, but arises from a particular mode of perception – one that conceptualises them as Other and as Strangers. Drawing on Foucault, he points to the ways in which nineteenth-century social science was much concerned with the construction of binary oppositions such as normal/abnormal, functional/ dysfunctional, in which disability was located in the category of the abnormal and negative. Such distinctions were given spatial expression in segregationist policies that confined the disabled – like the mad and the feeble minded – to special, separate institutions. Modernity is closely linked with these dividing practices.

The visual, Hughes (1999) argues, has a primacy in modernity that is rooted in the positivist epistemology of vision, in which sight is seen as affording access to the world in a direct and unmediated way. But, as Foucault and others have shown, vision is itself a social practice. Observation is not neutral. The gaze is socially constitutive. Eyes are instruments of power. To be looked at is to experience the play of power over the surface of the body. The very visibility of bodies enabled people to make assumptions on the basis of what they see. For disabled people, the surrounding culture provides little in the way of protection against these evaluations, which are internalised in damaging ways. Resistance lies in returning and challenging this gaze, but such responses are difficult. They need to be struggled for, as activists in disability politics who use forms of cultural combat, attest. Within the scopic regime of modernity, the paradigmatic see-ers are male, white, non-disabled. It is 'their' depictions of the world that are taken as constituting the 'truth'. Though their accounts are presented as neutral, they are in fact rooted in particular sorts of social experience and particular sorts of bodies.

The role of medicine is important here, embodying as it does a particular sort of able-bodied masculinity. This extends beyond the practices of medicine in defining and clarifying disabilities to the practitioners themselves. Until recently, accepting disabled people for medical training was as unthinkable as accepting women had been earlier. As we shall explore in Chapter 5, doctors are themselves embodied practitioners, and their bodies show forth ideas about the body and its worth more generally. Though medicine is overtly rooted in biology and the scientific assessment of bodies, it also contains unacknowledged aesthetic elements, in which ideals of bodily perfection are associated with concepts of health, wholeness and moral worth (Hughes 2000). The culture of sport and physical exercise, as it developed out of the nineteenth century, forged another, but associated, set of links between physical perfection and morality. The modern Olympic movement, drawing on the ancient Greeks and their valuation of the body, was imbued with ideas that connected an idealised, particularly male, body with concepts of virtue, morality and human worth. Riefenstahl's depiction of the athletes of the 1936 Berlin Olympics was not simply fascist in inspiration, but drew also on a longer tradition within the Olympic movement. It is for this reason that the political agitation to allow paraplegic athletes to compete as part of the mainstream games has had particular resonance, directly challenging the implicit values that lie behind the Olympic ideal. Here the discourses of medicine, morality and aesthetics flow into one another, reinforcing the cultural links between normality, truth, beauty and wholeness in ways that are damaging to the esteem and status of disabled people. More recently the rise of consumer culture with its emphasis on the visual has added a new twist to these cultural associations. Idealised images of the body surround us in modern commercial culture (though they have effectively been eradicated from High Art). This acts to fetishise appearance, so that beauty and good looks have become templates of morality, images of the ideal life, and with that primary sources of validation and invalidation (Hughes 2000).

Though Hughes emphasises the significance of modernity in his analysis, it is clear that the meanings attached to disability in the historic past have also been negative. As far back as Shakespeare and Richard III, disability has been presented in popular culture as embodying malevolence, jealousy and hidden spite; and these themes resonate through modern films also; for example in the James Bond series or in other media presentations (Kriegel 1987, Longmore 1987). The other principle cultural association of disability is with pathos, as in figures like Tiny Tim or Smike. Certain impairments or identities tend to recur in this cultural repertoire – epilepsy, restricted growth, 'cripples', 'lepers' – suggesting, Tom Shakespeare (1994) argues, that they have particular cultural resonance and utility. Drawing on Sontag and her account of illness as metaphor, he suggests that disabled people operate as ciphers for feelings and processes that non-disabled people cannot deal with, and that are projected on to disabled people, who then become in Hevey's words 'dustbins for disavowal' (Hevey 1992).

Freak shows provide an example of this. A form of popular entertainment common in America and Europe in the nineteenth and early twentieth centuries, they were a cross between the zoo and the museum (Thomson 1996, 1997). Frequently they displayed disabled people, whose 'monstrous' bodies and 'animalistic' appearance served to challenge the boundaries of the human, and as such acted to buttress embodied versions of normal identity. Here, Thomson argues, 'the disabled figure operates as the vividly embodied, stigmatized other, whose social role is to symbolically free the privileged, idealised figure of the American self from the vagaries and vulnerabilities of embodiment' (1997, p. 7). There was often a gender and race dimension to these shows, with their depictions of grotesque versions of femininity, as in the Bearded Lady, or of racialised groups, as in images of roaring Savages accompanied by white keepers; and these exhibitions acted to buttress and privilege certain social identities, notably those constructed around white supremacy and the traditional gender order.

Freak shows died out by the second half of the twentieth century, but disabled activists argue they live on in the presentation of disabled people in charity fundraising. During the 1980s and 1990s, the broadcast media in Britain discovered the attraction of charity appeals, such as Comic Relief, Children in Need and the Telethon. These typically featured able-bodied people having fun raising money for what were depicted as brave, but tragic, victims of illness or misfortune. Disabled activists argued that such images demeaned disabled people, constructing them as weak and pitiful. The fun and games involved, moreover, pointed to a recurring contention of disabled activists: that non-disabled people get a great deal out of helping the disabled, and that we need to question their motives if disabled people are not to be 'used' in this way. In Britain the issue came to a head in 1990 when the Telethon was picketed by more than 150 disabled demonstrators, using anarchic tactics to satirise the proceedings (Hevey 1992).

A similar challenge was presented to charity advertising. This had grown in significance in Britain in the 1980s under the influence of more professional marketing strategies. Hevey (1992), himself a disabled photographer, deconstructs the content of these adverts. They typically take the form of a dominate image, accompanied at the bottom by a much smaller space for text. The image is passive and conveys hopelessness and distress; the text is active and hopeful, pointing the way forward through cure or intervention by the charity. They are almost always in black and white; whereas commercial adverts are in colour. This is because charity adverts sell fear – commercial ones desire. Adverts work by getting you to buy into the lifestyle portrayed. Charity adverts work in reverse. Fear is their motivating force. Shakespeare (1994) draws parallels between charity adverts and pornography in the way they operate. Both use processes of objectification, whereby the gaze is focussed on the body: passive and available for scrutiny. Particular parts of the body are exaggerated: sexual parts in pornography, flawed ones in charity ads. The viewer is manipulated into an emotional response: desire in pornography, pity in charity. Initially the charities defended their approach, arguing that such images work, and that it is necessary to evoke pity and fear to get people to give. But more recently they have acknowledged the criticism and modified their images, giving a greater stress to positive aspects; and in this they have responded to a wider cultural shift.

Over past 20 years there has been a discernible rise in positive images of disabled people in the media. TV programmes and films have begun – tentatively – to portray disabled people in more rounded and less stereotypical ways. Above all, the more grotesque and demeaning depictions have become increasingly unacceptable. As important as these cultural changes, however, have been legal ones. In Britain the Disability Discrimination Act 1995 has had a profound impact on the way in which disability is treated, making it unlawful for businesses and organisations from 2004 to treat disabled people less favourably than others, requiring them to modify their premises and services. The Act draws strongly on the social model with its emphasis on access and civil rights, and can be seen as an exemplification of its approach.

Disability, eugenics and the new genetics

The use of selective abortion to screen out disabled foetuses has become an area where disabled activists and medicine have come into conflict. As we shall see, views on this differ within the disability movement. In order to understand the debates, however, we need to set the issue in the historical context of the eugenics movement and the related, though different, Nazi policy towards the unfit, for the history of this still colours the debate. It is important here to distinguish the various strands. Eugenics was a movement concerned with improving the genetic make up of the population, encouraging the fit to breed, and discouraging or preventing the unfit from doing so (Kelves 1986). It is different from the current use of selective abortion of impaired foetuses based on pre-natal testing. This may have a eugenic intent, but only weakly so. It is this policy that is largely in issue today. Eugenics also needs to be distinguished from a third phenomenon, which is the Nazi euthanasia policy. It is part of the horror of the Nazi period and of the related Final Solution, that these different elements are often confused.

Eugenics flourished the late nineteenth and early twentieth century in Europe and North America (Kelves 1986). It was driven by fears that the declining birthrate among the middle classes was leading to 'national suicide' in the form of a population that was differentially born to groups that were regarded by middle-class eugenicists as unfit. In the early part of the twentieth century, there was a widespread belief that the numbers of 'feeble-minded' and 'mental defectives' were increasing; and they were seen as lying at the root of much immorality and crime. Families of below average income and social character were seen as the chief source of such 'defectives'. Eugenics always had a strong class – and, particularly in America, race – dimension. Eugenicists tended to identify human worth with the middle-class qualities that they themselves possessed (Kelves 1986). In general they equated merit with intelligence; and the development of the early intelligence tests enabled such judgements to be given a scientific air.

The dominant approach was voluntarist, reliance being placed on education, moral exhortation and birth control aimed at encouraging the fit to have more children and discouraging the unfit from doing so. Increasingly, in the early twentieth century, however, a more interventionist approach developed, resting on compulsion and focussed on preventing the unfit from breeding by the use of marriage restrictions, sexual segregation in institutions and compulsory sterilisation. These developments were particularly marked in the United States, where from 1907 onwards state laws provided for the compulsory sterilisation of a range of individuals: criminals, epileptics, the insane and idiots in state institutions (Kelves 1986). By the end of the 1920s, sterilisation laws had been passed in twenty-four states. Sterilisation on eugenic grounds was also enacted in Sweden, Finland, Denmark, Germany, Switzerland and Japan (Barnes and Mercer 2003). Britain did not follow the American lead; and Kelves (1986) notes two differences that he considers significant in explaining the contrast. First, American legislatures and courts were more willing to consider the expert testimony of eugenicist doctors and scientists, whereas the British tradition afforded them no special status. Second, the British eugenics movement had always contained social radicals. Indeed eugenics was originally seen as a progressivist movement breaking down the barriers of class and wealth that prevented biologically desirable unions. These groups were ideologically opposed to compulsion.

In Germany the laws were more sweeping than in the US, and more vigorously implemented. In the 3 years after the 1933 Eugenic Sterilisation Law, some 225,000 people, mostly feeble-minded, were sterilised. Subsidies and grants were paid to biologically sound couples who produced children. In its early years, the eugenics movement had not been anti-Semitic, and some of its leaders were Jewish; but from the mid-1930s onwards, Nazi racial and eugenic policies merged. Public information films were shown in which doctors described their eugenic work as part of the struggle for race and nation. The asylums were deliberately opened to public viewing so that people could see, what was presented to them as, the impact of past failure to take active eugenic measures. Burleigh (1994) describes the way in which this hardening of the moral climate made possible the discussion – albeit in secret – of the killing policy, under which the asylums became killing centres. Many of the personnel involved in the killing squads were later transferred to work on the Final Solution, and the euthanasia policy is frequently interpreted as a precursor of the Holocaust.

After the war, Western countries wanted to forget this past. Eugenics fell into disrepute, and the sterilisation legislation was quietly repealed. Scientifically the basis of eugenics had been eroded. Work by Penrose and others had established which disabilities were indeed genetic, enabling a better grasp on those that were not, or only weakly so (Kelves 1986). The idea that the children of mental defectives would automatically be so themselves was shown to be wrong. It was also recognised that categories like the 'feeble-minded' or 'mentally defective' contained a range of conditions, with a variety of underlying causes, most of which had nothing to do with genetics. Eugenics, in the version that underlay the interwar movement, came to be recognised as a pseudo-science.

This history is, however, important because it forms the background to current debates concerning the new genetics and the role of selective abortion. The development of genetic knowledge in the last 20 years and the success of diagnostic tests such as ultrasound now mean that a large number of impairments can be detected in the womb. This has occurred concurrently with the growth, since the 1960s, of the acceptability of abortion generally, so that a woman with an impaired foetus is now routinely offered a termination. For many disabled activists, this practice represents an assault on the worth of disabled people and their lives, implying that they too were better dead, buttressing the wider cultural disparagement of disabled people. Selective abortion, from this viewpoint, is simply the old Nazi policy of euthanasia and eugenics in new guise.

Shakespeare (1998), himself a disabled activist, rejects this, arguing that selective abortion does not constitute eugenics as such – at least not in its strong version. He distinguishes between 'strong eugenics', where population-level improvements are sought through the use of state interventions to control reproduction; and 'weak eugenics', promoting reproductive selection on the basis of individual choice. It is only the second that is at issue today. He supports the capacity of parents to make free choices, though he questions the context in which they make such choices, noting that their decisions are not made in a vacuum, but are heavily influenced by the views of the doctors who present the evidence of the tests, most of whom, he believes, strongly support selective abortion as a means of achieving their aim that all women should have unimpaired babies. Eugenic outcomes are, therefore, an emergent property of genetic and other forms of screening.

For those disabled people who oppose *all* abortion on moral or religious grounds, opposition to selective abortion does not pose additional problems; and they join those opponents of abortion who have raised concerns about what they term the drift towards designer babies, in which foetuses are selected or rejected in order to achieve desirable features. But many – indeed probably most – disability activists are also supporters of reproductive rights, and for them the issue does present a conflict between the interests of disabled people and women. These tensions have resulted in the situation where some doctors or individuals who oppose social grounds for abortion will *only* abort on the basis of malformation; and some disability activists support free abortion in all cases, *except* those involving an impaired foetus. In Britain, the legislation in relation to abortion currently makes a distinction between the status of the impaired and the un-impaired foetus, allowing termination up to the time of birth in relation to the former (Human Fertilisation and Embryology Act 1990). Many activists who do not oppose all abortion argue for the removal of this as discriminatory (Bailey 1996, Shakespeare 1998).

For some disability activists, the issue is a straightforward one of oppression, and Hubbard has argued that attempts to screen out impairment medically make no more sense than trying to screen out blackness on the grounds that racism is a problem for black people. Shakespeare (1998) disputes this, arguing that there is nothing intrinsically difficult about being black. The problems associated with it are entirely cultural. But in the case of disability there may be intrinsic problems, and these need to be recognised and evaluated. These intrinsic problems relate directly to the body. Some impairments cause suffering and premature death. Shakespeare suggests that we need to adopt a more nuanced view, recognising a continuum of impairment, running from deafness, which involves no pain though some social disadvantage, and where selective abortion should not be supported; through restricted growth, involving social prejudice but only minor physical problems of an orthopaedic character; to problems like Tay-Sachs disease, involving suffering and early death, where abortion may be legitimately considered.

Disability and sexuality

Sexuality is a crucial component in self-identity. Sexual agency is a defining element of full adulthood in modern society, more defining, many would argue, than having a job. But disabled people – particularly those born with disabilities – are often denied this. Assumptions are made that they are asexual or, as Shakespeare and his colleagues (1996) express it, 'sick and sexless'. Expressions of sexuality by disabled people are subject to similar social discouragement as are other non-standard forms. As with gay or lesbian sexuality, displays of affection or desire in public are frowned upon. Young women, in particular, suffer from barriers to being sexual. In the UK the report of the King's Fund study of disabled women's sexuality *Sexual Health and Equality* (Gillespie-Sells *et al.* 1998), revealed the limited expectations placed on disabled young women to be sexual or to have sexual feelings.

Despite its centrality to human experience and identity, sexuality has not been at the heart of debates around disability. Professionals have traditionally regarded it as less important than practical matters. They often shared the sense of unease or embarrassment at the topic that is common among family members. Even the disability movement has not given the issue central prominence. 'Sexual rights' are rarely articulated within the movement (Shakespeare *et al.* 1996), and this is despite the fact that sexuality is the source of some of the deepest forms of oppression and personal pain, a form of exclusion that is hard to talk about.

For many disabled people, particularly those whose disability dates from birth or childhood, one of the most profound barriers to being sexual comes from the impact of medical experiences. From early years, many disabled people become accustomed to the privacy of their bodies being intruded upon, as they are examined, displayed, prodded and photographed. One disabled women with a progressive condition described how as she became more disabled, so her body increasingly became public property (Shakespeare *et al.* 1996). As a result, many become adept at disassociating themselves from what is happening to their bodies, and learn to see themselves as ugly. Micheline Mason describes the impact of such treatment:

> My memory is basically of a whole series of experiences of being very coldly and formally mauled around...I was never told I was nice to look at or nice to touch, there was never any feeling of being nice, just of being odd, peculiar. It's horrible. It's taken me years and years to get over it. (Sutherland 1981, p. 123)

Such experiences leave a legacy of distance and absence from the body that is the very reverse of an erotic sense of the self.

In the past it was commonplace to photograph disabled people naked. Mason describes the distress she felt when subjected to this at the age of 11. She had not been told that she would have to take off her clothes and stand exposed in a hospital g-string while two men photographed her (Sutherland 1981). Such medical practices, Shakespeare and his colleagues

(1996) argue, lie along a continuum of bodily invasion that extends to outright sexual abuse. They recount the testimony of one disabled woman who described how doctors lifted her nightdress and poked and pushed her body in front of a crowd of people. For her there was no real difference when subsequently the hospital porter did the same thing to her for his sexual gratification. Disabled people have long been victims of sexual abuse, particularly in institutions where the lack of autonomy, depersonalisation, and isolation from the surrounding world encourage regimes of power in which bullying and intimidation are endemic. Regular sexual abuse by both staff and other inmates has been common in such settings. More recently, with the move to community settings and the franker recognition of issues of sexuality and of sexual abuse generally, these patterns have begun to be exposed and tackled.

New work has begun to recognise the sexual needs of disabled people. Much of the literature, however, remains framed within a medical discourse. Many of the authors are doctors or other forms of therapists, with a primary focus on physical problems. But sexuality extends far beyond the mechanics of sexual performance. Shakespeare and colleagues argue that it is important to avoid a narrow essentialist view, whereby sexual problems are seen as an inevitable outcome of impairments and where the focus is placed solely on individual physical difficulties. The major part of the problem comes, they argue, not from these, but from prejudice and discrimination: 'for most disabled people, it is not how to do it which causes the main problems, it's finding someone to do it with' (1996, p. 99).

For disabled activists, part of the difficulty comes from the fact that sexuality is not recognised as a basic human need, unlike housing or education which are fully acknowledged within the service system. Disabled adults are often denied the privacy necessary to develop intimate relationships. Shakespeare and his colleagues (1996) argue that this failure to prioritise matters that are highly significant in the lives of most adults reflects a failure to regard disabled people as fully human. It is clear, however, that this also reflects the problems that public services generally have with sexuality. Sexuality belongs in the realm of the private, the hidden, the intrinsically intimate. It may relate to parts of lives that are concealed because they are secret, disreputable and transgressive. In either case, it is clearly at odds with the bureaucratised world of service delivery.

Responding to the sexual needs of disabled people thus poses problems for services. Some of the more radical solutions proposed by disability activists are controversial. For example, sexual surrogates have been provided in the Netherlands, though their role has been one of enabling disabled people to gain sexual experience and confidence, this sets their service within a therapy model of which some disabled people are critical. Facilitated sex, mainly masturbation, has similarly provoked controversy. It is clear that it does happen, though mainly as part of the twilight world of unofficial activity at work. One anonymous contributor to *Untold Desires* (Shakespeare *et al.* 1996) did argue for such help as a normal part of the needs of daily living, and something therefore that careworkers should provide, indeed should be required to provide as part of their job description. It is very unlikely that local authorities or other service agencies would be willing to incorporate such a service. To require it of staff would raise serious questions concerning their civil rights. It is also hard not to believe that this is a gendered response, with male clients requiring help from female care assistants.

Gender and disability

The experience of disability is refracted through gender. This means that men and women, though they may suffer the same forms of impairment, experience their meanings and consequences in ways that relate to wider constructions of masculinity and femininity. For example, though being attractive is important for both men and women, aesthetic norms bear more heavily on women. Their bodies are expected to conform to the ideal more closely, and deviation from this is more negatively judged. Many disabled women experience the appraising gaze of the non-disabled, evaluating what is 'wrong' with their bodies, in a particularly destructive way (Lonsdale 1990). It is difficult to turn this gaze around. It was for this reason that some disabled women took the controversial step of posing nude for *Playboy*, aiming to assert thereby the value of their bodies and their sexuality. However, as with other attempts at resistance through transgressive acts, it involved considerable ambiguity, and has not, by and large, been endorsed within the disability movement. Certain aspects of femininity, however, may mean that disability can in some senses be easier for women than men. The passivity of traditional femininity can mean that 'being helped' is less discordant for women. Masculinity by contrast is traditionally associated with strength, dominance and action (Connell 1995). Men can experience disability as weighing particularly heavily on them, dooming them to a lesser and damaged form of masculinity. Being in a wheelchair, below the level of others, having to be helped and waiting for assistance are all erosive of traditional masculinity. This is particularly so where sexual functioning has been compromised or lost. The primacy of the penis in male sexuality means that loss of capacity in this area can be experienced as devastating, and something that extends to the sufferer's subjective estimation of his social status also.

Seymour (1998) uses the parallels with sport to explore the gendered politics of disability, focussing in particular on rehabilitation culture as it relates to spinal injury. Sport is a powerful social institution through which male hegemony is constructed. Through sport, statements about power become literally embodied, so that over time the bodies of men and women are transformed physically by the social structures of gender. Sport empowers men physically and socially; but acts in reverse in relation to women. These physical manifestations of social relations define men as holders of power, and women as subordinates. Not all men engage in sport, and since its performance is demanding, only a minority can succeed in it. Its significance, however, lies less in the performance than in the values it embodies (Seymour 1998). Sport supports a wider masculinist ideology of competition, aggression and striving; and all men are able to engage with this through the spectacle of sport. Sportsmen are associated with particular bodily presentations and characteristics centring on strength, control, reliability, aggression, tenacity, discipline, competence. These ideas are internalised by men, influencing the ways in which they think about and experience their bodies. Detached from their original source, these qualities come to be seen as the natural attributes of men. Ideals of physicality thus come to inform the presentation of the male body in social contexts where physical strength is not required. Men typically use their bodies more powerfully than women in social situations, and the effectiveness of such masculine styles of interaction underwrite power relations across a range of settings. Attempts by women to copy such outward expressions of power in the workplace, as McDowell (1997) shows in her analysis of the phenomenon of 'Big Swinging Dicks' of corporate finance in the City, are doomed to failure, as they come up against the profoundly embodied nature of power in men's lives.

This gendered model of physicality provides the background to rehab culture. The Stoke Mandeville approach, which has dominated the field, itself developed out of the Second World War, and battle metaphors permeate its language. Seymour describes the atmosphere on the spinal unit as 'institutionally chauvinist', with female staff differentially focussed on helping male patients. In this culture, sport is consciously used to build up strength and confidence, and men are advantaged by the physical nature of their masculinity. Here wheelchair athletes represent the elite. The para-Olympics have been so successful precisely because they celebrate a form of physicality that is valued in the able-bodied world. They act to separate off young, fit disabled men from other, and implicitly lesser, groups of disabled men and women. Their success improves the situations of some disabled people by presenting them in an advantageous context, at the same time as marginalising others, not able to meet these exacting, and gendered, standards. The very wish of young, strong disabled men to escape the demeaning connotations of disability can thus have the effect of entrenching certain groups the more fully in them. This is a point that is made in a more general context by Connell (1995) in his analysis of hegemonic masculinity and the ways in which it privileges certain male groups, at the expense of others.

There is also a double standard in relation to sexuality. Men in wheelchairs are able to attract women; while Seymour argues men do not value or want women who are visibly disabled or in a wheelchair. The pattern is compounded by gendered assumptions around physical servicing. Within heterosexual relations, women traditionally provide men with care, and such forms of assistance thus fit more easily within relations where it is the man who has the disability and is helped, rather than the women. As Lonsdale (1990) shows, women who become disabled are more vulnerable to desertion than are men. The British OPCS studies of disability of the 1980s found that, among the working-age population, disabled women were twice as likely to be divorced or separated as men.

The double standard extends to relations with care staff also. Seymour (1998) notes how the rehab unit, where the majority of staff were female and patients were male, displayed a form of organisational sexuality, similar to that of secretaries and bosses, in which sexuality, as Rosemary Pringle (1989) showed, is interwoven with routine labour processes. As a result, intimate relationships between male patients and female staff were not uncommon. Sexuality and sexual pleasure are central to well-being and self-esteem, and for some men the experience of a form of sexual intimacy with nursing staff was an important part of the healing process, allowing them to reintegrate their sense of self and of bodily being. Nurses were particularly valued as partners because they did not require elaborate explanations around bowel and bladder issues; and their acceptance of the situation and the person provided many men with an important transition back into self-esteem. No comparable experience, however, was available to women on the unit.

It is clear from other testimonies from disabled men that sexual relations with female care staff are not as uncommon as official accounts of the work might suggest. *The Sexual Politics of Disability: Untold Desires* (Shakespeare *et al.* 1996) contains a number of accounts of sexual experiences with care assistants, some brief, others long-lasting. In all cases the disabled person was a man. It appears that such experiences in reverse are rare, and they run the risk of being defined as – and perhaps of being – abusive rather than pleasurable or enhancing. The power dynamic of traditional heterosexuality means that for disabled men to engage in such relationships is relatively safe, whereas for women it presents new forms of vulnerability. As with many issues in relation to gender, the patterning is asymmetrical. We will return to this in Chapter 7 when we look at the issues of cross-gender tending in relation to carework.

Conclusion

The cultural analysis of disability presents many of the same challenges to public policy as ageing. Exploring the social construction of disability and the disabled body enables us to see the ways in which public policy has been centrally implicated in the processes of its construction. Since the nineteenth century, disability has been constituted within the discourses of public welfare and organised in institutions and agencies that created regimes of classification and segregation in which the bodies of disabled people were marshalled and ordered. These processes were carried forward in the twentieth century by the network of charities and other organisations dealing with a variety of distinctly defined disabled groups, making provision for them in specific and ordered ways. Above all, the medical profession, with its systems of knowledge and its practices of power, has been centrally involved in defining the nature of disabled bodies, and with that the lives that such persons might be permitted to live. Though such interventions have, by and large, been benign in intent, their impact has at times been more questionable. The disability movement in recovering the histories of these processes has been able to use them to challenge both current patterns of provision, and the role of professionals in determining these.

Cultural accounts of disability also allow us to address some of the most deeply felt forms of oppression experienced by disabled people, those relating to the body, and to issues of sexuality and self-worth. Earlier approaches rooted in the social model in many ways rendered such subjects unspeakable, compounding the sense of the isolation and otherness that many disabled people, particularly those who have been disabled from birth, feel. Cultural writers have enabled us to refocus attention on these issues and on the disabled body – not in an essentialist way, but in one that explores the meanings with which it has been inscribed. Tracing these historically, through institutions like the freak show, also enables us to see the ways in which current responses to the disabled can also contain aspects of objectification and disparagement. Culturally informed analyses have also helped to put issues around sexuality and gender onto the service agenda.

Lastly, the new emphasis on identity and identity politics characteristic of the cultural turn has acted to reinforce the demand for a greater user-focus within public welfare discourse. Disabled activists, together with mental health users, have been in the van of such developments. Such demands not only rely strongly on the reworking and extension of civil rights discourse, but also draw on an assertion of the centrality of subjectivity and personal experience, and a demand that these should be acknowledged within the service system, indeed that they should actively drive choices within it.

Chapter 5

The Body in Medicine and Health Care

There is hardly an aspect of medicine that is not centrally concerned with the body, its treatment and management; indeed from some perspectives, the body represents the whole subject of medicine, its very ubiquity meaning that no aspect of medicine or health care is untouched by questions of its interpretation and construction. In this chapter, I will concentrate on four areas. Each, in its different way, illustrates some of the tensions within health care in regard to the body; and each rests, to some degree, on an alternative conceptualisation to that presented within dominant orthodoxy. The first part of the chapter will explore the historical emergence of the dominant paradigm of modern medicine, and the ways in which it has rested on a particular conceptualisation of the body. The rise of anatomy and the growth of dissection are crucial in this, and we will explore the implications of these techniques for the treatment and understanding of the body. The growing use of dissection in the late eighteenth and early nineteenth centuries produced pressure on the supply of bodies, and in Britain this resulted in the Anatomy Act which in the nineteenth century effectively commandeered the bodies of the poor for medical dissection. Direct links were thus made between the state, poverty and organ sequestration. These still resonate today in the debates around organ donation, proposed policies for assumed consent, and the emergent commercial traffic in organs rooted in Third World poverty. How we view body parts is still a sensitive matter in medicine, and I will discuss the ways in which these debates illustrate some of the enduring conflicts around rival meanings of the body in health care.

Medicine focusses on the object body of science. But this is far from how people experience their own bodies, even when they come within the orbit of illness or health care. In the second part of the chapter we address the dissonances that patients experience between their own sense of embodiment and the day-to-day practices of the hospital, which rest on a very different conception. We then turn to the third theme, the world of doctors and nurses, exploring the ways in which direct work on the body is managed and conceptualised within their professional practice. This lays the foundation for the later discussion of bodywork as an occupational category in Chapter 7. Doctors and nurses do not just deal with bodies, but are also themselves embodied subjects, and we will explore the implications of this for how they are represented and how their own embodiment interacts with their practice. Lastly we will discuss the nature of alternative medicine and the ways in which this reverses and challenges some of the meanings of the body found in orthodox accounts.

The medical construction of the body: The dominate paradigm

The emergence of modern medicine in the eighteenth and nineteenth centuries was accompanied by a change in the conceptualisation of illness and of its relationship to the body. In the Renaissance and early modern periods the dominant approach was that of the 'sick man', in which illnesses existed at the level of the person, resulting from an imbalance or disorder in the body or the life (Jewson 1976, Porter 1997). Such imbalances, often described in terms of the humoural system, manifested themselves in a diversity of symptoms. From the mid-eighteenth century onwards, however, this account began to be replaced by one that focussed on distinct conditions, or on diseases affecting specific parts, or systems, of the body. The individual character of the patient became less significant as illness was increasingly conceptualised at the level of objective physiological processes observable and explicable through scientific method. The body increasingly came to be conceptualised as a machine, made up of its component parts and systems. The arrival of Germ Theory at the end of the nineteenth century reinforced this, establishing how illnesses like cholera or tuberculosis were bacteriological in nature, the product of neutral biological activities occurring in the body rather than, as had previously often been supposed, wrong ways of living or humoural imbalances.

Ways of knowing the body also altered. In the late eighteenth century, dissection and anatomy laid bare the architecture of the body, displaying its systems, exposing its functioning parts, establishing what Foucault (1973) termed the 'anatomical atlas'. The body in medicine was increasingly constituted by this anatomical gaze (Jewson 1976, Armstrong 1983, 1995). The practice of dissection also helped to shift the individual physician's perception of the body towards a more distant and disengaged mode, playing a key role in allowing doctors to acquire a degree of clinical detachment. New forms of investigative technique in the nineteenth century, like the stethoscope, allowed the medical gaze to penetrate deeper into the living body. This was extended in the twentieth century, with the development of medical microscopy, X-rays, endoscopy and a range of more advanced imaging techniques. The rise of bio-chemical understandings further extended the medical gaze, as the body was increasingly conceptualised at the level of cells and of bio-chemical processes. These developments were paralleled institutionally with the emergence of the teaching hospital and the laboratory as a specialist sites for the exercise of the new scientific techniques on which modern medicine rests. The body has thus come to be constituted within medicine in a particular way: one that is objective, scientific, emotionally neutral and reductionist. This is at the heart of the current bio-medical conception.

Some qualification needs to be made to this account. Medicine is not monolithic. Modern medicine contains a variety of approaches and practices that rest on a plurality of understandings of health, illness and the body. Significant parts of medicine, furthermore, do not accord well with this account; and many doctors are themselves critical of the limitations of the bio-medical model. Different doctors and specialisms are differentially positioned in relation to the ideological core. That it remains the core, however, is evidenced in the ranking of specialisms within medical culture, in which highest status is accorded to those areas like neurology or cardiac surgery that relate most clearly to the bio-medical paradigm, and least to those on the periphery of the model, like psychiatry or public health medicine, that attempt, or are forced, to engage with different conceptualisations of illness and medical practice.

It is also important to recognise that this scientific account of the body forms the basis of modern medicine's capacity to diagnose, alleviate and cure. Modern bio-medicine is powerful because it is able to effect powerful and significant change. Pre-scientific medicine offered various forms of symbolic ordering and comfort, but could do little to cure. It is only in the twentieth century with the rise of scientific medicine that it has been possible to produce significant improvements in relation to the body and its ills. This fact should not be forgotten in our exploration of some of the limitations of the bio-medical model.

Dissection and the use of body parts

The rise of anatomy was crucial in the development of the new medical paradigm, and in the section that follows, I will explore the history of conflict around dissection, and in particular around the problems in the nineteenth century in sourcing an adequate supply of corpses for medical use. These conflicts illustrate tensions between the emergent scientific model of the body, and embedded feelings around the status of the corpse as a former human being. They also throw up questions of public policy and of the role of the state in regulating the supply of bodies and body parts. As we shall see the solution chosen produced a new relation between the state and the bodies of citizens – at least the bodies of the poor. Though dissection today is no longer a public issue, debates about the use of the body after death have not gone away, but have resurfaced in relation to organ donation and retention, and the role of the state and the market in facilitating or controlling this.

In Britain up until the nineteenth century the only legitimate source of corpses for dissection was the annual grant by the crown of four bodies of hanged felons to the Barbers and Surgeons (Richardson 1987). Dissection, since it dismembered the body, had the effect of denying the criminal a final resting place in the form of a grave; and it was thus part of a regime of exemplary punishment in which the bodies of criminals were subjected to mutilation and destruction, on a par with practices like drawing and quartering. The connection with punishment is important because it means that when dissection became the fate of people dying in poverty, the connotations were with criminality.

From the mid- to late-eighteenth century, pressure on the supply of corpses grew. The new private anatomy schools needed a steady supply of bodies, independent of the annual grant, which was now wholly insufficient (Richardson 1987). Corpses began to acquire monetary value, and a lively trade in dead bodies and body parts was established. Surgeons entered into contracts with condemned men to acquire their corpses after death. Body-snatching and graverobbing became common. A distinguished surgeon like Sir Astley Cooper could boast in the 1820s, that for a price he could obtain the corpse of anyone he wanted; and he did indeed obtain those of formal patients on whom he had operated and whose cause of death interested him. Such work was done secretly, and without the consent of relatives. The situation was complicated by the fact that graverobbing had an uncertain legal status, since the English Common Law does not recognise property in a dead body; and its theft, though deplored, was not a crime. The rich could protect themselves by vaults, iron coffins and cages over the grave; the less well off might band together to pay for graveyard walls or a parish watchman, particularly in districts close to the anatomy schools; but none could feel wholly safe.

By the 1820s, there was growing pressure from the medical profession over the issue of supply (Richardson 1987). Doctors found themselves engaged in underhand and semi-criminalous contacts in order to obtain bodies; and faced by prices they regarded as extortionate. The public was increasingly outraged by the activities of the resurrectionists. In 1828 a Select Committee of the House of Commons was set up, dominated by the interests of the medical elite and the concerns of the well-to-do. Various solutions were proposed, including the importation of corpses from abroad – then as now in relation to body parts, 'abroad' offered a useful means of sanitising the issue. The main proposal, however, was to commandeer the bodies of the poor. Radical opinion on the issue was divided. Many radicals saw dissection as part of the march of the intellect, and an integral part of social progress. Superstition and sentiment in these areas, particular when linked to religious or clerical opposition, were seen emblematic of ignorance and prejudice, and therefore to be resisted. Some were alert to the class element in the proposed legislation; but, by and large, radicals sided with science and the medical elite.

Discussion was overtaken, however, by news of the horrific murders in Edinburgh by Burke and Hare. Edinburgh was a centre for medical education and thus of dissection. Burke and Hare were not resurrectionists, but lodging house keepers; and after receiving a large sum of money for the corpse of an old person who had died in their lodging house, they realised the value of such bodies and embarked on murders to obtain corpses for sale. They were brought to justice, and Hare was hanged in 1829 after Burke had turned King's Evidence. There was, however, a strong suggestion of complicity on behalf of some Edinburgh doctors. The murders precipitated government action, and in 1832 the Anatomy Act was passed. This resolved the problem by commandeering the bodies of the poor. Those dying in Poor Law institutions whose relatives did not, or could not afford to, claim the body and had no money to pay for a funeral were sent for dissection. The Act was thus a sectional piece of legislation that replaced a situation where the bodies of all classes were at risk, to one where only those of the poor were (Richardson 1987).

As such it needs to be seen as part of a wider set of changes associated with the coming of industrialisation and the emergence of class society. In its way, it is as key a piece of social legislation as the Poor Law Amendment Act 1834. The Anatomy Act of 1832 can indeed be interpreted as an advanced clause of the New Poor Law, and as such part of a wider assault on the status of the poor and poverty, reversing older, more paternalistic, attitudes and substituting harsher regimes in which poverty was effectively criminalised. Dissection, that had for centuries been used to punish and stigmatise the bodies of criminals, was now applied to the bodies of the poor. Richardson describes the Anatomy Act as a 'class reprisal against the poor' and part of a wider 'symbolic degradation of poverty' (1987, p. 266). The Act was hated and feared by the poor, and contributed to the wider hostility to the Poor Law. To die destitute was not just to lack the means of a decent burial, but also to risk the possibility of dissection. Such fears underwrote widespread popularity of burial clubs and insurance schemes among the poor. Fear of a pauper's death lingered in Britain well into the post-war era (Richardson 1987, Hussey 2001).

By the 1960s the issue of supply was no longer pressing because of the growth of donation. Until the interwar period, the donation of bodies by people in their wills was largely unknown, but from that period on there was a steady growth in such gifts, accelerating in the post-war period: in 1934, bequests represented about 3 per cent of dissections; by 1940 it was

6 per cent; and by the 1960s, 70 per cent and upwards (Richardson 1996). Currently more bodies are bequeathed than are required – about a thousand a year (Department of Health 2004).

Behind this shift in attitudes to donation lies a profound change in feeling about the body and its disposal in death that is paralleled in the growth of cremation, which becomes the majority practice during this period (Jupp 1997). Though cremation is not contrary to Christian belief, and is now endorsed by the major denominations, its growth is clearly associated with a decline in belief in the afterlife and a weakening of the hold of religious faith in the culture. Though the belief in a bodily resurrection always posed problems about the nature of the body that was to be resurrected and its connection with the decaying remains of the corpse, it did underwrite a culture of attachment to the personal remains and to the place where they were laid. The practice of burial endorsed the idea of the continuity of the person with their bodily remains after death. Phrases such as 'laid to rest', 'sleeping', and the tending and beautifying of the grave supported this sense. Cremation by contrast effectively eradicates the body, and is linked to the sense that the long-term existence of the corpse has little meaning.

Richardson (1987) also attributes the greater willingness of people to donate their bodies to the growth in collectivist sentiment of the post-war years in Britain. People identified with the NHS and saw it as an altruistic enterprise that deserved their support and donation. Donating bodies for medical training was seen as a positive action and one that some at least were willing to contemplate. Pressure on bodies has also reduced, however, as a result of changes in the nature of medical education.

Though dissection has ceased to be the issue it once was, questions about the body and its uses after death remain. Now the issue is not corpses for dissection but body parts for transplantation. Before discussing this, and the ethical and policy issues that it raises, I want to explore briefly the recent 'scandals' at Alder Hey hospital, for this again illustrates some of the difficulties raised for public policy by the conflicts between the meanings of the body as perceived by doctors and by the lay public, in the form of relatives.

Alder Hey

Alder Hey is a specialist hospital in the Liverpool area where in the late 1990s a scandal arose concerning the retention of the organs of dead children without the permission of their parents. The story that emerged in the public inquiry reveals a tale of mismanagement, obfuscation and incompetence on behalf of the Trusts and the university, compounded by the behaviour of a rogue pathologist (Alder Hey 2001). But behind this lies a more general issue concerning the clash of cultures between doctors and relatives regarding the treatment of the body and of body parts.

The removal and retention of organs has been a long-standing and widespread practice in teaching hospitals and research centres in Britain and elsewhere. What marked Alder Hey out was the extent of the activity under the regime of a new pathologist Dr Van Velzen (Alder Hey 2001). When parents discovered that parts of their dead children or babies had been retained without their knowledge, there was outrage and distress. Had the hospital dealt with their concerns openly and sympathetically, the matter might have ended, but it did not, and the full extent of the collections and their mismanagement only emerged piecemeal, with parents having to endure multiple funerals, as new parts were discovered. Alder Hey and its collections became a running issue in the British media in the 1990s.

The story presents a complex of issues. The fact that it involved children was clearly significant. The fears and anxieties of parents are staple food for the tabloid press, as can be seen in the treatment of paedophilia, childhood illness and risk generally. It was not always clear, however, that the public at large shared the parents' estimation of the case. Many felt that the press played up the story, and that those parents, while understandably distressed, were over-reacting. The case also revealed an arrogant and cavalier attitude among doctors towards the bodies of children. The medical culture at Alder Hey treated consent as a formality, something that was undertaken in a sketchy and sometimes railroading way. Few parents understood that they could refuse, and most assumed that 'tissue' represented small scientific samples, not whole organs or body parts.

Behind this failure of good practice, however, lay a deeper cultural divide. It is clear than many doctors regarded the bodies of dead patients as in some sense belonging to the hospital and to medicine. The transition of the body into the hospital as a site of scientific endeavour seemed to accomplish an additional transformation in which it assumed the characteristics of the medical body, neutral, fragmented, cellular, so that the removal of parts of the body in death for scientific study became a natural, and above all reasonable, expectation. The nature of the parts involved was also clearly significant. 'Tissue' implies small amounts, dealt with in a scientific way, anonymised and reduced to the levels of cells. What caused most distress to parents was the idea of whole body organs, particularly symbolically sensitive ones like the heart, or ones associated clearly with personhood like the head. Scientifically there is no distinction to be made here, but emotionally there clearly is.

The resonance of the issue cannot be understood without acknowledging its ghoulish qualities. Beneath the rational debate about organ retention, or the trade in body parts, lies a deeper sense of unease. These are indeed visceral subjects. The report of the enquiry (2001) reflects something of this. Though its tone is measured and professional, there is an underlying sense of anger and outrage. The report of Alder Hey recounts how some specimens were in such a poor state, with tongues floating free, that they had to be cleaned up before they could be returned to parents. The photographs of the various decaying Victorian storerooms where the containers were piled up, and the account of opening unlabelled plastic containers to find a brain or head, all convey this sense of revulsion. Van Velzen himself emerges as a strange figure. Many of the problems related to his personal rudeness and arrogance, but there is also a vampiric quality to his pointless accumulation of vat after vat of organs.

The case was significant because it hit the headlines and led to a widespread review in Britain of policy and practice in relation to organ donation. It became clear that the retention of organs was a common practice in many hospitals, but one that proceeded with little in the way of legislative or other guidelines. In response, the Department of Health embarked on a policy consultation, and in 2004 the Human Tissue Act which strengthened the principle of consent was passed.

The case also resonates with two other areas of scandal or public concern. In Germany in the 1980s it emerged that medical schools were still using body specimens and tissue deriving from the Nazi executions and from the euthanasia policy, and revulsion was expressed at this direct bodily continuity with the past and its crimes. Pressure built up in the 1990s and in a number of research institutes and universities, specimens were removed and reburied (Hogle 1999, Peiffer 1999, Schmidt 2002). There are parallels also with the growing demands from former indigenous or colonial peoples for the return of bodies and body parts from Western ethnographic museums and research centres. Such demands are linked to struggles for respect and recognition; and they have provoked a wider review of the treatment of bodies and body parts within museums and beyond (Hogle 1999). We noted earlier the history of Sarah Bartmann, the Hottentot Venus, and the final removal of her remains from display in the late 1980s. Evidence of growing public sensitivity to such displays has, however, to be set against the recent fascination with dissection and body parts within popular culture, high art and the media more generally, where their transgressive nature has made them the centre of artistic exploration, as well as sensationalist displays like that of Van Hagen with his exhibition of dissected and plasticised corpses engaging in human actions like basketball.

Organ donation and transplants

Since the 1980s, the westernised world has witnessed a growth in the use of transplantation within medicine, whether at the level of major organs such as heart liver, kidneys or smaller tissue parts such as corneas. Demand is, however, outstripping supply, and this has created debate within Western countries around questions of donation and consent. It has also created a subterranean, worldwide traffic in body parts, in which organs pass, largely from the bodies of the poor into those of the rich.

Only a small proportion of deaths potentially yield organs for transplantation. In general, the patient needs to have been on a ventilator in the period prior to death, which has therefore to be registered by brain stem tests. This is a relatively small number of cases, and one that is declining. The British Medical Association (BMA), reporting an audit of potential donors in intensive care over the period 1989–90, estimates that only 38 per cent of such cases resulted in donation, so 62 per cent did not. Given the small potential numbers, this was a significant loss. Similar results have been reported in the Netherlands, Spain and Canada (BMA 2004). Elective ventilation provides one way around the difficulty, involving the ventilation of certain patients in a coma, or close to death, for a short period after brain stem death in order to harvest organs. This was tried briefly in the UK, but stopped in 1994 when the Department of Health declared it illegal. The law which is designed to protect people who are not competent to make a decision for themselves declares that medical procedures may only be undertaken which are necessary and in the patient's best interests: any other intervention is unlawful. In some cases organs, like kidneys, can be removed from non-heartbeating donors in the period immediately after death, so that those who die of cardiac arrest on the wards, or are declared dead on arrival, can sometimes be donors.

In the case of kidney donation, however, it is possible to obtain organs directly from living donors. In the UK in 1999, some 16 per cent of kidney transplants came from such a source (BMA 2004). Current legislation in Britain requires that all live donors must either be a close relative or, if not, obtain specific prior approval from the regulatory body. Live donors are increasingly spouses or partners; and in these cases specific approval is required.

In 2004 the BMA reviewed the principal potential means of increasing supply in the UK. Some relate to procedures and administrative structures, or to co-ordination and training. The issue of consent is, however, perceived as a major barrier. Britain currently operates an opt-in system that requires prior permission or the consent of relatives. In about 30 per cent of cases, this is refused. Increasing the numbers of people who carry donor cards or have registered consent is one option, but attempts to do this over the last 20 years have not been successful. The BMA report notes the importance of addressing residual fears and objections that the public have in relation to the status of death indicated by brain stem tests. Fears have also been expressed that 'Do Not Resuscitate' notices are being used to obtain organs, though this is based on a misunderstanding since, with only a small number of exceptions, once the heart has stopped beating, the organs are no longer of use.

In Britain the policy debate centres around whether to move from the current opt-in system to one based on opting-out in which there is a presumption of consent and in which donation can proceed unless the deceased has registered a prior objection, or one is raised by relatives. A number of countries, notably Belgium, operate such a system. Meaningful comparative evidence concerning the effect of such a shift is hard to obtain, as rates of successful donation and transplant are subject to factors other than consent. The BMA supports such a move, arguing that it is reasonable and appropriate to assume that people would wish to act altruistically and to help others after their death. It is certainly true that some 70 per cent of the population have reported that they would be willing to donate their organs, though only 20 per cent carry a card or have registered permission. It is hard to evaluate how far these discrepant figures simply suggest a failure to take action, and how far they reflect deeper feelings that the public is unwilling to register openly. It is certainly the case that a Department of Health survey in 1999 found that 50 per cent of the population did not want any change in the current arrangements around consent; 28 per cent wanted a move to presumed consent; and 22 per cent expressed no preference. The British government currently has no plans to move to an opt-out system. In the interview given in 2004, a junior minister, Rosie Winterton, perhaps echoing the earlier history of dissection, stated that the State does not own the bodies of citizens, and it can only obtain them by gift (Radio Four, Today, 15 January).

The trade in organs

Western governments and professional bodies have, by and large, refused to countenance a direct trade in organs, though there have been and are pressures on them to do so, and it is clear that such a trade exists and that it is highly profitable. Its extent is hard to gauge, since it is largely covert. As with dissection in an earlier age, it forges direct links between the upper strata of bio-medical practice and the lowest reaches of the criminal world. The chief source of information on the trade comes from Berkeley Organ Watch established in 1999 (Scheper-Hughes 2000, 2001a,b).

The trade is global, and patients sometimes travel to countries where organs can be sourced. Cohen (2001), for example, describes the growth of medical tourism in India, where First World facilities have been built close to international airports, and also close to Third World supply, in the form of individuals desperate enough to sell body parts. This practice applies particularly to kidneys, since living donation is possible, indeed favoured by some recipients as it ensures freshness. Though the Indian government passed a law in 1994 to make it illegal to buy or sell organs, there is a flourishing black market located in criminal circles and controlled by owners of for-profit hospitals. Cohen (2001) describes rural sellers as mostly men usually in debt, needing to support a family or pay a dowry; and urban sellers as mostly women, often destitute as result of a husband's unemployment or desertion. In some countries the state is directly involved, effectively commandeering the bodies of former citizens who have ceded their rights through crime. In China, the state systematically takes organs from executed prisoners (Scheper-Hughes 2000). These are used either to reward politically well-connected citizens, or commodified and sold to patients in Hong Kong, Taiwan and Singapore. Though officially denied, it is estimated that some 2000 prisoners per annum are used in this way. Some within China argue that such use is a social good, a form of enforced public service, and one that may allow a family to redeem its honour. In other countries under politically corrupt regimes, for example Argentina during the dirty war, organ removal took place in secret, but with the implicit connivance of the state. There are also well-attested cases of organ theft and medical malpractice around death under such regimes (Scheper-Hughes 2000, 2001a,b).

For Scheper-Hughes, the trade in organs is a symptom of the corroding force of global capitalism in which all aspects of life are reduced to the status of market commodities. The traffic in organs follows modern global routes of capital and labour flows, and conforms to established lines of social and economic cleavage. There is also a race element in this. Christiaan Barnard in the 1960s used to boast that there was no apartheid in organ transplantation in South Africa, but the reality was that the majority of hearts came from poor, black men in the townships, transplanted into the bodies of rich, white men. Today transplant flows run from South to North, from poor to rich, from black/brown to white, and to some degree from women to men (Scheper-Hughes 2000). There are parallels here with that other trade in bodies: the trafficking of women and children for sex work; and similar issues arise in relation to power, exploitation and the Othering of sources of 'goods' that are illegal or semi-legal in the rich home country.

From the neo-liberal perspective it is axiomatic that the market provides the most effective way in which to allocate scarce goods, including body parts. Proponents of regulated sale argue that organs are no different from other parts like blood, skin and corneas that are already traded (at least in some parts of the First World), and that objections rest on the basis of irrational distaste for inner body organs by lay people. Individuals need incentives to donate to overcome indifference or aversion, and financial ones are the clearest and best. The sale of organs represents an exchange in which both sides must gain sufficiently to engage, and high prices will attract more supply. These arguments have been most clearly articulated in relation to kidneys where live 'donation' or sale is possible, but neo-liberals have also developed proposals in relation strategies like a future's market in organs or discounts on health insurance for those willing to donate in the event of sudden death (Fox 1996, 2003, Murray 1996).

There are three broad areas of objection to these arguments. The first concerns the limits of market transactions. Though neo-liberals advocate the primacy of the market as the central mechanism of society, large parts of the social world and of social relations fall outside its remit, organised around different principles. We do not allow all things to be traded. We do not, for example, permit the buying and selling of votes or of legal verdicts. Western societies do not allow the purchase of a bride. Nor can we alienate from ourselves certain basic citizenship or human rights: we cannot sell ourselves into slavery, or agree to our murder. Significant parts of social relations thus lie outside the cash nexus. This is particularly so in relation to health care, where in the majority of Western countries, access is determined by need and governed by the collectivist principles of the welfare state or social insurance, not primarily by the market. To sell organs is to convert one sort of good – the human body – into a different sphere, that of the market (Murray 1996). Traditionally we keep these separate. That is part of why there is a widespread revulsion at the idea of the trade in organs.

Second, bodies are never just things, but are closely linked to identity and personhood. Corpses are never simply treated as garbage: all cultures have taboos and rituals concerning their management. The sale of organs tries to transmute a relationship that is one of intimate social and moral connectedness into one that is like that towards a used car, a source of spare widgets (Murray 1996). Fox points to our deeper unconscious feelings in these areas, arguing that organ transplants uncover the emotionally charged symbolic and anthropological meanings that we attach to our bodies and their parts: subterranean feelings, non-logical perceptions, compelling images, tenacious myths. She argues that we should listen to these and not allow ideas of medical scientific progress to catapult us beyond their reach (Fox 1996, p. 258).

Lastly the neo-liberal market model is based around ideas of contract and free choice. But these potential market relations are embedded in social realities that are far from free or equal. We have already noted how the global trade in organs follows established social and economic cleavages, and we only have to think of urban slums in South America or rural poverty in India to see that these are far from free or autonomous choices. A market place for organs exploits the desperation of the poor, turning their suffering, not into something that should be addressed, but an opportunity for gain, a new sort of good to be 'mined' and exploited by the First World.

For Scheper-Hughes the trade in body parts is quite simply a form of 'late-modern cannibalism' (2001a, p. 1).

The patient's experience of embodiment

Biomedicine constructs the body in a particular way, bracketing off certain features of human existence and abstracting and focussing on others (Madjar 1997, Crossley 2003). It is a constructed reality, but such is the status of its institutional and scientific base that it has achieved primacy, at least over large parts of public discourse. In this section we will explore some of the challenges that have been presented to this account from the perspective of the patient's own experience of embodiment, and from writers working within the phenomenological tradition.

The biomedicine account is far removed from our everyday experiences of ourselves and others. Medicine rests on the objectification of the patient and his/her body, and largely ignores subjective and embodied experience. Under its gaze, the person becomes a body, an object, a site of physical and causal processes, of health care interventions. Doctors are taught to lay aside or sift the patent's narrative in such a way as to see below what is often presented as a subjective and mistaken account, seeking the signs of an underlying condition. Kleinman (1988) argues that modern medical practice drives the doctor's attention away from the lived experience of the patient, and with it from key dimensions in how illness should be understood.

In a state of health, we experience the body in an unconscious way, as the phenomenologically absent body of everyday life (Leder 1990, Williams and Bendelow 1998, Madjar 1997). Health is a state of 'organic silence' (Herzlich 1973, p. 53). But illness and pain call forth awareness of the body, bringing it into perceptual consciousness, as our gaze turns inwards on the body and how it works – or does not work. We experience corporal betrayal as the disappearing body of everyday life is replaced by the malfunctioning, *dys* – appearing body of pain and illness (Leder 1990). The alienating nature of pain shatters the self, cuts you off from others, imprisons you in the body.

Since the 1980s and Kleinman's pathbreaking account of patient's narratives, there has been a growth of work that explored the experience of illness and the body from the perspective of the patient, some written by doctors or sociologists who have themselves suffered from illness (Sacks 1984, Scambler 1988, Kelly 1992, Frank 1995). Cancer has in particular been the subject of an extensive lay literature. Within sociology, work on pain (Leder 1990, Bendelow 1993) and on chronic illness (Bury 1982, 1991, Lawton 2000) have been particularly influential in refocussing the analytic framework on the lived experience of the patient. Much of this is concerned with the shattering effect of illness and treatment on the sense of self. Kelly (1992) and Madjar (1997), for example, in their explorations of colistis, chemotherapy and burns recount the fear, shock and revulsion experienced in relation to the post-operative body, particularly where interventions have resulted in disfigurement that means that the patient can no longer relate to the face in the mirror, or where the boundaries of the body have been disturbed in socially transgressive ways as in ileostomy. In treatments like chemotherapy, the body becomes a battleground. Patients are rendered powerless and vulnerable as they are made subject to invasive and disturbing procedures. A major theme in these accounts is the difficulty of regaining a sense of self in the body, and some people are so changed and overwhelmed by their experiences that they never do (Madjar 1997). Lawton (1998) describes the ultimate in such processes of alienation in her account of 'dirty dying' where patients effectively gave up all pretence at personhood. Others are more successful and manage to rebuild a new relationship with their bodies.

Pain is particularly significant here since it both reduces the person to the body and alienates them from it, destroying the sense of self and cutting the person off from others. Writers on the body tend to be critical of Cartesian dualism and its legacy for how we talk about and experience the body, but the split between mind and body can have benefits for those in pain, or in extreme old age or sickness, where the route of bodily transcendence offers one of the traditional ways to achieve a measure of personal resolution and integration. As Williams and Bendelow (1998, p. 160) comment, while

> at an *analytical* level the study of pain and suffering demands the dissolution of former dualistic modes of thinking, in drawing attention to the relatedness if self and world, mind and body, inside and outside, it must also confront and account for the 'enduring power and qualities of these dichotomies at the experiential level of suffering' (Leder 1990).

The very subjectivity of pain also underpins its unsharability (Madjar 1997). Health care professionals are often unable or unwilling to hear the patient's expressions of pain – laying them aside in their search for clinical signs, or in their need to make their jobs bearable. Kleinman (1988) notes how having the reality of one's pain questioned is one of the recurring experiences of the chronically ill. Chronic pain patients are among the *bêtes noires* of doctors, regarded as hostile, demanding and undermining of their health care. Their failure to get better challenges the rationality of medicine. Health care professionals are also reluctant to acknowledge the ways in which they are themselves inflicters of pain (Lawler 1991, Madjar 1997). Many diagnostic and curative procedures are painful and distressing, but this is at odds with how professionals – particularly nurses – like to present their work, with the result that there is a tendency to downplay or deny the patent's expression of pain or distress.

The practices of the hospital and health care professionals can also intensify the sense of bodily alienation. Hospitals are versions of Goffman's Total Institution (1961) in which patients are made subject to the institution in directly bodily ways, loosing their personal identities, becoming the Carcinoma in Bed Three. All aspects of their bodily lives become open to comment, review and record as they are required to expose themselves on demand and to perform bodily acts, like dressing and undressing, washing, eating, sleeping, excreting, under direction and according to schedule. Their bodies become inscribed with hospital meanings, from the identity bracelets to the specially purchased 'nightwear' required for life in the hospital. Their time becomes non-time as they learn to wait upon the time of the doctor (Frankenberg 1988). Their space becomes reduced to the temporary space of the bed and the locker; and even their command over the space of their bodies becomes uncertain.

Bodywork in health care

We now move to the subject of the body within the day-to-day practices of health care professionals. Health care involves working directly on and through the bodies of patients: assessing, diagnosing, handling, treating, reviewing and monitoring bodies. A large part of the work is therefore a form of bodywork. We will explore this occupational category more fully in Chapter 7, but in this section, I want to focus on the ways in which the bodywork element has been incorporated and evaluated within the professional practice of doctors and nurses, reflecting in particular on three recurring features of such work: that it is ambivalent work; that it is, in general, lowly regarded work, that those with high status aim to avoid or transcend; and that it is gendered work.

Though doctors focus on the bodies of their patients, their contact with them is circumscribed, framed within a particular set of symbolic values. Medicine shares a long-established set of assumptions whereby status is marked by distance from the bodily, and there is a clear dematerialising tendency within which the work is organised. Historically, the elite physicians of the seventeenth and eighteenth centuries aspired to be like gentlemen, scholarly advisors to their wealthy patients; and they avoided direct physical contact except of the most fleeting kind. This was left to the lower orders of apothecaries and barber-surgeons. Something of this is still present in the practice of doctors. Doctors touch and handle the bodies of patients in the course of the elite activities of investigation and diagnosis, or in ways that are mediated by high-tech machines, but they do not, by and large, deliver hands-on bodily treatment or care. That is left to lesser – and gendered – occupations such as physiotherapists or nurses. This is, of course, partly explicable economically through the division of labour, but not wholly so. Symbolic relations are also involved, in which status is expressed by distance from the bodily. Part of the drama of the traditional ward round in which the bodies of patients are prepared and presented by nursing staff is about protecting the status of doctors by providing a consciously limited frame within which the body is examined: the relevant parts of the body are prepared and exposed; the space in which the encounter takes place is closely defined; the time spent limited, before and after, arrival and exit clearly marked (Strong 1979). The exception to this is, of course, surgery where manual activity and skill are highly prized. But surgery also takes place in a clearly defined symbolic space; on a body that is typically anaesthetised; and the activity is bracketed off by clothes, masks and gloves. These, of course, play a vital role in asepsis, but they also act symbolically to separate off the event and the contact. Doctors thus do perform bodywork, but in ways that are designed to mitigate the otherwise demeaning connotations of manual labour on bodies.

Nursing is ambivalently positioned in relation to these ideas: in some ways endorsing them, and in others challenging and reversing them. Like medicine, it operates within the context of biomedicine and the concept of the body enshrined within that. It also displays elements of the dematerialising tendency referred to above, whereby status is marked by distance from the bodily. Nursing work is organised hierarchically; and bodywork is typically relegated to the lowest levels of staff. And yet, at the same time, nursing also contains an undercurrent that values the element of bodywork, and indeed uses it to assert a different and independent practice from that of dominant medicine. These tensions around the evaluation of bodywork have been part of nursing since its inception as a distinct occupation in the nineteenth century, and they relate to many of the central debates concerning its character and status (Davies 1995, 1998, Savage 1995). Currently these find expression in the conflict between holistic accounts of nursing and those rooted in an emphasis on technical skills and the division of labour.

Within the holistic account, nursing knowledge is seen as something distinct, that goes beyond the rationality of science. Lawler (1997) argues that nursing rests on a plurality of ways of knowing: 'nursing's knowledges are ontological (and felt), intellectual, performed and expressed' (p. 33). They tend towards narrative form, emphasising that which is irreducible, personalised, contextual, and meaningful only in gestalt. It is 'embodied knowledge'. Savage (1995) similarly sees nursing as embodied, resting on a fusion of intuition and experience, a non-intellectual form of knowledge that unites the mind and the body, the physical and the existential. It has its own knowledge base and techniques. Central to these is the ability to bring care and comfort to the patient. Nursing has techniques to make the patient comfortable, to refocus them away from pain and bodily fragmentation and to reaffirm them as sentient individuals. The body focus is central in this, for what nursing aims to do is integrate the two bodies: the object body of science and the lived body of individual experience. In this context, bodywork has a special value because it offers an opportunity for closeness and the expression of care, as well as an opportunity to try to redress the fragmenting experience of medicine. Advocates of holistic nursing see bodywork activities like bathing, washing and dressing, not as low-level tasks that should be relegated to a junior or untrained staff, but as a central element in nursing, something that should be done by trained nurses as an integral part of their care for the patient.

This reversal of values is sometimes linked the sacralising discourse in nursing, in which nurses present the bodywork element in heightened and semi-sacred terms, as a laying on of hands, or symbolic washing away of pain and sickness (Wolf 1988). Part of the symbolic work of nursing, it is argued, is to mediate the pollution inherent in dealing with sick and incontinent bodies and to transform these tasks through a heightened language of love. As we shall see, the nurse's own body and its symbolic presentation is used to help achieve this reversal. In this way, the meaning of dirty work is reversed, and given a special, exhaulted value. It is a reversal that remains, however, highly unstable. Dirt, incontinence and vomit have a powerful materiality to them that acts to undermine such symbolic strategies. This aspect of nursing work also has an evanescent quality to it. Like the discourse of 'care' to which it relates, it is hard to capture within the conventional categories of work. In particular it eludes analysis in terms of the kinds of rationalities that dominate health care currently. It is for this reason that nursing has found it difficult to articulate its role within a health care system increasingly dominated by the discourses of managerialism (Lawler 1997).

Holistic interpretations of nursing present an idealised account. In reality nursing is not always positioned so clearly on the side of the patient and the expressivity of the body. Nurses are also involved in disciplining and controlling bodies in directly Foucauldian ways. The hospital ward is a closely controlled regime in which the bodies of patients are ordered and regulated. Hospitals impose rules on the body and its expression. In the past the physical regime of the ward was strict, with bedclothes pulled tight, possessions tidied away and visitors warned not to sit on the bed. Nurses were, and are, agents of such control, disciplining and ordering the bodies of patients, making them subject to the regime of the institution.

Nursing has also become subject to a sharper division of labour under the impact of economic rationality and managerialist direction in health care. This has resulted in a growth in the use of grading and skill mix. Trained nurses are increasingly found in managerial and technical areas, and basic bodywork is consigned to semi-skilled staff. This economically driven agenda is not out of tune with nursing values, or at least some of them. Nursing has always been a hierarchical occupation, and nurses share with medicine the wider cultural estimation of bodily work. Nursing displays elements of the dematerialising tendency referred to above, so that as individuals rise up the hierarchy, they move away from the basic body-work of bedpans and sponge baths towards skilled high-tech interventions; moving from dirty work on bodies to clean work on machines. The highest echelons of nursing – management, teaching, research – involve no contact with bodies at all. Dunlop (1986) argues that the academicisation of nurse training has introduced an aetherialising and theoretical approach that represent a further flight from the bodily.

The emphasis on high-tech skills is linked to the professionalisation project. Since its inception nursing has struggled politically, both within its own ranks and more widely, with questions of its status, in particular its putative status as a profession. Technical skill and specialist knowledge are two key elements in such a claim, on a parallel with the classic profession of medicine (Parsons 1954, Freidson 1970). The professionalisation project is thus closely linked to the division of labour and the devaluation of bodywork element in nursing, which is seen as something that any untrained person could do, at least under supervision, and thus not part of professional work. The claim of nursing to professional status has been a long-running issue. The debate within sociology, at least in its original form, has run out of stream, superseded by the understanding of the key role that gender plays in the constitution of nursing as an occupation and, indeed, in the constitution of the concept of a profession. Davies (1995) argues that nursing is not so much a profession or a quasi-profession, as an adjunct of a gendered concept of profession, in which nursing functions to make possible the gendered work of medicine, enabling it to present itself as rational and masculine, and to gain the privileges that come from this. (The fact that many doctors are now women does not detract from this analysis. It is the gendered nature of the occupation rather than the gender of the person who occupies the post that is significant here.) Nursing is structured in terms of what medicine leaves out, does not see, or does not want to deal with: aspects of the patient that are too mundane or too lowly, or that are not directly germane to its scientific project. The care of the body is part of this. In this, nursing is like that other classically gendered occupation, the secretary, who similarly sorts out and smoothes the way for her boss, supports and enables his work, deals with emotions and bodily needs and acts as an informal channel of contact and information (Pringle 1989). It is personal work that draws on a range of skills, but these remain unaccredited, naturalised – like caring – in the characters of the women who do it. It is because secretaries perform this work, that bosses are able to continue to act in a disembodied unemotional way, and present their work in terms of the abstract ideal (Davies 1995).

Organisations like health care are deeply gendered and embodied. Images of men's and women's bodies pervade organisational processes (Acker 1990, Davies 1995), so that advantage, disadvantage, exploitation, control, action, emotion, meaning and identity are patterned through and in terms of the distinctions between male and female. According to the official organisational logic, jobs are abstract slots into which persons of either sex can be positioned. But Acker (1990) argues this is not so. Indeed the very concept of a job is gendered, both in that it rests on assumptions about a gendered division of labour and the separation of the public and private spheres, and in that it assumes a particular gendered organisation of domestic life and social production. This gendered division of labour, as we shall see in Chapter 9, is part of the sub-text of the rational and impersonal character of the public sphere.

Embodied practitioners

Most writing on the body in health care focusses on the bodies of patients, but we need also to look at the ways in which practitioners are themselves embodied. A number of writers have noted the ways in which nurses' bodies are presented in popular culture in a distinctive way, dicotomised as angels or tarts. Nurses' uniforms with their quasi-religious origins, headgear, pale colours and white aprons have traditionally been used to reinforce the sense of them as ministering angels. At the same time, the nurse's body has long been a focus of male fantasy, presented in the sexualised terms of the black stockings and busty aprons of Carry On films and strippergrams. Nurses by virtue of their intimate involvement with the body are assumed to be sexually knowing in relation to their own bodies. Porter (1992) argues that nurses are more singled out than other female occupations for being the butt of such sexual stereotyping, suggesting that the key lies in masculine fears concerning female intrusion into physical aspects of life and the person that are normally kept guarded. Nurses' potential intrusion into the body is thus countered by demeaning the nurse's own body.

There is a long tradition of the binary presentation of women as pure/ impure, relating to both bodily and moral preoccupations. Bashford (1998) in her account of the origins of the new nursing in the nineteenth century emphasises the way in which this new social role was rooted in ideas about the bodies of nurses. Young, middle-class, chaste women were to come into the space of the hospital to cleanse it of dirt, drunkenness and disorder; their bodies, clean, pure, disciplined and demonstrating the possibility of moral and physical cleanliness. She argues that women's bodies were a specially evocative symbol here since they always contained – like the hospital – the possibility and threat of pollution. Women's purity was always in a precarious state and constant guardedness and care was needed to ensure that it remained so. The nurse's body thus came both to symbolise the sanitarian enterprise and to be the means of achieving it.

Nurse training has never been simply about formal education, but has always contained a strong element of disciplining and moulding behaviour, both on the ward and outside. In the past nurses were expected to live under discipline, in nurses' homes under the control of senior nurses and hospital directors. In their work they were made subject to the regulation of detail and of bodily stance, the ordering of repetitious work, the precision of command, and hierarchical observation: all of what Foucault terms the 'political anatomy of detail'. Nurses still identify being professional, not with autonomy or discretion as other professions do, but with acting according to professional precepts and discipline. Nurses are thus both agents and objects of institutional discipline. Their bodies are controlled, disciplined and trained, and they in turn act as agents of control in relation to juniors and patients.

Though these bodily images are perhaps easiest to see in relation to nurses, they apply also to medicine. Christopher Lawrence (1998) has explored the ways different forms of knowledge have been embodied in depictions of the physical appearance of doctors. From the seventeenth century there has been the tradition of representation whereby physicians are presented as lean and bookish, in contrast to the stout vulgarity of surgeons. These differences reflect the historical development of the different branches of the profession and their claims to legitimacy and distinction, with physicians emphasising their links to the universities and gentlemanly connections, and surgery associated with practical hands-on work of the barber-surgeons. Even after surgeons had established a more elite status, popular presentations continued to depict them in the same visual terms as butchers: stout, coarse and fleshly. These historical embodiments still resonated through modern medicine, underwriting what Lawrence (1998) terms the 'tribal lore' of British and American medicine that physicians and surgeons can be distinguished by their corporeal and mental qualities. Physicians are stereotypically lean, aquiline, bookish, inscrutable and solitary; while surgeons are muscular, bluff, practical, theatrical, gregarious and ever ready for dramatic interventions.

This bodily imagery has implications of the position of women in the medicine as Hinze (1999) shows in her exploration of the symbolic universe that underpins the hierarchy of medical specialisms. Looking at the ranking of prestige she found that medical specialisms were organised along lines of gender, and that the bodies of doctors were described in gendered terms that reflected this. Bodies that occupy the top posts are described as action-oriented, macho and technologically sophisticated; while those at the bottom as passive, less physical and more affective. The perception of the different specialisms is also grounded in symbolic body parts that are themselves gendered. Surgery, for example, was described in terms of being a specialism that needs 'balls'; a heroic occupation that involved working long hours, bold and dramatic interventions, often deploying military metaphors. This poses difficulties for women who chose male specialisms, and who have to perform male behaviour, at the same time as avoiding negative judgements for doing so. Similar tensions around bodily presentation occur in other male-dominated occupations such as corporate banking (McDowell 1997) and the military (C.L. Williams 1989). The representation and imagery of different specialisms is thus not gender neutral. It both acts to keep women out of the best specialisms and gives voice to the silent symbolic, embodied world of gender that shapes the structure of medical specialisms into a ladder, with a masculine top and feminine bottom, regardless of whether male or female bodies occupy the rungs (Davies 1998).

Bashford (1998) similarly explores the ways in which ideas of embodiment affected the sorts of work that women doctors were allowed to do in early years of their entry into the profession, largely confining them to work with women and children. Whereas it was acceptable for women nurses to care for men, it was not acceptable for women doctors to do so. The reason lies in the very different relationship between the doctor and the patient and the nurse and the patient. 'So loaded was the doctor–patient relationship in subject–object and active–passive terms, that the very idea of women doctor implied a quite intolerable objectification of men' (Bashford 1998, p. 93). Special anxiety focussed around the idea of female doctors examining or pronouncing on male genitalia, though no similar constraint applied to male doctors in relation to their female patients. Nurses, by contrast, whose characters were understood in terms of self-sacrifice and self-effacement, posed no such threat.

These feelings coalesced particularly strongly around the dissecting room. The thought of women engaging in dissection disturbed deep levels of taboo in the nineteenth century in relation to gender and the body. Jordanova (1989) argues that dissection is a strongly sexualised practice: phallic, penetrative, in which the corpse represents the quintessence of the female object-body. Indeed she points to how depictions of dissection in art commonly presented the corpse as female, made all the more so by jewellery and flowing hair, though in reality most corpses were male. Paintings of dissection chime with other nineteenth-century depictions such as that of

Science unveiling Nature, in which the latter is again represented as the body of a woman. The gaze of the dissector is the gaze *par excellence*, since there is no possibility of the corpse looking back (Bashford 1998). The scientist or the doctor can look as long, and as deeply, as he likes. In the nineteenth century, how could a woman take on such a role?

Anatomy was a masculinist activity, one integral to the development of the self-identity of the medical profession (Petersen and de Bere 2005). The practices of the dissection room, served as a male bonding ritual, socialising neophytes into masculine culture. The thought of dissection undertaken by women students thus becomes a focus of hostility and anxiety in the nineteenth century, and angry protests were raised against the practice (Bashford 1998). These were not just the product of the exclusionary practices whereby male students sought to protect their knowledge, space and elite professional status by excluding women, but also reflected deeper fears. Women dissecting breached deeply felt taboos. It implied the use by women of knives to cut into the body; and Bashford draws on Pringle and Collings' discussion of butchery and of cultural taboos (1993), showing how the practice of cutting meat has historically been sexualised, with the knife standing in for the phallus. In the nineteenth-century medical context also, knives were loaded with symbolism: 'In the context of the gendering of nineteenth-century medical practice ... the knife is too phallic to contemplate its use, its appropriation by women: knives belong to men' (Bashford 1998, p. 120). Such feelings underwrote the encouragement of women doctors away from surgery and towards specialisms that did not involve cutting open the body.

Since then, changes in the culture and practice of medicine have led to a questioning of the primacy of dissection in medical education. Increasingly it has been replaced by other ways of learning in the form of 'live and virtual anatomies' which as well as teaching about the structure of the body are designed to introduce students to issues of personality, social character, lived experience, interpretations of bodily feelings and subjectivities (Petersen and de Bere 2005). These new emphases rest on a sense that medicine, as practised within the orthodox model, has lost contact with the lived experience of the patient, and the particularity of the individual and their body. One of the areas where these have remained central is alternative medicine.

The body in alternative medicine

Alternative medicine is not a unified practice, but covers a diverse set of therapies and interventions. Cant and Sharma (1999) estimate some 160 therapies are currently on offer in Britain. Various systems of classification – none wholly satisfactory – have been proposed in terms of their scope, knowledge-base, organisation and character. The single most significant factor uniting alternative therapies is, however, their socio-political status in relation to dominant medicine. It is against that orthodoxy that they are defined. What counts as alternative medicine thus will and has varied; the boundary is permeable.

The category needs to be understood historically in relation to the emergence of dominant orthodox medicine. Medicine in the eighteenth century and earlier had been an open and diverse system of therapeutics with no clearly delineated orthodoxy, and with a variety of practitioners – physicians, barber-surgeons, apothecaries, midwives as well as lay persons – providing herbal and other traditional remedies. Even those clearly within the medical profession practised in heterodox ways (Cooter 1988, Saks 1992, 1994, Porter 1997). By the late nineteenth century this situation had been transformed with the emergence of a culturally unified, formally organised and exclusionary medical profession based on the new scientific medicine. The Medical Act 1858 was pivotal in Britain, conferring on orthodox doctors the exclusive right to call themselves 'medical practitioners'. The institutionalisation of orthodox medicine was further reinforced in Britain by the National Health Insurance Act 1911 and the NHS Act 1948 that forged a link between orthodox medicine and the state, and greatly expanded the scope of institutions in whose organisation and delivery orthodox doctors had the dominant role. Currently alternative medicine in Britain remains governed by Common Law, and is neither endorsed nor forbidden. At various points in the last two decades attempts have been made to extend state regulation to at least parts of the sector. Parallel developments have occurred in other Western countries, resulting in slightly different legal and institutional status (Gevitz 1988, Cant and Sharma 1999).

Relations between alternative therapies and orthodox medicine have fluctuated. In recent years there has something of a rapprochement between the sectors, illustrated in the growing use of the term 'complimentary medicine'. Orthodox medicine has, by and large, been willing to incorporate aspects of practices like acupuncture where they have proved effective and where orthodox accounts of their working have emerged. Other therapies such as osteopathy have in large measure been 'tamed' or incorporated particularly in the United States, and made acceptable and ancillary to medicine. Others, such as aromatherapy, are tolerated as harmless. Some alternative therapies have sought state regulation and aspired to work alongside orthodoxy. Others have remained more radical and alternative in character. There is a recurring, though not inevitable, process whereby therapies, reacting from a sense that they have become too like orthodox medicine – too bureaucratic in their training, too subservient to bio-medical concepts, neglectful of principles like self-healing – return to their roots. The revival of lay homeopathy in 1970s in reaction against the medically qualified homeopaths is an example of this.

The sector is increasingly popular. Cant and Sharma (1999) estimate that at least a quarter of the population in Britain now has some level of involvement. Comparable figures exist in other Western countries (Eisenberg *et al.* 1998). Users are drawn to it for a variety of reasons. Many come for relief with chronic conditions where orthodox medicine has failed to alleviate symptoms. Some turn to alternative medicine for grave conditions like cancer where cure is not possible, but the aim is to improve the quality of life. Many seek a more personalised response than that typically offered within mainstream health care; and the perceived failings in the way orthodox medicine is delivered is a major recruiter for the sector. For some, alternative medicine is part of a wider set of beliefs and alternative life-styles. But Sharma (1992, 1996) suggests that most users adopt a fairly pragmatic approach and that their involvement should not be read as a radical turning away from orthodox medicine. The majority continue to use both systems. She alerts us to the danger of relying too heavily on accounts of the sector presented by practitioners who inevitably emphasise the theoretical and ideological element in their practice.

The growing popularity of alternative medicine needs, however, to be set in a wider cultural context. Alternative therapies have experienced a major period of expansion since the 1970s in association with a disparate set of cultural ideas broadly termed New Age or 'counter cultural' (Rozak 1971, Campbell 1987, Heelas 1996). Though these have been current in Western culture since the nineteenth century, they experienced a upsurge in the late 1960s and early 1970s when they were linked to a range of new social movements constructed around the politics of personal life, particularly in relation to feminism, sexuality, spirituality and the environment. They are frequently found in conjunction with practices like vegetarianism; and the growing popularity of that diet mirrors the growth in interest in alternative medicine (Twigg 1983). Alternative medicine itself has close links with vegetarianism; and a vegetarian diet is frequently seen as part of the treatment. These ideas that emerged in the 1970s have now been diffused into a wider, less distinctly alternative culture in which complimentary medicine is part. Underpinning them are certain central themes, focussed in particular around concepts of nature, wholeness and well-being. These resonate through the sector, and have implications for how the body is represented and managed within the field.

Coward argues that the body in alternative medicine is distinctive. It is the: 'vigorous body of perpetual renewal, the perfectible body which has no affinity with disease or darkness' (1989, p. 50). She regards this as an inversion of the earlier Christian conception of the degenerate body after the Fall which was seen as part of the burden of humanity, something prey to illness and death, so that it was only through the soul that one could transcend this world of corruption and loss. The body in alternative medicine, she argues, is the perfectible body, naturally good and healthful, and that it provides the basis for a form of secular, health-based salvation that links across to themes within modern consumer culture.

Alternative medicine aims to treat the person as a unified entity of mind, body and spirit. The body is seen as integral with the person, so that one cannot attend to it without exploring the state of that person more widely. This can not only mean material factors like diet or exercise, but also emotional, social and spiritual functioning, all of which are deemed relevant to determining why the person has become ill, and how they might be made better. Sickness is thus more than just a set of physical symptoms, but something rooted in the whole person and their wider environment. This holism often involves a spiritual dimension; indeed it is closely linked with the emergence in the west of 'spirituality' as a new social space, replacing the earlier focus on religion. Once again this is in contradistinction to orthodox medicine which developed in a way that is strongly secular; indeed the emergence of modern scientific medicine is one of the major breaking away of spheres that rent what Berger (1969) has termed the 'sacred canopy' of the pre-modern world view thus helping to create the modern secular world. Medicine has always had a strongly materialist, anti-metaphysical aspect. From the Middle Ages, medicine as a profession had a reputation for being irreligious, despite the personal piety of many doctors. It was seen as involving a reductionist form of knowledge, that involves a corporeal rather than spiritual focus.

Alternative therapies often contain ideas about the particularity of the patient and of the patient's body – of who and what they are – so that treatment is specific to that person. This can be seen within homeopathy with its concept of the patient's 'constitution' as something that is distinctive to them, and knowledge of which is central in determining doses. Again this contrasts with the way in which scientific medicine tends to treat the body, in which responses are in large degree seen as resting on a common physiology in which the body is seen as anonymous and generalisable, at least at the level of its cellular structure.

The emphasis on the person of the patient also extends to that of the practitioner, who is more readily deemed part of the interaction than is the case within orthodox medicine. The personality of the therapist or healer, his or her gifts or even bodily state, can be a significant element, not just in diagnosis but also in treatment. This is most true of therapies like spiritual healing, and can also be an element in more concrete forms of therapy. Alternative medicine contains strongly charismatic elements in which the personal relationship with the healer plays a significant role.

Once again modern scientific medicine does not traditionally operate on this basis – at least officially. The doctor is not primarily conceptualised as an individual in the interaction; and the relationship is characterised in terms of distance and personal neutrality. Medicine has, of course, always recognised the role of the doctor, and his or her personality, both in terms of special insights and qualities of personal empathy, and medicine is very aware of the placebo effect in which the personal charisma of the doctor can be important. However, it remains the case that scientific medicine aspires to perfect repeatability. The logic of the double blind RCT – the gold standard of modern medicine – rests precisely on eradicating these aspects.

Alternative medicine draws heavily on concepts of Nature and the natural. The body is regarded as naturally self-healing. These ideas are not absent from dominant medicine, but they are not emphasised to the same degree and are tempered by a greater belief in forceful intervention, in the form of drugs, surgery or other scientifically based treatments. Alternative medicine regards the natural healing power of the body as the real source of all alleviation or cure; and the aim of therapy is to work alongside and strengthen this force. The nature of the encounter is also one in which the body is used in a particular way. One of the characteristic features of alternative therapies is their use of direct touch, though the use of this varies. One of the consequences of the direct hands-on character is that the body of the therapist is significantly involved: it is their hands, their pressure, their physicality that is actively engaged. Just as the personality of the therapist can be significant, so too can their body, as a transmitter of healing presence. Again this contrasts with the dominant tradition of modern medicine in which the doctor and his or her body is rendered distant and neutral.

In drawing out the contrast between the body as conceptualised and treated within alternative and orthodox medicine, I have inevitably dealt with both systems in a schematic way that overemphasises their coherence and exaggerates the differences between them. As we have noted, modern scientific medicine is not a unitary phenomenon, but like alternative medicine, it contains a diversity of ideas and practices. Few GPs or psychiatrists, for example, would have difficulty in acknowledging the significance of the emotional and social life of the patient in his or her illness. Similarly many orthodox practitioners claim to practice in a holistic way. Medicine is also by its nature pragmatic, interested in what works, and this is once again a source of plurality and heterodoxy, in which ideas that are more characteristic of alternative schemes of thought can be included; and we have seen how orthodox medicine has incorporated elements from alternative therapies, like acupuncture or osteopathy, where they are deemed to have worked.

Conclusion

Medicine is one of the key institutions of modernity, located at the heart of modern culture. The way in which it constructs the body is, thus, of central significance for how it is perceived, managed, understood and experienced, both within the health care system itself, where medicine provides the central paradigm, and more widely through society, where its prestige and capacity to articulate and explain bodily matters means that its discourses occupy a dominant position. But as we have seen, medicine constructs the body in a particular way – one that is scientific, neutral, fragmented into its functioning parts, conceptualised at the level of cells and bio-chemical processes, and from which the element of meaning has been removed. The history of modern medicine is the story of the gradual replacement of transcendental, meaning-laden accounts of health and illness by neutral, scientific ones, and we noted in Chapter 3 on age how this also has implications for how old age – and death – are understood, and to some extent experienced, in modern societies.

But this dominant medical account is in many ways at odds with how the body is experienced and known, even within health care. Bodies – and body parts – are never just neutral things, and we saw how this has implications across a range of policy issues: the historical sequestration of corpses and the current retention of body parts; questions of presumed consent and the role of the state in determining this; and debates concerning the commodification of the body in a world-wide trade in organs. In each of these cases, there is a disjunction between the way in which the body is constructed within the dominant scientific paradigm, and the ways in which it is experienced, understood and valued within the wider culture.

Tensions around the meaning of the body also affect policy issues in relation to questions of human resources within the health care system. We saw how they resonate through debates concerning the nature of nursing, in particular its status as a profession and the role of the body and of direct work on it in this. Holistic nursing theory reasserts the value of such bodywork as part of its focus on the experiential body of the patient, but the predominant culture of health care does not supports this view. The growth of skill mix and division of labour, and the increasingly technical emphasis in nursing, means that such activities are sidelined, regarded as low-level, unskilled, not requiring a trained nurse. The increasing influence of managerialism within health care has also undermined these holistic perceptions. Nursing has not been successful in articulating the embodied nature of its work in the face of these trends. It is important here to recognise that nursing is itself ambivalent about these bodily activities. It shares the wider estimation of them exemplified in the dematerialising tendency whereby status is marked by distance from the bodily. Moreover, its own practices are not always so clearly located on the side of the patient and his/her embodiment. The holistic account of the body in nursing is an idealised one; and the profession is also closely involved in ordering, disciplining and controlling patients, producing the 'docile bodies' of Foucauldian analysis. We have also seen the importance of recognising the role of the bodily in relation to doctors and nurses themselves; for they too are embodied practitioners, and the ways in which they use their bodies, how they locate themselves within the larger symbolism of the body, has implications for how their practice is understood and evaluated. In particular it has implications for issues around the gendered character of these occupations.

Lastly, for many patients the experience of modern medicine – particularly hospital-based medicine – is a disjunctive one, involving not just pain but also dislocation, objectification and a denial of their sense of embodiment. A significant part of the distress that many patients feel in their encounters with hospitals and health care derive from failure to address the body as an experiential entity. Indeed, as we noted, part of the appeal of alternative medicine lies in the way that it rests on a different concept of the body and of the relationship between the patient and the practitioner. Alternative treatments emphasise the individuality of the patient and his/her body. They allow for greater personal empathy between the patient and the practitioner, an empathy that can extend into bodily contact through the use of techniques like touch or massage, in which the person, and indeed the body, of the practitioner is an acknowledged part of the exchange. We should not exaggerate the attraction of alternative medicine and the concept of the body that underlies it. Most who use it do so on a pragmatic basis that does not imply the repudiation of orthodox medicine. There are also questions to raise about efficacy. And it is important to recognise, as we noted at the start of this chapter, that the dominant scientific model of the body that underpins modern medicine, though open to criticism, is also the source of its unprecedented capacity to intervene effectively, to diagnose, alleviate and to some extent cure.

Chapter 6

Diet, Health and the Body: Obesity and Eating Disorders

In this chapter, I will explore the territory of health, eating and the body, concentrating on two areas: eating disorders and obesity. Both have become significant arenas of public health concern, and both illustrate the ways in which private troubles around the body, weight and weight control link to larger policy issues. In Britain, public health since its inception in the nineteenth century has been concerned with the structural factors that support or undermine the health of the population, and food has been an important element in these debates. Food raises the classic public health issues around the relationship between the State, the individual and the forces of capitalist production as they act on and shape the lives and bodies of people. There are also important links to be made between diets and dieting and the wider culture of consumption in which the body and its appearance assumes new significance, raising further questions concerning the representation and evaluation of the body in high- or postmodernity.

The links between public health and diet are not confined to these themes. The British Government has been concerned with questions of food and health, particularly in relation to the diets of the poor, since the nineteenth century, when food assumed a place in the wider Condition of England debate (Burnett 1979). In the early twentieth century, the focus moved to questions of national efficiency with the fear, particularly in the wake of the Boer War, that poor diets were undermining British military capacity. In the 1930s during the Depression, the diet of the poor, particularly the unemployed, again became the focus of concern, with the work of nutritionists and campaigners like Boyd Orr exposing the levels of malnutrition in the population (Smith 1999, A.S. Williams 1999). This work fed into the wartime development of food policy, particularly in relation to rationing which for the bottom half of society represented a significant improvement on their pre-war diet (Zweiniger-Bargielowska 2000). The emphasis began to change, however, in the 1960s and 1970s with the shift in understanding of *mal*nutrition away simply from inadequate intake, towards problems of excess. This evolution in public policy away from a problematic sector of society – the poor – towards the whole population was in line with the development of the New Public Health (Ashton and Seymour 1988) which aimed to focus on structural factors determining healthy and unhealthy

99

lives in the population as a whole. Concern with the diets of poorer people has not, however, gone way; and there is a large literature that has explored the degree to which it is possible – or rather not possible – to sustain a healthy life on benefits, particularly for children (Nelson 1993, 1999, 2002, Dobson 1994, Dowler and Calvert 1995, Leather 1996, L. Morris 1996, Piachaud and Webb 1996, Dowler *et al.* 2001, Dowler 2002).

The British government has also been involved in the nation's diet through the links that have been established between eating and health. Again the concern is a long-established one, but it has come into new prominence as statistical evidence has mounted over the last 20 years concerning the links between diet and patterns of disease. For example, it is now estimated that diet is a factor in about 40 per cent of cancers, rising to 80 per cent in relation to the large bowel, breast and prostate (Doll and Peto 1981, Cummings and Bingham 1998, Key *et al.* 2002). Diet is also implicated in coronary heart disease, stroke and diabetes (Baggott 2000, Mann 2002). Obesity, as we shall see, is also associated with poor health outcomes.

In general, government involvement in diet remains at the level of education and exhortation. Food is largely seen as a market good, though of course government is involved indirectly in this market through its role in agricultural subsidies, in planning and regulation (Gardner 1996, Wrigley and Lowe 1996, Duff 1999, Marsden *et al.* 2000, Marsden *et al.* 2000, Atkins and Bowler 2001, Barling *et al.* 2002). However, there are occasions when government is more directly involved through either setting standards or actual provision. In Britain, the school meal service provides an example of this. Developed on a charitable and voluntary basis in the nineteenth century as a means of alleviating poverty and malnutrition, the service was expanded after the Second World War to encompass all state schools (Burnett 1979, Rose and Falconer 1992, Webster 1997, Gustafsson 2002). School meals in the post-war era exemplified the values of the British welfare state: dull but nutritious; universalist, in part at least; and worthy, but lacking in choice. But with the shift in political values in the 1980s with the Thatcher government, schools were encouraged to reduce costs and to outsource provision to commercial caterers. Nutritional standards were abandoned; vending machines encouraged. The model of provision was to mirror that of the market. Since then, as we shall see, rising concern over childhood obesity has put this free market policy under critical spotlight. Current government policy in Britain is concerned with reversing at least some of these changes.

Eating disorders

Eating disorders encompass a range of problematic conditions in relation to food, of which anorexia nervosa and bulimia are the most common.

Anorexia is a form of self-starvation, that can be life-threatening. It has one of the highest rates of mortality for any psychiatric condition, estimated at 13–20 per cent at 20-year follow-up (Howlett *et al.* 1995). Bulimia nervosa, involving self-induced vomiting and purging, can occur in conjunction with anorexia, or as a condition on its own. It is associated with binge eating in which gross amounts of food are consumed regardless of need, pleasure or hunger, often alone and accompanied by feelings of self-disgust, anxiety and depression. Bulimia is found in association with a range of body weights.

There is little systematic data on prevalence of such disorders in the general population. Even within health statistics, evidence is patchy; and many who suffer from eating disorders never become visible to health professionals – indeed their wider cultural significance lies in the fact that they represent exaggerated versions of behaviour that is common within the population. As a result, it is not always easy to define the exact point at which normal dieting or bingeing becomes a disorder. The Royal College of Psychiatrists estimated in 1992 that in the UK about 60,000 people may be receiving treatment for anorexia or bulimia at any time (EDA 2005). Howlett and colleagues (1995) estimate the prevalence of anorexia among women at around 0.2 per cent, with prevalence around 1 per cent among teenage schoolgirls. Hoek (1991) in a Dutch study of primary care established a rate of anorexia of 6.3 per 100,000 of the population, and of bulimia of 9.9. King (1986), with a similar UK population, estimated 1 per cent of patients had bulimia, with a further 3 per cent displaying partial symptoms.

Eating disorders are a phenomenon of modern society. Though anorexia was first identified by Gull in 1858, it was a rare condition; and it is only in the last three decades that its incidence has increased markedly. This is likely to be a real increase and not simply the product of greater levels of recognition, though these may play a part. Some writers have attempted to read the condition back historically into earlier centuries. Bell (1985), in his *Holy Anorexia*, argued that medieval saints exhibited these symptoms. Such attempts are, however, essentially mistaken. As Bynum (1987) shows, the meanings of phenomena like medieval self-starvation are specific to their historical and cultural settings, and need to be interpreted in the contexts of medieval women's relationships to food, religion and the body more generally rather than simply read off in a modern context. The current manifestation of anorexia is similarly historically situated, and requires similar cultural analysis to make sense of its meanings.

Eating disorders are strongly gendered. The great majority of sufferers of anorexia are female: the widely quoted ratio is 10:1, though the basis for the estimate is unclear. Bulimia and binge eating also appear to be more common among women, though the gender balance seems to be slightly more even. Anorexia is often associated with adolescence, but is also common among women in their twenties and thirties. It used to be associated with middle-class girls and with educational success, but this has been questioned, and the condition itself may have spread to other groups.

Gender is central to both the phenomena and the analysis. It was the work of feminists across a range of disciplines that originally brought the topic into view. This developed initially in the context of feminist reworkings of psychoanalysis and psychotherapy (Bruch 1973, Orbach 1986), but it extended into a wider social and cultural analysis. Within this feminist literature, a broad consensus has emerged, though with differences in emphasis (Chernin 1981, Robertson 1992, Bordo 1993, MacSween 1993, Hepworth 1999). Eating disorders, especially anorexia, though forms of individual sickness, reflect wider preoccupations in culture – what Bordo (1993) captures in the phrase 'psychopathology as the crystallisation of culture'. They represent, in exaggerated form, practices in relation to the body found more widely in society, specifically around ideals concerning self-control, consumption and bodily perfectionism. Eating disorders reflect the paradoxical situation of women in modern society, presenting a working through at the individual bodily level, of tensions in relation to women's wider social position. They are both a rebellion against contemporary femininity and an exaggerated adherence to aspects of it. The type of body pursued – exaggeratedly thin and stripped of fat – and the practices used to achieve it – the severe imposition of control – are both significant in its understanding. The condition has both psychological and social/cultural significance, and its explanation needs to be pursued at a number of levels. Some feminist writers emphasise the psychodynamic aspects, looking at the function of the behaviour as much as the meaning, and emphasising aspects like power struggles within the family, problems between mothers and daughters. However, even where they do emphasise individual aspects, it is always within a context in which gender is not taken as given, but seen as something deriving from social and cultural structures.

Over the last century, the desirable body shape for women has changed. In previous eras, generous flowing curves and abundant flesh were favoured, unsurprisingly in societies where supply of food was not always secure and where wealth was associated with bodily size. But from the 1920s onwards Western society has favoured a slimmer, more boyish shape (Sterns 1997). Fat has come to be evaluated negatively in terms of sexual unattractiveness, slothfulness and low social class. In an age of family limitation and growing involvement of women in the labour market, abundant, visible fertility is no longer in tune with aspirations. The slim physique is also associated with youth; and the pursuit of slimness is part of the wider culture of anti-ageing discussed in Chapter 3. Visual representations in the media have followed and amplified these trends, with heavy pressure on women at all costs to be slim. Women in the public eye who put on weight are held up to ridicule in the popular press who act as the 'fat police', enforcing the body ideal. Among models, in particular, the trend has been for increasingly thin bodies. The form of body favoured is semi-androgynous, with slim hips, flat stomach, defined muscles and long thin legs, although with breast augmentation this can be artificially feminised, presenting the paradox of a lean stripped body with full breasts. Women are thus presented through the media with forms of bodies that are not just aspirational but literally unachievable, except through surgery.

Physical looks have been central in the evaluation of women's worth for centuries. What has changed, however, is that women are increasingly surrounded by a visual culture saturated with images of perfection. Unsurprisingly women record higher levels of dissatisfaction with their appearance and their bodies than do men (Tseelon 1995). Women have traditionally been identified with their bodies in a way that men are not, and they invest much more of themselves, and of their time and effort, in attempts to produce a desirable appearance. Women internalise the male gaze; and with their greater knowledge and preoccupation, create within themselves an exacting connoisseur – a task master all the more exacting since 'he' is schooled in all the refinements of femininity (Lloyd 1996). This turning in of the critical gaze, which is common among women, is particularly important in the understanding of anorexia, which needs to be seen as an even harsher form of such self-policing.

Eating disorders present a paradoxical phenomena, involving both complicity with, and rebellion against cultural norms around the gendered body (Benson 1997). MacSween (1993) argues that women in creating anorexic bodies are synthesising contradictory aspects of their social position, transforming the public and social conflicts around gender into the private and individualised setting of their bodies. Parallels are often drawn with hysteria, another historically situated disease, in which the structural limitations placed on women's lives resulted in behaviour that embodied both submission and rebellion (Showalter 1987, Ussher 1991). Nineteenth-century hysteria contains both an exaggerated version of contemporary femininity, in which women were frail, irrational, emotionally volatile and thus unable to cope with the strains of education or of public life, and a rebellion against such ideas through wildness, sickness, lack of decorum and control. Anorexia, like hysteria, can be seen as a form of gender rebellion, though a profoundly dysfunctional one.

One of the paradoxical features of anorexia is the way in which it is linked to women's growing success in the public world; and a number of writers have presented the condition as a form of self-limiting, in the context of competing demands on women in the public and private spheres. For Chernin (1986), the tensions relate in particular to mothers and daughters, and the contradictions posed to young women of seeming to exceed and, thus reject, their mothers through their own success, a theme that echoes Bruch's (1973) earlier analysis in terms of over-compliant daughters. Educational attainment is seen as significant because it presents a conflict between pursuing individual success, which may seem to revolve around rejecting affiliation, and taking the more 'feminine' route of subordinating the self to the wishes and desires of others.

Other writers emphasise the tensions arising from competing demands placed on women in the public sphere. There is an inherent contradiction, MacSween (1993) argues, between the ideal of individualism presented to women in terms of the pursuit of success, and the ideal of femininity that demands the reverse. Men can be, and are, non-gendered subjects, representing the neutral as much as the masculine. Women, however, are never ungendered in this way. They are their sex; are their bodies; never generally representative but always specifically female. Though individualism is presented as gender neutral, it is fundamentally masculine. Reconciling the hidden incompatibility of the two ideals of individualism and femininity poses central difficulties for women. The anorexic body of adolescence can be seen as a dysfunctional attempt to resolve the problem through the creation of a gender neutral individualism within a female body.

The imposition of control is a central feature of anorexia; and the struggle for self-mastery, a recurring theme in anorexic accounts. Controling the body is one of the traditional requirements of femininity: women learn to watch how they behave; how they sit, eat or otherwise comport themselves physically. Women, particularly at adolescence, can experience their bodies as a sources of embarrassment and betrayal (Frost 2001). In particular women's bodies are disciplined in relation to sexuality and its overt expression. Women learn early that they need to exert control over their bodies and their desires, if they are to be acceptable. The other face of this control is fear and disgust with the aspects of the self that are required to be controlled. These processes have their parallel in relation to appetite. In anorexia, appetite is the enemy, and elaborate rituals are adopted by sufferers in order to control and deny it. In MacSweens's reading of anorexia, appetite comes to stand for an encroaching and alarming femaleness that threatens to destabilise the neutral, androgynous self. Anorexia represents a fear of the Female, perceived as demanding, needful, out of control, and since women in patriarchal culture are not allowed to have autonomous desires, female desire, if asserted, becomes voracious and overwhelming. The feared insatiability of women in relation to sex is thus transformed into a feared insatiability over food; and control of the mouth and of the appetite become means of imposing control over these alarming desires.

For Orbach (1986) the denial of food is part of a wider denial of emotional neediness. Women's emotional needs in modern society often remain unmet. Women are atuned to meeting the emotional needs of men, and in such a way that they remain hidden from public view – to the extent indeed that men themselves often remain unaware of them. It is not that men are not emotionally needy, it is just that their needs are likely to be met (Orbach and Eichenbaum 1983). Women, by contrast, rarely receive comparable emotional support, and because their needs are unmet, they experienced themselves as needy and voracious. Mothers are often ambivalent in the face of their daughters' needs, that seems to echo and reflect their own. Girls learn to regard their legitimate wants as signs of neediness and excess, things to be denied and controlled.

Though gender is central to the understanding of eating disorders, the conditions also reflect wider cultural themes. Since the Greeks, Western culture has contained a set of meanings around the rejection of food as a means of transcendence. In this Platonic tradition, the body is identified with confinement and limitation, its grossness and earthliness contrasted with the purity of the soul. The body is seen as alien, not part of the essential self, something that weighs the person down and from which the soul seeks to escape (Bordo 1993). At worst, the body is an enemy, a source of betrayal, of desire and confusion, something that must be mastered and disciplined. Control of food, especially certain sorts of food, becomes a means to this. Red meat, through its association with the flesh, was traditionally seen as something that stimulated the passions; and it was often avoided by those seeking a higher spiritual life, for example within Western monasticism or later Christian and eastern-derived spiritual movements (Twigg 1983). These ascetic purificatory themes find their echo in the accounts of anorexics, who similarly speak of rising above the body, of purging its grossness and fatness, of feeling clear, pure and light. Adopting a vegetarian diet is a common stage on the way to anorexia. This is not to argue that anorexic ideas are the same as those of Platonic, medieval or later Christian writers, but rather to recognise that these dualist themes run as an undercurrent through Western culture and contribute to the variety of meanings that are currently available in the negotiation of the body. For Turner (1984) what is significant is the way that older religious ascetic ideas have been transformed into modern secular versions. People now discipline and control their bodies – and their lives – not in pursuit of religious ideals but secular, consumerist ones.

Eating disorders also need to be located within pervasive ideas about self-mastery and control. In an increasingly anomic and globalised world, in which people feel they have little purchase over the forces that determine their lives, the body can represent a small area over which they feel they can exercise control. Working on the body, pursuing dreams of beauty or bodily perfection, offers space for self-determination. One of the central aspirations, even fantasies, of modern society is that of taking control of one's life and self. A vast self-help literature supports the dream that by one's own effort one can be successful, happy, healthy – and dieting is a classic component in this. Women in particular are prone to displace onto their bodies other discontents, believing that if only they could lose a stone, their lives would be transformed; and the self-help literature is full of advice on losing weight and remaking appearance. For men, the parallel expression can be found in extreme exercise regimes or body building. Just as the bodies of anorexics offer a grim parodic version of acceptable femininity, so the built body of the bodybuilder with its bulging muscles represents an exaggerated version of masculinity incarnate (Lloyd 1996, Benson 1997). Like anorexia these are modern 'epidemics of the will' in which the desire for self-mastery and control achieves exaggerated proportions.

Lastly these bodily practices are linked to the dynamic of consumption. Women in particular strive after standards of appearance and bodily perfection presented in advertising and the media that cannot ultimately be met, but whose pursuit can be displaced onto products associated with such ideals. The body has thus become a major site for consumption, with a proliferation over the last two decades of products aimed at the body. The earlier focus in the cosmetic and toiletry industry on the face has shifted to the body as a whole, with the elaboration of creams, gels, lotions aimed at its improvement and enhancement. A minor industry has developed around the eradication of cellulite – a condition unknown until the 1980s. The slim ideal is part of this new bodily perfectionism.

We now come, however, to the paradox concerning modern diets. Though we are surrounded by images of slim, perfect bodies, as a society we are increasingly fat. The cultural messages may be in terms of stringency and the need to achieve a slim stripped body, but it is clear that they are not being heard or not being acted upon, effectively at least. As we shall see, average weight is increasing steadily across all Western societies. If modern society is indeed so preoccupied with slimness and bodily perfection, how can this be so? Is there a discrepancy in the evidence, or the interpretation?

It is certainly the case that the evidence of obesity does challenge some of the more culturally based accounts that stress the significance of bodily perfectionism in the negotiation of modern identity. Much of the work around the cultural significance of eating disorders draws on theorising for which the evidential base is somewhat weak; and the postmodern emphasis on representation presents the danger of focussing on imagery rather than actuality. Such media-based approaches also tend to privilege the concerns of young middle-class urban elites, with their accounts of gyms, body culture and the postmodern search for identity through consumption and the body. These themes are found across the fashionable media, but the extent to which they actually operate within people's day-to-day lives is more questionable. Many who write on the topic of eating disorders within the broad remit of cultural studies are themselves drawn from these social groups. The contrast between the preoccupations of cultural critics and the realities of body weight in the general population may provide us with a warning about the limitations of such analyses and the need to temper theorising with critical evidence.

There is, however, a second way to resolve the apparent paradox, and this is by exploring the way in which the two elements are linked. Both represent a situation in which eating has become problematic. The social disciplines and constraints of earlier eras have weakened, leaving individuals more isolated in determining the pattern of their lives, including eating lives. People are thrown back on their own resources, so that constraint increasingly has to be imposed from within. For many, however, the constant requirement to achieve such individualised self-control is too demanding, and their weight drifts up. For others, the imposition of self-control takes over, and the situation spirals down into the malign one of anorexia. The reasons why this happens are rooted in individual psychology, as well as the wider social milieu. The paradox of perfectionism and failure may, thus, not be a paradox at all. Consumer society is driven by such discrepancies between the images and the realities of people's lives. Rising levels of obesity do not mean the population is unconcerned with weight, or not engaged with the culture of slimness. It simply means that their aspirations are not being achieved, for reasons that we will explore in the next section.

The rise of obesity

Obesity is commonly defined in terms of Body Mass Index (BMI). By this, 47 per cent of men and 33 per cent of women were categorised as overweight in the UK in 2001; and 21 per cent of men and 23 per cent of women as obese (Social Trends 2001). This means that the majority of the population, some 68 per cent of men and 56 per cent of women, are above desirable weight. These figures have been rising steadily. The prevalence of obesity in the UK has tripled since 1980 and is set to rise further. Overweight is more frequent among men than women, though women have slightly higher levels of obesity. Weight increases with age, though obesity is growing faster among the young. Obesity is associated negatively with socio-economic levels (Social Trends 2001). This is particularly the case among women. There is also a 'race' dimension. In the US, obesity is more common among Black and Hispanic women, and in the UK among Black Caribbean and Pakistani women (NAO 2001). The trend towards obesity is worldwide, to the extent that the World Health Organisation (WHO) has termed it a 'global epidemic' (WHO 2000). The WHO now regards obesity as a 'non-communicable disease', one closely linked with modern Western lifestyles, and spreading, it seems, inexorably from the developed to the developing world. Developing societies can now exhibit the twin problems of rising obesity for some groups, in conjunction with undernutrition for others.

Body Mass Index has been criticised as a measure. In health terms, the form in which fat is stored in the body can be as important as the level of fat, with upper- and mid-body fat more problematic than lower body; and for this reason, some studies include a waist measurement. BMI also varies between ethnic groups: Polynesians, for example, have a lower proportion of body fat than do Caucasian Australians with the same BMI (WHO 2000). It is also culturally based to some degree at least. Evaluations of ideal weight reflect ideas about the body and its desirability; and we have already noted how these have changed historically. In the past abundant flesh, particularly in women, was seen as a sign of health, fertility, good looks and wealth; and these positive evaluations are still dominant in many developing countries, where an attribution of obesity would not be recognised. Some writers suggest that such judgements represent a colonial practice, based on white Western body norms that favour the slim, ascetic and disciplined body. They argue instead in favour of what is seen as a richer, fuller and more sensual version of the body that accepts and celebrates physicality, particularly female physicality. The definition of obesity is also questioned by fat advocates in the West, particularly in America, where such groups have challenged the negative portrayal of larger people and argue for their civil rights (Bovey 1994, National Association to Advance Fat Acceptance 2005).

It remains the case, however, that obesity measured by BMI is linked with poorer health outcomes. WHO (2000) reports an almost lineal relationship between BMI and increased levels of morbidity and mortality, though the nature of the link is complex. Problems associated with overweight include Type 2 diabetes, hypertension, myocardial infarction and cancer of the colon. In the case of diabetes, obesity increases the chance of contracting the condition by a factor of 5.2 in men and 12.7 in women; in the case of hypertension by 2.6 and 4.2; and cancer of the colon by 3.0 and 2.7 (NAO 2001). The National Audit Office estimates that in 1998, 18 million days of medically certified sickness in Britain were attributable to obesity and its consequences. Thirty thousand deaths were attributable, representing 6 per cent of all deaths that year. This compares with 10 per cent for smoking. Obesity is thus a major public health concern.

Weight is the product of the balance between calories consumed and energy expended. The exact physiology of the body in relation to weight gain is complex, and not fully understood (WHO 2000). Bodily regulation acts to even out intake over the short term. There are also mechanisms that mean that steady weight gain or loss may be followed by a static phase where a new balance is established; and this may underlie evidence that persistent dieting can contribute to the problem. Basal metabolism also varies between individuals. However, it remains the case that the primary factors determining weight are food intake and level of physical activity. Both of these have been subject to significant change over the last 30 years.

In relation to food intake, much of the problem concerns what has been termed 'passive overconsumption', the unthinking consumption of large numbers of calories, associated in particular with foods high in fat. Fat is crucial because it has the highest energy density of all foods, combined with a pleasing mouth feel. The physiology of the body is also such that it is easier to overconsume food high in fat (WHO 2000). Appetite control signals in relation to it are weak, and often too delayed to prevent high intake. Less energy dense foods allow time for appetite signals to operate, making it harder to overconsume. Though the body responds strongly to sweetness, it does not appear to overwhelm appetite control to quite the same degree. The combination of sweetness and fat is, however, a very strong inducement to consume.

Offer (2001, 2006) argues that difficulties around overconsumption are part of a wider set of problems in relation to the growth of short-term pleasure time horizons and the erosion of the culture of self-control in the post-war era. This can be discerned across a range of behaviour – sexual, dietary, economic in terms of savings ratios and levels of public investment – in which people are increasingly reluctant to restrain current consumption in favour of future benefits. These represent what he terms 'myopic choices' in which people act in ways that will result in adverse consequences even though these are foreseeable. The immediate gratification of eating is thus preferred to the delayed one of normative appearance in the form of a socially approved body size. In the post-war era, affluence brought a flow of new and inexpensive rewards. He argues that these rewards arrived faster than the disciplines of prudence that might constrain their pursuit, with the result that self-control in relation to a range of goods, including food, declined in this era.

A major part of the problem derives from the nature of the food industry in capitalist society (Nestle 2002). Manufacturers operate in the context of abundance. Food consumption is now relatively inelastic: there is only so much food that people in the West can be persuaded to eat. Corporations thus compete for what is a limited market. Profits lie in selling products with a high value added, ideally based on inexpensive ingredients. Sugar and fat are both cheap and highly attractive. Salt is also valuable to manufacturers since it too is cheap, enhances flavour and, through its capacity to bind water, bulks up processed foods. Manufactured food, and especially fast foods, rely heavily on these three ingredients.

Food producers spend large sums of money on advertising and promotion, mostly in relation to fast food and highly packaged, processed foods where the big profits lie. Seventy per cent of money spent on food advertising in the US goes on convenience foods – candy, snacks, soft drinks and desserts.

Only 2.2 per cent is spent on fruit, vegetables and beans (Nestle 2002). Fruit and vegetables are not promoted because they do not support elaborate processing and yield low profits. Food manufacturers have also had clear incentives to inflate portion sizes. It has been more profitable, particularly for fast food providers, to focus on size rather than price. The marginal cost of ingredients is small; and such strategies enable them to create an image of abundance and good value. In the post-war era, McDonald's biggest hamburger inflated from 3.7 ounces to almost 9 (Offer 2001). McDonald's Supersize meal now contains 1304 calories, with over 44 grams of fat. Whoppers, giant portions and double helpings are strongly promoted. Large portions are now ubiquitous in America. One of the key differences between the United States and France, which has the lowest level of obesity in Europe, is portion size, which is larger in the US in every setting (Nielsen and Popkin 2003). All of this supports what Nestle (2002) terms an 'eat more' culture that encourages overconsumption and obesity.

Since the 1960s, nutritional advice has been a battleground of competing interests, with particular conflict around labelling and dietary advice. As Nestle shows in her analysis of the US, food producers have consistently attempted to weaken and manipulate dietary advice given by government and health agencies. The Department of Agriculture has been caught between its responsibilities to protect agriculture and to advice the public about health and diet. Similar tensions occurred in the UK, where the primary government body dealing with food in the post-war era, the Ministry of Agriculture, Fisheries and Foods (MAFF), focussed its concern almost exclusively on agriculture and food production; and it presents a classic example of capture by producer interests (Smith 1989). Since then, partly under the impact of food scandals like the one involving BSE and the loss of confidence among the population in the government's regulatory role, MAFF has been broken up, and the Food Standards Agency established with a much clearer public health remit.

The food industry often tries to obfuscate the nutritional messages, encouraging confusion among the public over the details of recommendation and the significance of new studies. However, as Nestle (2002) shows, the broad nature of advice has been, and remains, clear: reduced intake of fat, sugar, salt and alcohol; increased fruit and vegetables; and substitution of unrefined for processed foods. It is just that this is unpalatable to the food industry. In particular the industry uses arguments about 'balance' to undermine nutritional advice. While it is true that no food is bad in itself and what matters is the balance of consumption, this is used by the industry to deflect criticism from specific foods and to undermine suggestions that people ought to eat less of or avoid certain foods. Crisps, hamburgers, pot noodles, sugar drinks can thus all qualify for being 'part of a healthy diet'.

The problem of obesity is compounded by the ubiquity of opportunities to eat in modern society. Food is now on offer across a range of settings: theatres, shops, museums, churches, libraries, pubs and stately homes. There is almost no public place where food, particularly snack food, is not available. This presents individuals with the requirement that they exercise constraint over their consumption on an almost constant basis. The opportunities – and thus the temptations – to consume are all around and all the time, no longer constrained, as in the past by limited outlets or set patterns of eating. Eating patterns have become more fragmented, both in the ways people eat and in the social structuring of meals. While the death of the meal announced by Fischler (1980) and its replacement by the 'empire of snacks' has been exaggerated, there has been a decline in the formality of eating patterns. Even within families, traditionally the classic setting for the 'proper meal' (Murcott 1982, Charles and Kerr 1988), there has been a growth in eating in shifts, with less emphasis placed on the shared evening meal around the table, as children's and adults' work and leisure timetables have become more complex.

More meals are taken outside the home. This is significant because such meals are typically high in fat and sugar. In the 1950s, six out of ten men in the Britain took their main meal at home at midday. In 1955 eating out represented less than 10 per cent of food outlays. By 1995 it had more than doubled its share of food spending, rising to 25 per cent in the Britain, and more than 45 per cent in US (Offer 2001). Half of American meals are now taken out of the home. People have much less control over and less knowledge of the ingredients going into such meals, making it hard to monitor intake. Portions are also larger than at home.

The way food is consumed is also more informal, with more snack foods, more grazing, eating in the hand from the wrapper rather than on a plate. Fast food is typically designed to be eaten in this way, often while walking along. Its ubiquity in the high street has helped erode earlier prohibitions on eating in the streets or with the hands. These patterns are again relevant because they make it harder to regulate or limit food intake. They speed up the rate of consumption, making it easier to overeat. Such eating is often done in conjunction with other things, like watching TV or films, again making it easier for passive consumption to occur. By contrast, behavioural approaches to losing weight emphasise the importance of set meal times, slow eating and making the food the focus of attention and enjoyment.

The other half of the weight equation concerns physical activity. Here again the nature of modern life conspires against people, who are less physically active than in the past. A range of labour-saving mechanisms like escalators, automatic doors, washing machines and hedge clippers mean that daily life is less physically arduous. Manual work is less demanding; and many such jobs have been replaced by service occupations. We have increasingly built an environment that supports sedentary lifestyles. Planning has prioritised the car over walking, and its use has risen as more and more venues, from shopping malls to cinemas, become largely inaccessible except by car. Foot transport is in decline. In Britain, the Department of Health data for 1998 suggests that 23 per cent of men and 26 per cent of women were sedentary, using the criterion of less than 30-minute period of moderate exercise per week. The WHO (2000) measures physical activity levels (PAL) giving values of 1.4 for sedentary; 1.55–1.6 for limited activity; and more than 1.75 for active. People living in cities using motor transport and doing non-manual work will typically have a PAL value of 1.55–1.60, and these figures are drifting downwards in all industrialised societies. It is a measure of the difficulty involved in increasing physical activity levels that in order to raise this value from 1.58 to 1.70 for an average weight man, he would have to add 20 minutes of vigorous exercise or one hour of walking every day, and this in a context where there is already a 24 minute exercise requirement built into the estimates.

The problems come together particularly sharply in the case of children. Childhood obesity has increased markedly over the last two decades. Obesity in 2–4-year olds has almost doubled in 10 years, from 5 to 9 per cent (Royal College of Physicians 2004). Between 1989 and 1998 in the UK, there was an increase in the proportion who were overweight from 15 to 24 per cent and obese from 5 to 9 per cent. The trend towards overweight has been observed among children younger than four (Bundred *et al.* 2001). In the US the prevalence of obesity among children aged 6–11 years has risen from 7 per cent in 1976 to 13 per cent in 1999, and among those aged 12–19 years from 5 to 14 per cent (American Obesity Association 2002). With this has gone a growth in weight-related conditions previously only associated with adults, such as high serum cholesterol, high blood pressure, Type 2 or late onset diabetes, which can no longer be termed such (Nestle 2002). There is a strong correlation between obesity and watching TV, so that one study suggested that the viewing habits of children convey more information about risk of early coronary heart disease than do conventional questions about family disease history (Nestle 2002). American children's diets are heavy in manufactured foods. Fifty per cent of their calories come from added fat and sugar (35 and 15 per cent respectively) (Nestle 2002).

The food industry targets children in particular in its promotions. Ninety per cent of food advertising screened during children's broadcasts in the UK is for foods high in fat, salt and/or sugar (Royal College of Physicians 2004). In the United States, TV programmes aimed at children are frequently sponsored by sweet, soft drink and food manufacturers. Teletubbies in the US are sponsored by McDonalds, who also feature their own children-friendly figure of Ronald McDonald who hands out toys and supports birthday parties. Coca Cola as well as sponsoring events send promotional gifts to 'teen influentials' like cheerleaders and sports players, with the aim that they will pass on the surplus to friends so that the product comes with a local peer endorsement (Nestle 2002). The aim is to build life-long loyalty. Similar promotions operate in the UK. Food and drink adverts are used to support educational TV in the US, which is beamed into schools in conjunction with adverts. Vouchers are also used to bring resources into schools. Walker's Crisps in the UK claim to have donated some 7 million books to schools as part of their voucher scheme; this requires the consumption of some 1.2 billions packs (*The Times* 3 March 2004). These forms of funding are particularly important in poorer neighbourhoods, where diets are already likely to be deficient.

Food corporations are also involved directly in school meals. In the US, in 1997 some 30 per cent of public high schools served fast food. From the school's point of view, it resolves the problem of providing a meal, gives students what they want, keeps them on the premises and may contribute to school funds. Some schools have signed contracts for 'pouring rights' whereby the school receives money for the exclusive right to serve a particular drink. By 2000, some 200 school districts had such contracts. In the UK, vending machines have similarly contributed to school finances. The growth in the consumption of sugary soda drinks is particularly problematic. Forty years ago, children drank water with their meals; now they drink heavily promoted fizzy drinks. The market for soft drinks in the US in the 1990s expanded four times as fast as any other category of food or beverage. Since the overwhelming intake is in the non-diet variety, this represents what Nestle terms 'liquid candy'. Americans now consume an average of 556 cans of soft drink per year, only 124 of which are of low calorie (Nestle 2002).

Children lead less physically active lives. This is partly the result of a general decline, but it is exacerbated by increasingly protective attitudes among parents arising from fear of traffic, paedophiles and other dangers in the social environment. As a result children are escorted to school or taken by car and only more rarely allowed out to play independently. In the decade between 1987 and 1996, the proportion of under-17s walking to school fell from 59 to 49 per cent (NAO 2001). The National Diet and Nutritional Survey of 2000 measuring PAL estimated that the majority of 7–18-year olds were 'inactive'. Schools also put less emphasis on physical exercise. During the 1980s and 1990s as part of the Thatcherite-inspired asset stripping, some UK schools sold off their playing fields. The demands of the national curriculum have also squeezed out sport: the proportion of young people spending more than 2 hours a week in curricular school sport fell from 46 per cent in 1994 to 33 per cent in 1999 (NAO 2001). English schools are at the bottom of the European league in terms of time allocated to physical education (Royal College of Physicians 2004).

The politics of ingestion

Responses to obesity raise classic tensions in relation to the role of the state, the individual and the forces of capitalist production. Though questions of weight can be presented as the product of individual choices, decisions concerning them take place in a social and cultural context that is shaped by wider forces. Prominent among these are the complex of economic activities that make up the food provider interest and the market relations within which they operate. Government in attempting to affect consumption finds itself in direct conflict with these. There are parallels here with government's dealings with other form of ingestion, notably tobacco, alcohol and, in a different category, recreational drugs; though each presents a slightly different goal in public health terms.

The ambivalence of government has perhaps been clearest in relation to the tobacco industry, where in the UK taxation created, in the mid-twentieth century, a symbiotic relationship between the Treasury and the tobacco producers that the public health lobby found hard to break (Calnan 1984, Taylor 1984, Viscusi 1992). Tobacco companies have been, and to some extent still are, important corporate interests – employers of large number of people and providers of many shareholder dividends. Governments have been reluctant to disturb this. Over the last 30 years different administrations in the UK engaged in a cat and mouse game with the industry, in the form of agreements, followed by requirements, in relation to advertising, warnings on packages, restrictions on sales. Government commitment was never wholehearted, particularly under Conservative administrations, and the tobacco industry used its money to create a powerful political lobby. More recently pressure from the European Union has been important in driving forward polices in relation to warnings and advertising bans. Government in Britain now accepts that smoking is wholly bad and that total cession is the aim, though it is still cautious in how far it can go in attempting to restrict people's choices. The discovery of passive smoking was a turning point here, because it has legitimated environmental strategies like work place bans. Though justified in terms of the protecting individuals otherwise exposed to smoke, their real importance lies in supporting the classic public health argument that interventions need to address structural rather than individual factors. Tobacco companies are also increasingly facing the possibility of legal action on a parallel with developments in the United States, where the companies have been forced into expensive settlements in the face of health care claims. Though the tobacco industry still attempts to fight a rear guard battle in the West, it has largely accepted that it has little future there, and that the Third World offers a more profitable setting, and one in which free market approaches are still untrammelled.

There is a parallel history of government ambivalence and control in relation to alcohol, though here the focus has been more on crime and public disorder than health impact. There is a long history in Britain of government attempts to control, license and profit from the sale of alcohol, through restrictions on outlets and hours, on access by minors, by control of advertising and promotions, and through taxation (Harrison 1971, Baggott 2000, Room *et al.* 2005). Here the public health aim is slightly different, not cessation but moderation. The message is also more complex, in that it encompasses concern not only with the more obvious problems of people who can be deemed 'alcoholic', but also the hidden difficulties of the now considerable proportion of the population who are drinking above recommended levels but without immediate and obvious damage. The drink industry is willing to acknowledge the first, but reluctant to recognise the second. Above all the drink industry is highly resistant to the classic public health argument that the best way to reduce problematic drinking is by a reduction in overall consumption. Baggott (2000) recounts some of the recent battles between government and the industry over recommended intake levels. Room and colleagues conclude:

> A stark discrepancy exists between research findings about the effective-ness of alcohol control measures and the policy options considered by most governments. In many places, the interests of the alcohol industry have effectively exercised a veto over policies, making sure that the main emphasis is on ineffective strategies such as education. (Room *et al.* 2005, p. 527)

In relation to food, the public health message is more complex. There is not the single focus that there is with tobacco and alcohol. The aim is a balanced diet across a range of consumption, though as we have noted the notion of 'balance' can be exploited by the food industry to blur the health message. So far government has preferred to pursue the issue at the level of advice on diet and lifestyles. In relation to the food industry there is a strong preference for codes of conduct rather than legislation. Government has been cautious, even fearful, of seeming to interfere in people's choices.

More recently, however, the problem of obesity has risen up the political agenda. There have been a series of reports and public enquiries in the UK and beyond (WHO 2000, NAO 2001, House of Commons Health Committee 2004, Royal College of Physicians 2004). The issue has even begun to impact on the Treasury in its new role under Gordon Brown as auditor of policy outcomes. The Wanless Reports on health care for the Treasury strongly endorsed the public health agenda as the only effective means of increasing productivity in relation to health. This included a strong focus on obesity (Wanless 2004). Newspapers and the popular media have taken up the issue, which manages to unite the personal concerns of readers with larger policy matters. Among the middle class there is an additional resonance, in that there is a marked class profile in obesity, and the issue thus offers opportunities to deplore the bad habits of others. Obesity now forms part of the cultural politics of class in which working-class habits of eating and parenting are singled out and stigmatised, allowing class prejudices to express themselves in directly bodily form.

The new political and media attention has meant that the food industry is worried. Chocolate bar manufactures are fearful that they will have to carry health warnings like those on cigarettes. McDonald's – emblematic of fast food providers – has seen its profits decline. It has responded by introducing healthy options – though these remain marginal to the enterprise. Fast food providers in the United States are particularly fearful that they may be subject to successful suits on a parallel to the smoking ones; and they have taken pre-emptive action promoting legislative changes that outlaw such claims.

Together these shifts in opinion have created a climate in which government is more willing to act, though it is notable that the current government in Britain is more confident in focussing on childhood obesity than that of adults. The rationale is in terms of the worrying increase in this group and the long-term health impacts, but it also reflects the fear of interfering in relation to adults. Government is confident in trying to affect the choices of children, but not adults.

We should perhaps ask at this point why governments are so reluctant to get directly involved in issues of ingestion. Why, when the evidence concerning the impact on health is so clear, do they shy away from action that goes beyond simply advice or exhortation? The key lies in the fact that all Western governments operate in the context of capitalism. They have no wish fundamentally to challenge the logic that underlies these relations. The public health agenda, if taken beyond simply exhorting change at the level of the individual, requires government to address the structural factors that underpin unhealthy forms of behaviour, and these include the influences of capitalist market production in the form of the food, drinks and other industries.

Being serious about changing lifestyles means facing up to the major economic interests in society that shape these. Government is highly ambivalent when facing such corporate power. Food production and retailing are important sectors of the economy; the food corporations are among the largest in the UK. They are powerful interest groups, and one that have in the past effectively colonised aspects of government. We noted earlier how the post-war history of MAFF was one of producer capture in which the interests of the food producers took primacy over those of the consumer. These corporations are, moreover, increasingly multinational in character, operating in a global economy that floats above the level of the nation state and its policy-making capacity.

It also means challenging the nature of free choice as presented by the market. Food is an area in modern Western society that is perceived in terms of free choice, a matter indeed of personal freedom. Apart from notable exceptions such as rationing in wartime or under conditions of famine, the primary distributional agent for food in the West has always been the market. Food is also closely linked to the self and the expression of choice, exemplifying family habits and virtues. People resent criticism or interference in these areas. For government, there is an added problem in that the primary health messages in relation to ingestion are negative. However much the health lobby tries to parcel it up in attractive, positive guise, the overall message is one of 'less': less alcohol, less fat, fewer calories, no tobacco. No democratic government wants to be associated with this denial of pleasure. For these reasons government is chary of seeming to offer advice, of 'interfering' or acting like the 'nanny state'. The phrase is particularly associated in Britain with the Thatcher decade and its critique of government intervention in all spheres. In the 1980s, Digby Anderson, a neo-right ideologue and founder of the Social Affairs Unit, coined the term 'food Leninists' to capture and vilify these impulses.

The presentation of public health strategies in these terms has found unlikely endorsement in the recent trend of academic analysis. From a Foucauldian or poststructuralist perspective, public health is indeed a regulatory regime, one focussed on the ordering and disciplining of individual bodies and the social body as a whole (Armstrong 1983). Its discourses are a version of power-knowledge, that endorses the creation of, yet greater, levels of surveillance, particularly through the expert regimes of doctors, epidemiologists and public health specialists. Public health enables the State to engage in moral regulation aimed at encouraging subjects to become self-regulating in regard to the body and its health in order to pursue society's broader aims, particularly in terms of productivity. It is certainly the case that public health is a form of surveillance, and one that fits well within Foucault's account of the rise of the social sciences as part of the disciplinary framework of modernity, focussed at the twin levels of the body and the population. Dieting, exercise and weight control are also clearly among the 'technologies of the self' that Foucault presents as central to the constitution of modern subjectivity.

The problem with such approaches, however, is that they inevitably play into the hands of the neo-liberal corporate agenda. By presenting public health as a form of state surveillance, such analyses endorse the perception of them as interfering and 'nannyish'. Postmodern accounts present public health in an essentially sinister light. Seeing it in terms of discourse also detracts from its status as knowledge. The possibility of empirical evidence and of public debate is thus undermined, and with that the possibility of interventions that might actually improve the health of individuals. All the evidence of the past 40 years suggests that smoking is seriously harmful to health. Presenting this in terms of discourse and surveillance erodes the power of the message, and plays into the hands of corporate interest. To this degree it represents a form of *traison des clercs*. As Taylor-Gooby (1994) argues in relation to postmodernism, such approaches leave the door open for what is in reality the predominate grand narrative of the current order – that of neo-liberalism and globalised corporate power.

Conclusion

Food and the body are intimately – indeed organically – linked, and we have seen some of the ways in which ideas about the body and its representation present issues for the ways in which food and diet are treated within public policy. Eating disorders and obesity both represent problematic responses to food, its provision and meanings, and both raise classic tensions in relation to public health and the intervention of the state. In modern society we are encouraged to see food as a matter of personal freedom and autonomy – an area of life which adults control for themselves. Food, with its intimate connectedness with the body, is closely linked to ideas of the self. It is also a significant source of pleasure. For these reasons, governments are often chary of seeming to interfere, preferring to leave the determination of food choices to individuals. But governments are inevitably involved in the area through the impact of food patterns on a range of health outcomes. Diet and dietary choices have significant implications for public health, and with that for the costs to the state of health interventions. Furthermore, food and food patterns cannot simply be seen as the products of personal choice, but are significantly shaped by the forces of capitalist production that dominate the provision of food in modern Western economies. Addressing public health concerns thus requires government to face up to powerful economic interests, and ones moreover that are increasingly supranational in character and organisation.

Chapter 7

Home Care: The Body in Domestic Time and Space

In this chapter we will explore the body in social care, focussing on the provision of personal care within the domestic space of home. Domestic life is ordered spatially and temporally, and this ordering intersects with that of the body in ways that have implications for the provision of social care.

Domestic life is structured around the care of the body: rising, washing, dressing, shaving, eating, drinking and excreting. These activities mark out and punctuate the day, giving it its rhythm and structure; indeed much of our sense of ontological security derives from this bedrock of bodily comfort, comportment and care. It creates routine and regularity at a directly physical level, underpinning our sense of security and ease. Such processes, however, take place by and large at a level below conscious thought or articulation. They are part of our taken-for-granted world – too trivial or too private for comment. Old age, sickness and disability, however, disrupt these patterns, forcing the body and its difficulties into the forefront of consciousness. Day-to-day habits that could once be assumed become increasingly problematic. This is the point at which social care with its formal regulations and alien logics comes into the lives and homes of older and disabled people, disrupting their spatial and temporal ordering, intruding foreign service rationalities, replacing the privacy of home and body with new and sometimes disjunctive intimacies. But before we explore this, we need to address the way in which social care has traditionally been conceptualised as non-bodily, and the consequences of this for our understanding of the sector.

The absent body of social care

As we noted at the start of this book, social care is an under-theorised subject, whose nature and remit is poorly defined. The ways in which it has traditionally been presented, however, often results in its being seen as non-bodily in nature. To a large extent social care is constructed in contradistinction to medicine. The relationship is, however, asymmetrical, in which social care stands for the lesser, unmarked category – medicine's poor relation. Like nursing in an earlier chapter, social care deals with those aspects of the patient that medicine leaves out, or prefers to assign to other, lesser professionals, typically aspects relating to practical needs or social or psychological functioning. As a result it has always had a somewhat residual character, encompassing those needs of the client or patient that are thought of as 'non-medical'; and these are often taken to mean 'non-bodily'. But this is not always the case. Certain aspects of social care are very bodily in nature – for example, help with bathing, dressing, toileting and eating. It is just that they relate to a different version of the body from that presented within medicine. Medicine, as we saw in the previous chapter, constitutes the body in a particular way, one that emphasises its nature as a subject of scientific study and intervention. Other versions of the body and of embodiment are sidelined. Within the hospital, these other aspects where acknowledged are often assigned to nursing. Once outside that defining medical locus, however, in the patient's or client's own home, they cease to be seen as medical or quasi-medical in nature, and are reconceptualised as 'social care' needs. These needs are also thought to be simple and day-to-day, and as a result not to require trained staff, unlike medical needs. Social care activity is indeed often defined in terms of those needs any lay person could meet, and these include basic needs around the care of the body.

There is, thus, a body in social care. It is just that it is an unacknowledged, untheorised one. There are no comparable professional discourses to those of medicine, or nursing, within which it is constituted. As a result the body in social care remains largely inarticulate, mute – a very concrete presence, but one that is not openly acknowledged within the discourses of the sector.

This brings us to the second reason for the neglect of the body within accounts of social care, and this concerns the nature of the professional groups dominant in the sector. Social care is constituted within the twin discourses of social work and managerialism, each of which in its different way is notably non-bodily in character. Social work has traditionally been the lead profession within the social care, providing its ideological base and elite personnel. Though many clients, particularly older clients, will not see a trained social worker, the key managerial posts within social services have until recently been held by professional social workers; and their discourses shape the ways in which social service activities are constituted. The ideological core of social work lies in casework and in therapeutic interventions focussed around relationship work. Though its practice is more diverse, this remains at the heart of its professional identity and claim to expertise. Work on the body is not part of this. Indeed social work traditionally regards the body as something that belongs to medicine, so that work on the body marks the limit of the social worker's remit.

Within social work, there is also a hierarchy of value in which work with children and families has higher status than with older people. In part this reflects a general ageism, in which children matter more than older people, and younger adults are thought to be more interesting and more capable of change. But it also reflects the nature of work with older people, whose primary needs are for practical help with daily living, not psychotherapeutic input. These needs are often bodily in nature, and they are largely met, not by social workers, but by low-ranking untrained staff. The fact that this is physical, bodily in nature, contributes to its lowly status within the social care hierarchy. It also contributes to its relative invisibility, and there is a tendency not to stress these features in an attempt to enhance the status of the sector.

Increasingly, social care is subject to managerialist interventions and discourses, exemplified in Britain by the New Public Management (Ferlie *et al*. 1996) and by the current political enthusiasm for target setting and measurement. These approaches, drawing on disciplines like economics, accountancy, organisations and methods that prize quantification, abstraction and emotional distance, are notably non-bodily in character. Indeed the body represents just those qualities of embedded, messy, concreteness that such analyses hope to transcend. Their advent in social care has, therefore, resulted in an even more abstracted, aetherialised account of the sector than that which obtained before – one that is very far from its day-to-day realities.

The third reason why the body has been a silenced presence in social care relates to the desire of agencies to protect the status of clients by not putting too strong an emphasis on the bodily nature of their needs. As we noted earlier, ordinary social life rests on being able to manage the body in such a way that it can largely be ignored. In the modern West, we are socialised to pass over bodily functions and needs in relative silence. Disability and old age, however, push the body into the forefront. Failures of bodily performance come to dominate public perceptions of the person, and this is particularly acute if the failure involves transgressing the boundaries of the body, as with incontinence. For these reasons, good practice in social care aims to down-play such problems, constructing the client as a feeling person rather than a failing body, the body in social care is seen as something to be transcended not emphasised.

All this, however, is at odds with what is increasingly the reality of social care. Within the British system, personal care now represents the main activity of home care. In the past, such body care was seen primarily as a nursing activity, something provided by the community nursing service – if it was provided, for access was very limited. But from the late 1990s under the impact of active community care policies, personal care has become part of mainstream social care (Means *et al*. 2002). Of course it was always part of social care in the context of institutional settings like residential homes. What was new, however, was its extensive deployment in home care. With this has gone the transfer of responsibility for bodily care out of the remit of health and into that of social care. The reason is largely economic: the substitution of nurses by low paid social care staff and, particularly in the British context, the transfer of financial responsibility out of the fully publicly funded health sector into the means-tested social care one. But one of the consequences of this is that the body has become the central focus of social care.

Personal care

Personal care involves nakedness, touch and the management of human wastes (Twigg 2000a). As such it transgresses normal social relations. Indeed personal care can be defined in terms of those things that an adult would normally do for himself or herself: washing, dressing and excreting. However rich we are, these are things that – at least in the modern West – we do for ourselves, typically alone or in the company of intimates. Personal care thus marks the boundary of the wholly personal and individual in modern life. Having to receive help in such areas transgresses social boundaries and undermines one's status as an adult. These things are normally only done for babies, and this fact underwrites the profoundly infantalising tendencies of 'care'.

Incontinence is a particularly powerful social marker here. Lawton (1998, 2000), Öberg (1996) and others have argued that modern culture is increasingly stringent in regard to the boundaries of the body and their dissolution, intolerant of the unbounded body of sickness and old age. Modern expectations demand that individuals present clearly defined, bounded bodies that reflect modern concepts of individualism and autonomy, and to fail to do so is to have one's personhood questioned. Incontinence thus breaches profound rules about the management of body in modernity. For many it marks the last stage of social life, the point beyond which it is no longer possible to take part fully and equally in society. These meanings affect the experiences of receiving personal care.

Personal care also involves direct hands-on contact. Touch is one of the most powerful forms of human contact, operating at a level beyond and below words, releasing emotion and underwriting human connectedness (Montagu 1986, Synnott 1993). Many older people, with the loss of intimate family and friends, live their lives in a context that is starved of touch. Personal care, though much of its touch is instrumental rather than expressive, does offer an opportunity for human contact of this deeper kind. In general the context of social care – at least for older people – is one in which touch is still fairly freely offered and received, and in which it is used to convey comfort and human warmth. Touch can, however, also be a vector of status and power, with the more powerful touching the less so (Henley 1973).

Personal care can thus offer an opportunity of the expression of not only care and comfort, but also of authority and control.

Personal care also involves nakedness and the exposure of parts of the body in ways that can be at odds with normal social expectations. Nakedness in the West tends not to be part of day-to-day social relations, but is a special state reserved for particular situations or relationships. Access to the body either by sight or by touch is socially structured according to rules relating to gender, relationship and social setting (Jourard 1966, Jourard and Rubin 1968, Henley 1973, Whitcher and Fisher 1979, Routasalo and Isola 1996). Some parts are relatively neutral, like the upper arms and back, and can be touched by a range of people. Others like the knees and thighs are less so. Breasts and genitals are in general off limits in all but erotic relations. These meanings affect the provision of personal care. In general, help with the more neutral parts of the body – arms, legs, feet and hair – is relatively unproblematic. Matters are, however, more sensitive in relation to private parts. Having to be washed in these intimate areas can be seen as humiliating and embarrassing – a further twist in the spiral of dependency; and maintaining independence and control over these parts can be an important dimension in self-esteem. It was striking in the bathing study (Twigg 2000a) how one part of the body – the back – did acquire acceptability. In the context of bathing and the often ambivalent intimacies it creates, the back has a special meaning, standing for the body in general, or at least for an acceptable version of the body, one that has a certain neutrality about it. It was the only part of the body that was spontaneously named by recipients; and they sometimes talked about the process of bathing as if it were confined to washing the back. The back is the part of the body that is both offered to the worker and is used to shelter more private and sensitive parts. It thus stands in for the public presentation of the body in the context of an otherwise sometimes discordant intimacy. The back was also the one part of the body where pleasure in touch was openly acknowledged. Recipients would describe enjoying having their backs scrubbed. In general expressing pleasure in touch was something that recipients were reluctant to do; it seemed in their eyes to suggest something that was not quite right, an ambivalent element that did not belong in this context of relative strangers. Presenting bathing in terms of scrubbing the back was thus a means of deflecting an otherwise disturbing intimacy on to a relatively neutral and public part of the body.

To be naked in a social situation, as recipients of personal care are, is to be put in a disjunctive context. One that is made all the more so by the fact that the nakedness is asymmetrical: the recipient is naked, while the helper is fully clothed. Personal care thus makes for a strange relationship: in one sense intimate and close, involving physical contact and access to the private dimensions of life; and yet, in another, a meeting of strangers in which the worker is paid to do a job and may never have seen the recipient before. The intimacy, moreover, occurs in a context that is forced, arising from disability, not choice, and a closeness that is imposed, not sought. This produces inherent discords in the relationship which is transgressive of normal social codes; and effort is needed on both sides to define its character and put limits on its intimacy. In this context, what clients said they wanted is a bounded intimacy, something that is close, but in a specialised and limited way (Twigg 2000a). They tended to prefer someone whom they had got to know in these particular circumstances, and where the relationship was defined by them.

As we shall see in the next chapter, personal care can be a classic site for the expression of Foucauldian bio-power, in which bodies are ordered, disciplined, cleaned, rendered docile and made subject to the regime of the institution, or of the worker's gaze. Washing and bathing can be part of this, and I have explored elsewhere the rival discourses within which bathing is located (Twigg 2000a). Some relate to pleasure and sensuality – and these can play a part in the experiences of home care, to a some degree at least – but some are linked to coercive cultures in which the body is made subject to regimes of control and domination, and these meanings are present in potentiality at least wherever bodies are cleaned, ordered and bathed. They form part of background noise to the provision. By and large, these Foucauldian themes are muted within home care; and later in the chapter we will explore one of the reasons why, looking at the ways in which the setting of home endows recipients with a degree of power that enables them to resist such meanings.

Spatio-temporal ordering: The body in domestic time and space

Home care takes place in a special space: that of home; and this affects the ways in which it is provided and the meanings that attach to it. 'Home' has been the subject of a large sociological and geographical literature, much of it rooted in phenomenological analysis (Allan and Crow 1989, Sixsmith 1990, Gurney and Means 1993, Massey 1994, Longhurst 2001). Three elements are generally recognised as central: privacy, security and identity. Home is the quintessence of private space, offering the capacity to exclude strangers and non-residents. Home is somewhere where you can shut the door on the outside world; and lack of privacy is one of the most disliked features of communal or institutional life (Allan and Crow 1989). The capacity to restrict access to only certain people, at certain times, also means that you can stage-manage social life, concealing the ways in which your home and life falls short of the domestic ideal. This supports the second meaning of home which is as a place of relaxation and freedom. Feeling 'at home' suggests a state of ease and the relaxed, informal bodily comportment that goes with this. Home is also for most people a place of security, a haven in a sometimes harsh world. This can be particularly important for older people who may feel vulnerable in public, exposed to the threat of falls, or frightening strangers, or ill at ease with the changes of modern life (Vincent 1999). Home by contrast is safe. It is also familiar, embodying the continuity of the self and its past, offering opportunities for the extension of the self in material decoration, objects and surroundings (Rubinstein 1989, Rubinstein and Parmelee 1992, Gurney and Means 1993). For many older people this has special resonance, summing up their lives, linking them to the person they once were, as well as embodying memories of a lost partner. Home, thus, stands for a complex of meanings around privacy, security and identity, in which features of the built environment embody, enable and reinforce particular social relationships and meanings.

It is important not to present too rosy an account. Home is not always as benign as the normative ideology suggests. As many feminist writers have pointed out, home for many women is as much a place of labour as of relaxation, somewhere one might seek to escape *from*, as much as *to*. For some, as the incidence of domestic violence shows, it can be a place of fear and abuse. For those without paid employment or extensive social contact, it can also be a place of loneliness and isolation. The meanings of home, thus, cannot be assumed in a blanket way, but intersect with particular experiences and social relationships.

Though home is a private space, it is itself ordered along a privacy gradient in which some parts of the home are deemed more private than others (Lawrence 1987, Munro and Madigan 1993, Pearson and Richards 1994). In general the most public parts are those adjacent to the front door, the lobby and the hall; the sitting room is slightly less public; the bathroom or bedroom even less so. Lawrence (1987) suggests that these gradations can be analysed in British culture in terms of a series of oppositions in which public/private map on to front/back, clean/dirty, special/day-to-day, and in which the parlour represents the clean/front/special space and the kitchen the back/dirty/everyday. Upstairs spaces are more private than down; and strangers are rarely invited there. These spaces shelter the body in its more vulnerable states – when resting or sleeping, when dressing or undressed, when naked or otherwise free of the formal constraints of clothes. Private acts like sex, excretion or body maintenance and care predominantly take place in these defined spaces.

This spatial ordering is not static but operates dynamically in conjunction with the body, so that the privacy of particular spaces is affected by the presence or otherwise of bodies within them (Gurney 2000). This is particularly clear in relation to a space like the bedroom which has additional charge of privacy when occupied. Similarly, bathrooms represent a no man's land of privacy: semi-public when empty, distinctly private when not. Bathrooms are indeed the only rooms in the modern house that have locks. Bodies and spaces thus interact, so that the ordered privacy of the home is reinforced by the ordered privacy of the body.

Home is also structured in terms of time, and the body is once again crucial in this. Body time is not only one of the most taken-for-granted dimensions of daily existence, but also one of the most profound, regulating and ordering our daily sense of self (Adam 1995). Our bodies are temporally organised in a complex of cycles and rhythms: neural pulses, heart beats, circadian rhythms and menstrual cycles, and their disruption can lead to distress and ill health, as the negative impact of shift work or jet lag demonstrates. Temporal order, as experienced at a day-to-day level of our bodies, is a fundamental source of security and well-being. This body time intersects with the social structures of the home to create domestic time. Domestic time, which gives form and definition to the day-to-day flow of experience, is punctuated by activity around the body. The start of the day is marked by rising, washing, shaving and dressing. Showering and bathing can also be used through the day as domestic rites of passage, marking out transitions between, for example, work time and domestic time, ordinary life and special occasions like parties. Changing out of work or school clothes can also be used to mark the shift into a different social state in a directly bodily way. Sleep represents a particular bodily state, one that again marks out the passage of the day, and is associated with specialised clothes (or absence of clothes) and by particular bodily comportment. Like bathing and washing, it takes place in a distinctive, private space – the bedroom. Food similarly acts to punctuate the rhythm of the day, or of longer temporal cycles like the week or the year. Other body activities like excreting are less clearly defined socially in their temporal pattern, treated fairly freely, in response to need. Within the world of institutional life, however, this is not the case, and many older people in residential homes and hospitals are toileted regularly at set times. It is a measure of the extent and rigidity of the time ordering of these places that an aspect of the body that is normally fairly freely structured becomes subject to close control and regulation.

The temporal ordering of the home intersects with the spatial, so that the structure of privacy is also affected by the temporal cycle of the day and week. In many homes, strangers are only admitted during limited periods of the day; and by the evening, the house may have moved into a semi-closed mode, when knocks at the door are not answered, and when residents may reconfigure the pattern of public and private space, allowing informal dress – slippers, dressing gowns and semi-nudity – to expand into spaces at other times treated more formally and publicly.

Spatio-temporal re-ordering

The coming of home care disrupts these ordered relationships, disturbing not just the social relations of the body, but those of the home also. Indeed the two intersect, so that the discordant activities of personal care disturb the ordered privacy of the home, presenting the wrong sorts of bodies in the wrong spaces. Just as personal care intrudes upon the privacy of the body, so too careworkers intrude on the privacy of the home, bringing alien rationalities into its spaces.

Service provision rests on a very different social logic to that of domestic life. Angus and colleagues (2005) analyse this clash in terms of Bourdieu's concepts of habitus and field. Habitus represents the durable pattern of dispositions that are deeply inculcated in daily life and that reflect the social position of the individual, or the material conditions to which they are accustomed. Such dispositions are corporeal in that they are embodied and materialised in postures, gestures and movements; though they also exist in aesthetic preferences, or in taste for food, clothes or decoration. They are enacted at a pre-reflexive level, learnt at the level of the body and not explicitly articulated. But the coming of service help into the home disturbs this. Service help is rooted in a very different 'field', that of 'health care'. As its logics become active within the home, disjunction arises between the habitus of care recipients and the new realities of their domestic surroundings. The transposition of logic derived from an external social field, that of 'health care', alters and disrupts the meanings and character of being 'at home'.

Illness and disability can certainly impose a radical re-ordering on the home, as bedrooms move downstairs, and sleeping arrangements collapse into areas of daily living. Bedrooms and bathrooms become semi-public spaces in which service personnel enter at will, and over which they may exert authority, reordering these spaces according to their own service logics. The clutter of equipment becomes dominant, with bedrooms and bathrooms overtaken by hoists, chairs and bedpans. Studies of hospital-at-home initiatives find that many of the presumed advantages of such provision in terms of its more domestic or homely character are in fact nullified by the dominance of health care imperatives and practices, as nurses come and go, and commodes, lifts and oxygen cylinder move in. As Angus and colleagues (2005) note, such objects profoundly change the aesthetics of the home, disrupting its sensory dimensions in terms of look, feel and smell. With their durable materials, functional appearance and easy-to-clean surfaces, these objects are not focussed on comfort or sensory enjoyment, but driven by the logic of expedience and standardisation. Many relate to bodily needs that are usually secluded and confined to special spaces. Commodes are particularly significant here, standing for permanent emblems of bodily disruption, turning bedrooms and sitting rooms into toilet spaces, and bringing the normally private act of excretion into public space. Just as incontinence breaks the boundaries of bodily behaviour, so the presence of the commode stands for the breaking of the normally spatial ordering of privacy in the home. The ordering of the body and of the home are interlinked.

The logic of home care also clashes with the temporal ordering of the body and the home. The time of service provision is in a clock-based, rationalised form, in which time is abstract, decontextualised and commodified (Adam 1995). It is the time of economic production, measured, cut up, allocated and costed. In this, staff work according to schedules that allocate distinct units of time to specific clients. They work in a time-ordered sequence, in which clients are dealt with in series, one after another and not in parallel. These time sequences map on to spatial ones, as workers move across the geographical territory they cover. But this is in conflict with the ways in which body time and domestic time operate. Body time is rooted in organic processes; it is fluid, experiential. Its timings cannot always be predicted; nor can it be accumulated in ways that the time of economic production can. Care tasks cannot be accumulated and dealt with efficiently in one go: you cannot save up going to the toilet for a week, and then do it just once. The body also has its own timings. It is not always possible to predict when someone will need to go to the toilet, so that it is difficult to mesh the regular, clock-based nature of service provision with the more fluid and unpredictable nature of bodily needs. The order of the body is also by its nature unstable, capable at any point of a radical return to disorder. Illness, or other failures of bodily performance, may suddenly present the worker with new unpredictable tasks, as the client who has just been washed and dressed vomits food all over their clothes just as the worker is leaving for the next client. Like everything that deals with the maintenance of states of purity and cleanliness, carework is fragile and unstable in character, closely linked to the particularity of the situation and the rationalities of service provision.

We have already seen the ways in which body time intersects with domestic time, so that many of its key markers are bodily in character. Again this poses problems for service delivery. Individuals order their day by such transitions and value their periodicity: they do not want to lunch at 11, or be put to bed at 3. Activities like bathing, as we have noted, can also act as domestic rites of passage marking out transitions between social states, and their timing is thus meaningful. People do not want to have baths or meals at meaningless times. This presents difficulties for agencies, however, who want to construct rational schedules in which clients are dealt with regularly, efficiently and in sequence. Domestic timings, moreover, tend to cluster at key points in the day: everyone wants lunch at roughly the same time; and these points are also ones when workers want to attend to their domestic and bodily lives. From the perspective of the recipients, workers would ideally come frequently and flexibly according to the requirements of the day. But this is in conflict with the traditionally ordering of employment in which workers expect to have clear blocks of work time, and not fragmented moments of intervention interspersed through the day. These problems around time and the body mean that it is hard to achieve economic rationalities in the context of social care.

The power of home

We now turn to the ways in which the ideology of home and the values of security, identity and privacy it embodies can endow clients with a degree of power, enabling them to resist, to some extent, the domination of careworkers and professionals, turning back that erosive gaze. Home is a space that belongs to the occupant, who can quite literally shut the door on unwanted intrusion. In the English context this has legal force in that social care agencies have no right of access. Workers enter this space on license – to some degree they are visitors. These values around home are widely recognised and endorsed – are indeed operative in the worker's own private lives, so that they are deeply entrenched socially. This is not to say that they are never ignored, but they are a significant element structuring the encounter. As a result home care workers operate in a space that does not wholly belong to them. Their place of work is another's home. Such meanings affect the power dynamics of the exchange, sometimes at a directly bodily level, underwriting the capacity of individuals to refuse interventions or treatments.

There was an example of such resistance based on place in the bathing study (Twigg 2000a). One of the community nurses recounted how he had a patient who refused to have an enema.

> [She] just wasn't prepared to have them. It was her home and she felt she was in control. And I got back to the day hospital who'd referred her and they said: Well she's never any problem with us. We just tell her it's time for her enema and she has it.

He felt at first that he looked foolish in the eyes of hospital colleagues:

> They thought that we were being quite inadequate about it, in that we weren't pushing hard enough. But it's all to do with that shift of power. The power was in this woman's hands and she, you know. She chose to exercise it. (Twigg 2000a, p. 84)

In her own setting, she was able to exercise control over her body and what happened to it in a way that was not possible in the day hospital. The case brings out the contrast with institutional settings. Here the space belongs not to the residents, but to the staff. It is they who are in charge and they who determine the rules. Significant parts of the home or institution – the office, the staff toilets – are out of bounds to the residents. Residents never really control these settings. Even their bedrooms, though notionally private, are constantly intruded upon.

Home as the embodiment of identity acts to buttress the power of the client. Surrounded by emblems of identity and connectedness – pictures of the person in the past, possessions that exhibit their interests and photographs of family – it is harder for them to be reduced by the processes of care. Possessions help put a limit on the depersonalising effects of care, particularly of a bodily sort, that can easily reduce the dignity of the individual, turning them into a body to be cleaned rather than a person to be respected. This contrasts again with institutional care. At their worst, institutions strip individuals of all possessions and identity, making them subject to anonymous and collective regimes, as described by Goffman (1961) in his account of the Total Institution. One of the classic features of such places is that people have no possessions, not even personal clothing, and the stripping of material objects becomes a stripping of identity. It is one of the marked features of the institutional life of older people, even more benign versions like modern residential care, that people end up with so little in the way of possessions after a lifetime of independent living. This absence underpins their re-constitution as a standardised, anonymous resident.

Time also affects the power dynamic. Home care visits do not last long. Even those receiving high levels of input spend the majority of the day alone or in company of relatives. This gives a tangential quality to the worker's presence in the home. As a result there are long periods when the domestic ordering of the home reasserts itself. Again this is in contrast with institutional settings where 'care' and the presence of careworkers extend over 24 hours a day, so that the resident is never free of them, wholly subject to their regimes, even in sleep.

It is important not to exaggerate the power of home. Recipients of home care are usually frail, sometimes confused and above all dependant on the careworkers in order to continue living at home. The workers are physically stronger and by and large more mentally robust. Personal care in particular exposes clients in bodily ways that undermines their personal authority, making the assertion of the self harder. Home can only tip the balance of power to limited degree. Its private setting can also be a source of vulnerability and danger. Care settings that are hidden from view have sometimes been sites of neglect and cruelty, as recent evidence concerning the extent of abuse of vulnerable adults in institutions in the recent past shows (Biggs *et al.* 1995, Glendinning 1997). In general the reputation of home care has been good, but caution is always necessary where activities are hidden from view.

Conclusion

In this chapter we have explored some of the complex ways in which the spatial and temporal relations of the home intersect with the materiality of the body, and the implications of this for the provision of care. Traditionally social care has been presented as non-bodily. There is no consciously articulated language of the body within this sector; indeed the dominant discourses that have traditionally constructed the field seek to avoid the topic. But as we have seen, it is not that the body is absent from social care, it is just that it is implicit, mute. One of the central tasks of new writing on social care is to redress this, and to bring the body back into analytic and professional view.

The process of giving voice to the body has implications for the support and training of workers. Careworkers undertake difficult tasks, involving subtle and complex interactions around the body, and as we shall see in the next chapter, they deal with many of the less attractive aspects of bodily life. But they do so in the context that offers little in the way of support or training. Failing to articulate the body is part of the reason for this. Recovering the body in social care also has implications for policy makers and planners, helping to get away from the overly distant and abstract account that has characterised of the field, enabling them to root their accounts and judgements more strongly in the concrete realities of care.

Work on the body also has implications for questions of power and authority, and in particular for the ways in which these inscribe the body. Insights deriving from Foucault alert us to just how powerful such forces can be. Activities which are presented in neutral terms, like getting someone bathed, may involve the exercise of power and control at quite a profound level. By and large, the context of home care is a caring one, but parallels with more coercive settings and institutions, and the practices that adhere in them, remind us of the potentially charged nature of these processes of body management.

Home also raises questions of identity. We have seen how practices of body care contribute to the ways in which identity is reproduced and sustained at a directly bodily level. Our domestic lives are profoundly body based, and the rhythms of bodylife play a central role in our sense of ontological security. There is a complex symbiotic relationship between the body and the spatial and temporal structure of home. Though this is true for all individuals, it is particularly so for older and disabled people whose lives may largely be confined to home, and more closely embodied in it. Home is indeed the centre of their life world and we need to be better attuned to this. Work around the body and its interlinkages with the spatial and temporal structure of home can help us do this. Again this has implications for training and for how services are provided.

Lastly we have explored the disjunction that can occur between the habitus of the home, and the logic of service delivery. The rhythms and periodicities of domestic life are largely at odds with those of the service world; and the body is a crucial site where these two logics clash. Bodytime and service time are in conflict. This has implications for issues around rationalisation of services, and indeed for the limits that are placed on this by the bodily nature of many of the tasks.

Chapter 8

The Bodywork of Care

In this chapter, we will explore the category of bodywork as it applies to the activities of staff employed in the social and health care sectors. We have already touched on some of these themes in relation to health care in Chapter 5, in particular in the sections concerning the embodied work of doctors and nurses. In this chapter, I will concentrate on social care, and the provision of personal care to frail, older and disabled people living at home. The chapter thus also links to Chapter 7 and its discussion of the management of the body in home care.

The main part of the chapter explores the nature of carework as a species of bodywork, concentrating on the ways in which work on the body represents the core activity of carework for frail and older people, and exploring the consequences of this for our understanding of the sector. One of the most prominent features of both carework and bodywork is its gendered nature, and in the second part of this chapter, I will explore how we might understand this connection. In doing so I will refer to some of the other key literatures within which the gendered nature of carework needs to be analysed, drawing on debates concerning the service economy, domestic labour, emotional labour and 'care'. Carework is a field where gender and 'race' intersect, and I will also touch upon the ways in which carework – and sometimes bodywork – is a racialised, as well as gendered, employment sector. Before doing so, however, we need to address briefly the nature of bodywork as an occupational category.

Bodywork as an occupational category

Bodywork is work focussed on the bodies of others – manipulating, touching, cleaning, adjusting and otherwise managing bodies (Wolkowitz 2002). The recipients of such work may diversely be known as customers, clients, patients and service users. Bodies thus form the object of the workers' labour. (I am excluding from consideration here the work that individuals perform on their own bodies as part of regimes of body maintenance or improvement.) Bodywork is an element in a range of occupations. Doctors, nurses, physiotherapists, careworkers, nannies, child minders, beauticians, hairdressers, alternative therapists, masseurs, sex workers and undertakers all engage in bodywork. As will be clear from this list, the contexts in which they operate and the discourses of the body in which their practices are located are very diverse; as are their occupational status. There are, however, certain commonalties that I have discussed elsewhere (Twigg 2000a). I will outline the main features of these briefly, before going on to explore their significance for the bodywork element in social care.

Bodywork is ambivalent work that can violate norms concerning the management of the body, particularly in terms of touch or visual contact. As such, it may require symbolic negotiation by means of distancing techniques, manipulations of eye contact, special clothes, aprons, gloves, distinct settings, rituals of privacy and disclosure (Twigg 2000a). Bodywork typically involves direct hand-on touch, often in a context of nudity or semi-nudity. Bodywork is often hidden work, performed behind the screens, in semi-private spaces. It is also hidden in the sense that it is often unarticulated, treated as obvious. Like the body itself, the work is often assumed; and this gives it a silenced, implicit quality that is sometimes used to justify regarding it as unskilled.

Bodywork lies on the borders of sexuality, and this contributes to both its ambiguous character and gendered patterning. Part of the ambiguity derives from the way it transgresses the territory of sex, involving as it does direct physical contact, often in circumstances of nakedness and sometimes giving rise to emotional closeness. Bodywork trades can find themselves ambivalently located in terms of public interpretation and evaluation; and symbolic and boundary maintenance effort is required to counter these sexualised meanings. 'Massage' is a classic example of this. Commercially, massage has come to imply sexual servicing, and is part of the sex industry; and yet it also has a legitimate existence as a therapeutic and beauty technique, and one indeed that has grown in popularity with the expansion of spa culture. Many practitioners therefore engage in symbolic boundary maintenance to mark out the limits of their activity. One of the ways in which this can be done is by locating 'legitimate' massage, by and large, in feminised settings; for it is women (or possibly men) giving massage to men that gives rise to the heavily sexualised interpretation. Feminising the meanings limits and controls this. Such bracketing off the sexual, and maintaining of psychic boundaries is a feature of many bodywork occupations. It is evident within medicine, for example, where techniques like bodily stance, avoidance of eye contact, deployment of screens and white coats are used to re-order potentially sexual meanings. The vaginal examination in health care provides a classic example of how the sexual connotations of a procedure can be symbolically and interactionally overridden. Similar techniques are deployed within nursing. These tend, however, to have a less stable quality to them as we noted in Chapter 5 in relation to the continued fantasy status of the nurse's own body.

Bodywork may also involve dealing with, what I have termed elsewhere (Twigg 2000a), the negativities of the body, negotiating the less attractive aspects of corporeal life. This may involve, for example, in beauty work dealing with the eradication of hairs, skin or other blemishes, or in nursing or carework dealing with human wastes. The latter in particular means that bodywork can be dirty work; and this links to the tendency for it to be demeaned and to be of poor status. Bodywork trades tend to come low in the occupational hierarchy, and often with an element of stigma attached to them. In this they share in the general cultural ambivalence about the status of the bodily that we noted in Chapter 1. When part of the work of high status individuals, such as doctors, as we saw in Chapter 5, bodywork is subject to a dematerialisation tendency whereby it is compartmentalised or bracketed off by means of symbolic procedures. Direct hands-on work in the health sector is often delegated to lesser, frequently feminised, occupational groups like nurses. Dirty work in relation to the body is in wider society differentially assigned to women; and this is part of a wider gender patterning.

Bodywork can, however, also be linked to pleasure and emotional rapport. Therapies and techniques that rest on it, such as massage, aromatherapy and spa culture generally, aim to create a zone of physical enjoyment and well-being in which the body is at the centre. Increasingly beauty therapies are not so much aimed at adjusting the body to norms of attractiveness, but achieving states of individual well-being (Black and Sharma 2001, Black 2002, 2004). Beauty therapy has become part of a wider process of ego-servicing in which women in particular engage in body rituals to gain pleasure, and in which the discourses of pampering and 'stress' play a prominent part. This new spa culture also draws on the ideas of alternative medicine with its emphasis, as we saw in the previous chapter, on wholeness and well-being, and linking these to a concept of individualised spirituality focussed on the body. Bodywork thus finds itself located at the centre of the new nexus of beauty/therapy/spirituality that has become a significant cultural construct in the early twenty-first century, particularly for women.

Bodywork is also ambivalently positioned in relation to power, caught in a dynamic that can tip either way, presenting the worker as either a demeaned body servant, subordinate to the customer/client in a directly bodily way, or as an exerciser of Foucauldian bio-power, disciplining and controlling the bodies of recipients. Bodywork contains both these potentialities. Which is to the fore depends on the meaning and status of the occupation and the particular dynamics of the exchange. In these power dynamics, 'race', class and gender can play significant roles.

Lastly bodywork is gendered work, in that it is differentially performed, and as we have noted to some degree also received, by women. Many of the occupations referred to above are feminised in character, and work on the body tends to be seen as female territory. This is not, however, always the case, and the category encompasses some occupations that are primarily male, for example barbers and undertakers, and to some degree also doctors, though their involvement as we have noted is symbolically circumscribed. Barbers, however, have their origins in a trade established to service the needs of men within the public economy at a time when men dominated this sphere, and when such intimate work by women would not have been acceptable. Undertaking has its roots in other male occupations like building and carpentry, as well as involving degrees of physical strength less common among women. As an occupation it does, however, link to the aspect of bodywork that is ambivalent, dirty, dealing with wastes, overflows and aspects of the abject that are exemplified in the corpse – though, laying out was, of course, traditionally a female occupation.

Bodywork is thus marked by being ambivalent, hidden work that tends to remain unarticulated within official discourses. It may breach social norms, and can require symbolic techniques to renegotiate these. It may involve dealing with the negativities of the body; and be regarded as low-level, dirty work. But at the same time it is also often associated with pleasure and emotional warmth. As such it lies on the borders of sexuality. It is also ambivalently placed in relation to the exercise of power. It thus falls within a wider set of dichotomies that locate it on the side of the intimate, emotional, physical, dirty, low level and female; as opposed to the emotionally distant, cerebral, clean, high status and masculine.

The bodywork of care

These features resonate through the bodywork of care. Carework is in general poorly regarded work, predominantly undertaken by people with few formal skills and a poor purchase on the labour market (Bates 1993, Skeggs 1997). It is badly paid, and its terms of work disadvantageous. Despite the aura of love and care that is sometimes associated with it, it has low status; and the bodily nature is part of this. Carework is dirty work in a direct and obvious way, dealing as it does with the less attractive aspects of the body that result from sickness, frailty and decline – with incontinence, vomit, sputum – substances emitted from the body of a polluting character and widely associated with disgust and social revulsion (Douglas 1966, Miller 1997). These general negative evaluations are compounded by the fact that careworkers predominantly deal not with babies or children, but with older people – a social category that is itself marginalised. These bodies take on aspects of the Abject. Kubie (discussed in Lawler 1991) moreover, argues that the bodies of the old are perceived as dirty, in a way that is not so with the young. There are also reasons, as we noted earlier, to think that modern Western society has become less tolerant of the unbounded body, more stringent in its expectations of the body, promoting an antiseptic ideal that is intolerant of bodily odours and secretions (Öberg 1996, Lawton 1998).

These feelings mean that those who deal with such bodies and wastes are themselves subject to ideas of pollution. Nursing has the advantage in this context, in that its status protects workers in some degree from dirty work designations. The tradition of the nurse's uniform with its starched white apron and 'angel' head-gear sets nurses apart, endowing them with a symbolically pure and exhaulted status, something reinforced by the sacralising discourses of the profession (Wolf 1988). These contribute to the special capacity claimed by nurses to deal with and transcend 'dirt' or pollution. Careworkers by contrast have few such symbolic resources to deploy. They remain much more closely compromised by the dirty work designation, and this contributes to the low esteem of the occupation (Cambridge and Carnaby 2000). Workers are often evasive about the realities of the work – obscuring it behind the language of 'care'; something that is also done by managers and policy makers, who as we noted in the previous chapter similarly tend to present it in an aetherialised, non-bodily way. Even within nursing, Lawler (1991) has noted similar processes. Although bed-and-bodywork comprises the core of nursing practice, nursing texts are traditionally reticent in describing it, treating it as 'obvious' or in some sense below comment. This has the consequence, however, of rendering what is a key aspect of the work hidden, literally unspeakable, contributing to a sense that this is slightly shameful work. Lawler (1991) also makes the important point that bodywork is hidden work, not only because of the wish to protect the dignity of the patient or client, but also from a desire to protect the status of the worker. Bodywork is potentially demeaning work, and nurses go 'behind the screens' to perform it.

Carework is also 'dirty work' in a second, more sociological sense, in that it represents aspects of work that society regards as necessary, but at the same time slightly shameful, at odds with its ideals and norms, so that it is demeaned and hidden (Emerson and Pollner 1976). Carework is 'dirty work' because it deals with aspects of life that society, especially modern secular society with its ethic of material success and its emphasis on youth and glamour, does not want to think about: decay, dirt, death, decline and failure. Careworkers manage these on behalf of the wider society, ensuring they remain hidden, tidied away into the obscurity of institutions or private homes.

Bodywork is by its nature intimate work, involving direct physical touch, sometimes in situations of nakedness or semi-nakedness. This means that it can be transgressive, disturbing normal social codes. One of the tasks of carework is to negotiate the intimacies of the body in ways that are acceptable to the client, and that – ideally – do not embarrass or demean them. Bodywork thus requires special sensitivity to people's feelings and to the symbolic structures within which bodily behaviour is encoded. Within the social care sector, however, this is something that is rarely taught or even articulated (Cambridge and Carnaby 2000). Carework is predominantly regarded as unskilled work; and workers are left to find their own way through these cultural thickets, as Diamond (1992) eloquently showed in his ethnographic account of working as a nursing home aide.

We have noted how bodywork occupations encompass trades like hairdressing, massage, the alternative therapies of new age-influenced spa culture that have a strong body-pleasing, body-pampering aspect. In recent years there have been attempts to encompass something of this in carework and nursing, offering forms of massage like aromatherapy, or beauty treatments like hairdressing and nail care in day hospitals and residential homes. The aim has been to provide a bodily experience that is focussed on pleasure, in a context where there is often little of this. In particular they offer opportunities for human contact at a bodily level. Nail and hand care, for example, allow for physical closeness, hand holding, massage and close attention to the person; and they can be particularly useful in dementia where it is hard to make contact verbally (Kitwood 1997, Ward and Duquin 1998). Similar techniques have also been used within holistic nursing and palliative care, as a means to redress the fragmentation of the body associated with serious illness and its treatment (van der Riet 1997).

Carework is also emotionally charged work. The reasons for this are complex, relating both to the situations of clients, their dependency, frailty, experiences of loss and the nature of the relationship between the client and the worker, in which familiarity and the passage of time can create a relationship of closeness and warmth. The bodily nature of care, particularly the physical intimacy of touch, can play a part in this. With the death of spouses and family members, many frail and older people live in a world where there is little in the way of human contact of a directly physical kind. Carework can provide this. But the physical contact of care can also be problematic and disjunctive. Physical closeness does not always produce or re-inforce emotional closeness in this context. The dynamic can spiral the other way. As Davidhizar and Giger (1997) point out in relation to nursing, touch is not always welcome; it may be intrusive or disjunctive. In particular intimate touch may be at odds with the specific nature of the relationship. We can see this in people's responses to the provision of personal care within informal, family-based care, where contrary to assumptions that are sometimes made concerning emotional and physical closeness, people often experience difficulty and embarrassment in giving and receiving intimate care, preferring to entrust the task to a paid worker or other more neutral figure (Daatland 1990, Parker 1993, Twigg and Atkin 1994). Intimate bodycare can be at odds with the character of the relationship. As we noted in the last chapter, what most recipients tend to want is a relationship with the worker that is not only warm and friendly, but also bounded in nature, defined by the specifics of the task and rooted in the nature of that relationship.

Part of the ambivalence around these areas of intimacy and relationships arises from their closeness to sexuality. We have already noted how body-work tends to be located on the borders of sexuality, so that bracketing off the sexual, and maintaining psychic boundaries is a feature of many of these occupations. In relation to carework, the issue may seem less central since the majority of recipients are elderly, and physical contact between them and younger workers is assumed to be asexual. Careworkers do on occasion have to deal with unwanted sexual advances from elderly male clients, but they are relatively infrequent and workers tend to shrug them off (Twigg 2000a). The clients are, by and large, weak and pose little in the way of sexual threat; and their behaviour tends to be interpreted as a symptom of mental frailty.

Among younger clients, however, the meanings are more ambiguous and the boundaries are less easy to maintain. As Cambridge and Carnaby (2000) show, intimate tending, particularly in relation to adults with learning disa-bilities, constantly gives rise to sexually ambiguous situations. In the bathing study (Twigg 2000a) one young male respondent reported how he found help with washing and showering sexually arousing, and he was anxious to hide this for fear of being accused of sexual harassment. Sexual servicing within formal services clearly goes on, though largely as part of the twilight world of sex at work. Evidence for this comes mainly from recipients not careworkers. As we saw in the chapter on disability, one disabled author describes a series of sexual relations he had with his care-workers. Seymour (1998) similarly notes the surreptitious availability of sexual servicing for disabled men on the spinal unit. In both these cases the activity was unofficial, secret and occurred on the edges of other sorts of bodywork. In both cases the flow of services was from women to men.

This raises the wider question of cross-gender tending, and asymmetrical meanings of this as between male and female workers and clients. Within the home care service the great majority of workers are female, as indeed are the clients. This means that the care system naturally delivers a pattern of supply and demand that is in accord with the dominant assumptions held by both clients and staff as to what is appropriate. Cross-gender tending by women for male clients in this context is regarded as unprob-lematic except in those few cases where female careworkers experience sexual expression that is unpleasant or threatening; and in these cases the work is typically transferred to a male worker. Women caring for women is also seen as unproblematic; and is regarded as raising no issues of sexuality. Males caring for males is also regarded as acceptable – at least by the agencies, for some of the male clients were less happy with the idea and preferred a woman. Many men are accustomed to being cared for by wives, as they have earlier been by mothers; and female careworkers are a natural continuation of that. Some men in the bathing study (Twigg 2000a) also expressed unease at the potentially homosexual nature of the encounter. This was reinforced by a related but slightly different perception that carework was not proper work for a man.

The one area of cross-gender tending, however, that is perceived as potentially problematic is the situation of male workers giving intimate care to women. This is regarded as breaching a taboo, and in general it does not happen within home care in the UK, though it does sometimes occur in residential care. Part of the meaning of this pattern concerns anxieties about sexual abuse. Cambridge and Carnaby (2000) in their review of intimate care for people with learning disabilities report how most agencies have responded to the risks of abuse in this context by instituting same gender polices for all intimate care. But as their review of evidence concerning the sexual abuse of people with learning disabilities shows, male perpetrators account for almost all recorded cases, and same sex polices do not address the 30–50 per cent of cases where the victim of the abuse is male. They also draw attention to the difficulties presented to gay- and lesbian-identified staff by the heterosexist assumptions that underpin such policies.

Most carework is about the provision of 'care' in the true sense, and is predominantly located in relationships of attention, concern and – often – mutual affection. But we need to recognise that care can also be a site of conflict in which two sets of people – workers and clients – both of whom suffer from a wider cultural disparagement, struggle to achieve autonomy and self-esteem. Clients struggle to resist the dominance of workers, and to maintain a fragile sense of self against the erosions of disability and old age. As we have seen in the previous chapter, the symbolic meanings of home can endow them with a certain degree of power. Workers, by contrast, strive to establish control over their work in the form of the lives and bodies of clients and to extract from this those elements of self-esteem and status that are available in an otherwise marginalised and poorly regarded employment sector. The bodily character of the work can be an element in this struggle.

Bodywork contains a power dynamic that has an ambiguous, unstable quality to it. It can tip either way, subordinating the workers in a particularly close and bodily way, or creating an agent of Foucauldian bio-power, disciplining and ordering the bodies of clients. Part of the tension arises from the master/servant dynamic that haunts these relationships; and this takes on an additional twist where the body is involved. Bodywork is demeaned work in part because it threatens the worker with the status of the body servant, the person who works on the body of another in a directly subordinated way. The very intimacy of the contact makes the subordination all the more personal. This dynamic also contributes to the low estimation of sex work. This is stigmatised not just because it violates cultural codes around sex, but because it involves subordination of a directly bodily kind, servicing the desires and demands of a client.

Something of these issues around domination is carried over into concerns that have been expressed regarding the role of Personal Assistants (PAs) within social care. PAs are helpers who are directly employed by disabled people to perform tasks of a personal nature that they are unable to do. They are seen, particularly by the disability movement, as preferable to workers provided by agencies or authorities since they are selected by disabled people themselves, and expected to act directly under their orders. They are thus servants, not agents of professional control. At the extreme they are regarded as bodily extensions of the disabled person's will: their hands and feet. Ungerson (1999) has critiqued this ideal, both in terms of the gendered realties that underlie it and the civil and employment rights of the workers. In general the PA model is only realised in social care to a limited degree; most social care is not delivered in this way. Even where PAs are employed, the kind of dominance and control that the ideology of the disability movement seeks is rarely fully achieved. Payment and employment terms do not wholly override the dynamics that traditionally adhere in situations of disability and dependence.

By and large, therefore, the dynamic works the other way. Again the body plays a direct part in this, for carework favours the exercise of bio-power of a classically Foucauldian type. Workers are younger, stronger and in general more mentally robust. Clients are frail and dependent on the workers to survive. Personal care involves nakedness, and in an asymmetrical situation in which the client is naked and the worker is clothed and dominant. It may involve incontinence or other socially embarrassing lapses in bodily competence, so that receiving help can be humiliating. Clients are very directly under the control of the workers by virtue of the bodily closeness. In such situations, it is hard to assert the self against the worker. Workers are very much in charge. These dynamics are all the stronger in residential care, where in addition the territory belongs to the workers. Lee-Treweek's account (1994, 1996) of a nursing home conveys the way in which bodywork operates in this setting. Workers struggle to establish control over the objects of their labour in the form of the bodies and persons of residents. In a context of harsh time constraints, this means organising, ordering and disciplining the bodies of residents, containing disruption and mess whether in the form of dirty substances or awkward emotions. In the back bedrooms of the institution the careworkers labour to produce the end product of the home in the form of what she terms the 'lounge standard resident'.

Carework and women's employment

Running through this account of carework is the dimension of gender. Carework is quintessentially women's work, and this links, as we have seen, to its character as bodywork. Before exploring this gendering more fully, however, we need to look at some of the other frameworks within which carework has been analysed. Four are particularly relevant here: service work, domestic labour, emotional labour and 'care'. As we shall see, these debates about gender also intersect in specific contexts with questions of 'race'.

Carework is a form of service work. The service sector now forms the largest part of Western economies, accounting in the US for 79 per cent of non-agricultural jobs (Macdonald and Sirianni 1996). Service work is intangible, marked by the fact that it is produced and consumed simultaneously. Though it encompasses a variety of jobs, including aspects of the highly paid professional work, the main focus here is on the 'emotional proletariat', those low-level service occupations that involve an element of emotional labour. Service workers are in the business of producing social relations, and the work demands not just the performance of labour tasks, but an attitude to the exchange. As a result, the personal characteristics of the worker are strongly linked to the job. The producer is to some degree the product. This means not just that the sector is marked in terms of who typically does this work, but that traits like gender, 'race', age and sexuality serve as a significatory function indicating to the customer the tone of the interaction (Glenn 1996). Women, for example, are expected to be more nurturing, and to tolerate more offensive behaviour from customers. People of colour are expected to be deferential and to take on more demeaning tasks. These service occupations, Glenn argues in the context of the United States, are so saturated with gender and race that they determine not just who does the work, but how it is done and in what context. Worker characteristics shape what is expected of the worker, how they adapt to the work and what aspects they will resist or embrace. Women are more likely to embrace the emotional demands of certain sorts of service work, as they fit with ideas of gender-appropriate behaviour. Heterosexual men by contrast resist these, regarding such 'feminised' emotional labour as demeaning. They either reframe the work to emphasise traditional masculine qualities, or distance themselves by providing service by rote, making it clear that they are acting under duress (Glenn 1996).

A service sector analysis in relation to carework brings many advantages. It helps us to focus on the front line where 'care' is produced and consumed as part of a dynamic interchange between the worker and the client. It enables us to relate to the intangible interactive character of the work: how this work is done is as important as what is done. Above all it allows us to explore the organic nature of the link between the job and the personal attributes of the worker, notably in this case, their gender, and also to some degree 'race'. But the service literature also presents problems. The struggle for dignity and respect is part of the traditional conflict of the work place, and much sociological literature about service work implicitly endorses this, locating its analysis within a critical, broadly Marxian, tradition that sides with the workers against their oppression and exploitation. Anderson (2000) in her analysis of paid domestic work positions herself clearly on the side of the workers against their 'mistresses'. Within this literature, resistance to the dominance of the bosses and the customers is recounted in terms of acts of subversion, refusals of compliance, withdrawal of warmth, covert or open rudeness.

This analytic stance becomes problematic, however, when applied to the situations of frail elders receiving help from careworkers. Here the traditional power dynamic of service work is to a large degree reversed. The workers are dominant and in charge. The clients are weak, dependant on them for survival. Service work can be seen as oppressive and exploitative of the workers since it involves the expropriation of their labour in the interests of profit, but in the case of carework, the end of the exchange is not primarily profit – though it can be involved where the service is provided on a commercial basis – but the provision of care, something that can be seen as a final end, of worth in itself. This does not mean that the circumstances of its delivery may not be oppressive of the worker – and the poor employment terms of most carework points to this – but that the power dynamics of the exchange need to be evaluated rather differently from those of other service sectors. Concepts of resistance by workers become more ambiguous here. Resistance to doing the job can mean acting in a cold unfeeling way, using denigrating language, rough actions. At worst it can mean abuse. Drawing on the parallels with other service sectors, therefore, needs to be done with caution, and with a recognition that there are key differences that locate these relationships within a different dynamic, and one that needs to be evaluated in specific terms.

The bodywork element of care and its gendered nature also needs to be set in the context of the revival of the domestic labour debate. Feminist analyses have traditionally seen the gendered division of labour in the home as an aspect of patriarchy whereby men obtain the services of women as wives and mothers, avoiding unattractive work in the home, and freeing themselves to concentrate their efforts on the field of paid employment and to achieve the dominance there that underpins their dominance in the home. Domestic labour is women's work not only because women do it, but because it reproduces gender relations between men and women. Class and gender intersect here. Middle-class women are subordinated within patriarchy to their husbands. Rather than challenging inequality in the home, they use domestic service to ease their burden, passing it over to women with less economic power. In the nineteenth and earlier twentieth centuries this enabled bourgeois women to resolve the contradiction between their status as refined, delicate, feminine, non-bodily, and the demands that they provide a comfortable domestic environment. More recently the tension has been between their status as professionals in the labour market – qualified, intellectual, managerial – and the demands of domestic labour, and this has resulted in the re-emergence of paid domestic work in relation to both housework and childcare (Gregson and Lowe 1994, Glenn 1996, Macdonald and Sirianni 1996). The availability of paid domestic labour thus acts to buttress male privilege by perpetuating the concept of reproductive labour as women's work, sustaining the illusion of a protected private sphere for women and displacing conflict away from the husband/wife towards the housewife/domestic (Macdonald and Sirianni 1996).

In many Western countries, this gendered and class-based division of labour takes on an additional racialised dimension (Anderson 2000, Neysmith and Aronson 1997). The pattern of racialisation varies, rooted in different histories, often of a post-colonial character, and different labour markets. The racialisation of domestic and service work is particularly marked in the United States where the long legacy of slavery still acts to structure the labour market along racial lines. Women of colour have historically been confined to the least desirable female jobs, concentrated in private household and domestic work and in technologically backward sectors (Feldman *et al.* 1990, Glenn 1996). In 1940, 60 per cent of employed black women were in domestic service in private households (Anderson 2000). Domestic work was naturalised in black women, and that association still affects how they are seen within the paid labour market. Women of colour are differentially found in low-level service and cleaning occupations; and this pattern extends into the care sector. Home care is heavily racialised: in states like New York, 96 per cent of home care workers are either Black or Hispanic (Donovan 1987, 1989). Similar patterns obtain in parts of Canada (Neysmith and Aronson 1997). Women of colour are also heavily overrepresented in the bottom echelons of health care, so much so that it has been suggested that there is no need for uniforms in the hospital: gender and race tell you all you need to know about the status of a worker (Macdonald and Sirianni 1996).

In Britain, there is a similar pattern of racial stratification in relation to low-level cleaning and service occupations, though it is more complex and fragmented as a result of past patterns of migration and the operation of local labour markets. Women of African-Caribbean descent are heavily overrepresented in the lower levels of the NHS and in carework, particularly in London (Mama 1992, Ward 1993, Ahmad and Atkin 1996). Paid domestic labour is similarly racialised, at least in parts of Britain.

The racialisation of domestic and carework needs to be set within the context of globalisation. Unlike manufacturing, low-level service jobs of a personalised nature cannot be exported. They have to be provided and consumed in the home country. Western economies cannot transfer these jobs to the Third World, but need to import labour to do them. Anderson (2000) and others have traced the flows of such female labour from the Third World and from the transitional economies on the margins of Europe into domestic service and carework in Europe and North America. Local workers are increasingly reluctant to take on these jobs. Part of the reason is the poor pay and conditions. But part also is the demeaned and personalised nature of the work. As Anderson (2000) argues, though domestic work is vital and sustaining, it is demeaned and disregarded.

Domestic work in the homes of others revives the old relations of master and servant. It was precisely to escape these that large numbers of women in the twentieth century moved out of domestic labour, where they were predominantly employed, into factories and offices, as such opportunities opened up to women (Burnett 1974). These employment sectors offered a contract-based relationship in which workers were not required to be personally subordinate, and in which home and workplace were separated. What is disliked about domestic service are the aspects of personal subordination, servicing the needs of another, doing the things they could do for themselves but choose not to. There is also an unlimited, potentially unbounded, quality to the work. The servant does everything that is needed, and shapes his/her work around the personal desires of the master/ mistress. At its strongest (most characteristic of live-in servants), it involves doing everything that is required, when it is required. Both these features are also characteristics of women's work within the family. Part of the meaning of domestic labour is to be under the thumb of the employer, and Anderson (whose focus is mainly on live-in domestic workers) sees the appropriation of the personhood of the worker, rather than just her labour power, as a key element in domestic service relations.

Domestic work, as Anderson (2000) argues, is part of the 'dirty work' of Western economies. Part of the 'dishonour' that attaches to it comes precisely from the fact that it deals in dirt and the body. It manages those aspects and clears them away. Paid domestic labour thus allows the privilege of being disembodied to men and to middle-class women, who are able to hire a racialised female labour force to do this work. Middle-class women are, as in earlier eras in relation to class, able to rid themselves of the burden of mundane physicality by loading it on to another Other group – in this case women of colour. Through racialised discourses these women are differentially associated with the body and with dirty work. Indeed, as Anderson shows, their own bodies are often made subject to ideas concerning contamination and dirt. 'Race', gender and class thus intersect, as we noted in Chapter 2, in complex, distinctive but often mutually supporting, ways. Rather than seeing them as additive aspects of oppression as earlier work tended to do, we need to understand how they interpenetrate and reinforce each other.

The third literature within which the bodywork of care needs to be located is that of emotional labour. 'Emotional labour' was the term coined by Hochschild (1983) to cover the feeling work that service workers such as flight attendants engage in as an implicit, but expected, part of their jobs. The term has proved widely influential, though it is used in slightly varying ways (James 1989, 1992, Lee-Treweek 1996, Gunaratnam and Lewis 2001). Hochschild's account contains the sense that this is work that is engaged in at the expense of the worker. It corrupts the authenticity of their lives: the mask eats into the face. But emotional labour is also often used in the more general sense to cover the deployment of emotion as an element in work – and as such it is part of the wider recognition of the role of emotions in the workplace (Fineman 1993). Emotional labour also contains a sense that it is the role of the worker to produce feeling states in the recipient; particularly in the context of certain commercial service settings like the airline or the expensive hotel, where the worker's role is to service and endorse the self-worth of the customer; and this links the analysis to the model of the servant that although in many ways obsolete in the modern world still implicitly structures some of its relations. It also gives the work a boundless, undefined quality, something that we have again noted in relation to the model of the servant and domestic service and that we shall note again in the conceptualisation of 'care'. This unbounded quality is a key element in the understanding of its nature as gendered work. Finally the aspect of emotional labour is not always at the expense of the worker. In the context of carework, particularly in certain harsher settings where the 'customer' is far from king, workers may use emotional labour not to service the egos of clients but to advance their own interests. Here emotional labour takes on a colder, more manipulative quality; and Lee-Treweek (1994, 1996) has explored how careworkers use emotional bribery to obtain the compliance of residents as part of their strategies for getting the work done.

Emotional labour is clearly an important dimension of carework, occurring in parallel with the physical labour of the work. There are also clear links between bodywork and emotional labour. We noted earlier how bodywork trades often involve aspects of emotion, using personal attention, touch and physical closeness to create a zone of pleasure and well-being. Carework without an aspect of emotional engagement would moreover be cold and mechanical. Emotion and bodywork, however, interact in complex ways. Physical closeness can create emotional closeness. But as we noted earlier, the association can also result in discordant, ambivalent feelings where bodily intimacy is at odds with social roles and personal relations.

Finally, carework has most commonly been analysed in terms of the debate on care. This emerged in the 1980s, primarily in response to the issue of informal care in the family; and it was part of a wider feminist focus on the unpaid work of women (Finch and Groves 1983, Ungerson 1987, Waerness 1987, Lewis and Meredith 1988, Graham 1991). The approach has been particularly valuable for the links it makes between women's unpaid work in the family and their role in the labour market, both in terms of their disadvantaged position, as a result of the double burden, and the limited sectors to which their skills and abilities are seen to be appropriate. Women are differentially employed in 'female' sectors that reflect and mimic aspects of their responsibilities in the home; and carework is a prime example of this. Ungerson (1993) has analysed the fluid boundaries between paid and unpaid work. The debate on care has also been important for the attempt to capture the unbounded, diffuse nature of care, and its relationship to women's work and lives, and this has extended the debate into political theory (Gilligan 1982, Balbo 1987, Tronto 1993, Larabee 1993). Though Waerness (1987) attempted to articulate the distinctive quality of 'care' as an alternative mode of rationality to that which sociology has traditionally focussed upon in its analysis of action, Thomas (1993) concluded that the concept, though important in alerting us to certain key relationships, had not proved successful as an overarching sociological term.

The conceptualisation of 'care' within this debate can also be problematic for the analysis of carework as a result of its roots in family relations and obligation. This can mislead in relation to paid work. Lee-Treweek (1998) argues that feminist accounts of care distort our understanding of paid carework which is better understood in the context of other forms of low-level, poorly regarded service work. This is a view shared by Anderson (2000) in relation to paid domestic work: though the tasks may be the same as when performed within the family, the social relations that structure the role are profoundly different. The word 'care' also presents problems. It implies that emotional connectedness is at the core of the activity and the social relations. Within the family this is, by and large, true; but within the context of work, it is not always so. Carework is bound by employment contracts, and these put limits on the emotional connectedness. Carework can also be performed coldly. In certain harsh, poor quality institutional settings, typically dealing with dementia, it often is. It only represents 'care' in the sense of tending. Lastly the word 'care' is also problematic because of its inherently sacralising quality. We noted earlier the ways in which it operates in holistic nursing discourse. It is difficult for people to be 'against' such a thing. Rather than allowing us to get hold of these difficult evanescent aspects sociologically, the language of 'care' can make the task more difficult.

A number of themes of relevance for the analysis of the gendered nature of carework emerge from this literature around service work, domestic labour and care. The first concerns the unbounded, unfocussed quality of much of it, built around responding to the needs and demands of others, whether practical or emotional. We have noted how this quality links back to the nature of women's work in the family, servicing the needs and desires of husbands and children. This is gendered work not just because women do it, but because it reproduces the gender order. It underpins both what women do in the family and the formal economy, and the unbounded, undefined terms under which they do it. This quality is central to much service work, particularly that which involves emotional labour, where the job requires not just the performance of tasks but implicates aspects of the personhood of the worker. This relates to the second theme which concerns the way in which the language of master and servant continues to resonate through these relationships, despite the superficial obsolescence of such terminology in the modern world. Once again the link to gendered relations in the family is crucial for the replication of these subordinated relations. The third concerns the way in which what is regarded as women's work in this service context often represents, as Anderson notes, the 'dirty work' of the economy. Its association with the bodily and with servicing the body is a key component in this.

Gender and bodywork

We can now return to the bodywork of social care, exploring the ways in which this can be understood as gendered work. The first link concerns the association that is frequently made within culture between the women and the body more generally. Women are often presented as more bodily in nature than men, defined by the processes of reproduction, caught up in tides of the body and of emotion. As such they have come to stand for the Body itself (Jordanova 1989, Lupton 1994). As we noted earlier men and women are often presented within an asymmetrically valued set of dichotomies in which women are associated with the body, emotion, the private sphere, and men with mind, rationality and the public world. These links are used to explain how bodywork is considered to belong 'naturally' to women. Women also represent the Body in term of male desire, the form of desire that is hegemonic in culture. They thus come to stand for sexuality itself. The control of sexuality often pursued through the control of women's bodies and access to them; and this has consequences, as we seen, for cross gender tending and access to bodies in carework.

Women and bodywork are also linked through the model of maternity. What women traditionally do for babies, they continue to do for adults in the context of the family, or by extension in employment. As we noted, for many men being helped in this way by a female careworker or nurse is not discordant, but is at one with earlier experiences in the family, and thus part of 'normal' gender expectations. Occupations like nursing have historically been constructed around gendered assumptions that have their roots in home-based body care (Reverby 1987). We noted earlier in the chapter on health care how the association of bodywork and bodily access is also embedded in issues of power and control. Bodily access is gendered, but part of the meaning of this concerns authority. Bashford's (1998) account of the difficulties presented by women doctors' surveillance of men's bodies in the nineteenth century illustrates this intersection. Access by nurses, by contrast, posed no problems in this context. Part of the gendered meaning of bodywork in care concerns its subordinated character.

The third set of links concerns the association made between dirt, pollution and women's bodies. Ungerson (1983) has suggested that the association of women with bodywork and body wastes reflects a wider cultural perception of their bodies as themselves dirty and polluted by processes of reproduction. Women are assigned to deal with such matters because they themselves belong to the realm of the body, its fluxes and wastes. Bashford (1998) makes a parallel point in relation to the new nursing that emerged in the nineteenth century. The very instability of the purity of the nurses' bodies made them potent symbols of purity and of the sanitary endeavour. These associations between the bodies of the workers and the nature of the work is also used to underlie the symbolic association of racialised groups with dirty work, particularly within colonial or racist discourse. We saw in Chapter 2 the ways in which colonial discourses constructed the Black bodies in terms of dirt, disease and primitiveness (McClintock 1995).

As important as the association of women (and racialised groups) with pollution are, however, the issues of power and status. Dirty work is by its nature demeaned and disliked, and those with power – by and large men, but also women who have been able to transcend their bodily ascription – manage to avoid it, handing it over to less powerful, typically gendered, but often also racialised, social groups. Gender privilege allows men to do this within the family, thus avoiding most of the dirty work of the household. This is why who changes the nappy, who cleans the toilet and washes the dirty underclothes has been the particular focus of feminist struggles within the family. This pattern of privilege extends to the economy also.

Men do do dirty work, but it is dirty work on machines, not bodies. Even within occupations like nursing that involve dealing with bodies, we can see this gendered pattern of evasion and transcendence. C.L. Williams (1989) in her study of non-standard gender occupations argues that nursing is work that is below or demeaning for men, and that this is closely linked to its bodily character, particularly the bedpan and shit cleaning aspects. As a result, men within nursing are encouraged and enabled to take the route out of such activity, up the ladder of managerial advance. Dirty work is seen as in someway 'unsuitable' for them; and the glass escalator of cultural assumptions takes them up and away. Something of the same processes operates in relation to social care, where men who enter the sector soon move away from the front line of bodycare. The discordant status as dirty work is not the only reason for this, but it is a powerful one.

Bodywork is thus naturalised in the characters and bodies of women. One of the consequences of this is that it tends to be treated as obvious, something that comes naturally and that does not require training, or indeed the wages that traditionally go with training. This also underpins the additional elements like emotional labour that are included as part of the hidden gender contract. These additional elements are deemed to come with the worker, something that is neither acknowledged nor paid for. This naturalisation of care in the persons of women also underpins the polar estimation of carework as both vital and estimable, yet low level and poorly rewarded. There are parallels here with the ways in which motherhood is traditionally presented in conservative discourse, as something of inestimable value, connected to love and self-sacrifice, and yet at the same time low level and marginalised. These patterns illustrate what has been termed the patriarchal feminine, that allows for the valuing and praise of female work but in ways that reinforce female subordination.

Lastly the assumption that bodywork is women's work is underwritten by commonly held beliefs about male sexuality. Hegemonic masculinity has traditionally constructed men as sexually predatory (Connell 1995, 2000), and limits are placed on their free access to bodies, mostly female but to some degree male also. Though there is, of course, considerable historical and cultural variance in this, the pattern is reinforced by the differential treatment of men's and women's bodies within culture generally. Again there is considerable variation in this; however, certain patterns do recur. Women's bodies have traditionally been prime sites for the exercise of patriarchy; and visual and physical access to them is often controlled and limited. The rules of modesty traditionally operate differentially between men and women, with women's bodies more shrouded, hidden from the male phallic gaze. This asymmetry has consequences for carework, underpinning the assumed pattern of cross gender tending that we noted earlier. It also underlies the concern among agencies about using male staff in intimate settings where access to the body is part of the work. The recent uncovering of the extent of sexual abuse in institutions in the past has re-inforced this. Male workers are still employed in carework with children and vulnerable adults, but there is often a sense that they would be ill-advised to stay too long in this work: it is fine for experience, but continued involvement may be suspicious. Once again this points to the ways in which the gendered patterning of jobs and men's exclusion from some of them acts to their advantage, propelling them away from poorly regarded employment, and from the dirty work of care.

Conclusion

In this chapter, I have argued for the importance of recognising carework as a form of bodywork. Doing so, I believe, elucidates key features of the work and allows us to locate its analysis within a wider conceptual framework, enabling us to trace the commonalities that attach to work on the body across a range of settings. Bodywork, as we saw, is marked by being ambivalent, hidden work, which tends to remain unarticulated within official discourses. It can breach social norms, and may require symbolic techniques to negotiate these. It can involve dealing with the negativities of the body; and it is often regarded as low-level, dirty work. But at the same time it is also often associated with pleasure and emotional warmth, and as such it lies on the borders of sexuality. It is also ambivalently placed in relation to the exercise of power. Exploring the ways in which these features also resonate through carework alerts us to key dimensions of it.

One of the most significant dimensions of carework is its gendered nature; and we have explored the complex interplay of features that constitute and mutually reinforce this association. The body plays a significant part in this. Currently carework across Western economies is predominantly provided by women. Though comprehensive figures are lacking for the UK, estimates suggest that considerably less than 10 per cent of the workforce is male. But pressure is likely to build up over the next decades in all Western countries in relation to labour supply. In some countries this is already being felt. The rising proportion of older people are part of the equation. But as significant has been changes in women's employment options in the late twentieth and early twenty-first centuries with the opening up of educational and other work-related opportunities. This threatens labour supply in traditionally gendered fields like nursing and carework, raising the question as to whether men might be used to do this work, particularly as traditional unskilled male jobs decline. There are certainly no inherent reasons why men cannot; and many currently do. But as we have seen the gendering of carework occurs at a number of levels. It is constructed around embedded assumptions about women – and to some degree men – and the bodily element is a central part in this. Exploring carework's nature as bodywork helps us to see some of the limitations that may be presented to using male workers; and it certainly points to some of the problems that are likely to arise in attempts to recruit considerable numbers of men into this work.

Recognising the centrality of the body also raises issues concerning the support and training of careworkers. As we have seen careworkers are asked to engage in complex and sensitive forms of intervention in relation to their clients, negotiating the rules of the body and its management. And yet, they receive little in the ways of support or training to do this. This reflects the general neglect of this group, and the disadvantageous employment context in which they work. Carework is a poorly resourced sector in the UK and elsewhere. Cost containment bears down heavily on it. There is little leeway in budgets for training; and almost no commitment to it among purchasers and commissioners. Partly this is because the work is assumed to be unskilled and obvious. But it also reflects the evasion of the bodily within official discourses. A double process goes on here whereby policy makers and planners, having erased the bodily from their own rationalistic and abstract discourses, unconsciously extend this to the services they plan and commission, so that the nature of these is not fully articulated or acknowledged. Workers are thus required to undertake their work within a zone of silence, their activities rendered 'unutterable' within the official discourses of social care.

To some degree the workers are themselves complicit in these processes, often choosing not to foreground the bodywork element in their accounts of their work, preferring to emphasise the 'nicer', more genteel, elements of emotional support and care. Foregrounding the bodily can have an ambivalent quality to it. It can lead to a greater recognition of the realities of the work and, with that, the need for support and training. It may lead to a greater recognition of carework as a vital part of the service system and something therefore requiring more in the way of accreditation and reward. But it may also act to the detriment of workers, exposing the nature of their work in ways that erode rather than enhance their status. At the moment careworkers have little in the ways of protection against the dirty work designation. They have few professional or other symbolic shields that they can deploy. Emphasising the bodily in their work without also enhancing and defining their occupational status may therefore be an unhelpful strategy.

Chapter 9

The Body in Public Space: Breastfeeding and Toilets

The focus of this final chapter is the body in public space, and within that the particular issues raised by the gendered body in public policy. I will take two examples to explore this: the public provision of toilets, and breastfeeding in public. Both represent responses to the needs of the body in the context of public space and both have implications for public health. I will trace the historical changes that have occurred around these issues, and the current responses of government and other public bodies; and in doing so, will raise questions about the nature of the body in public space and in particular about the kinds of bodies that are acceptable in such settings. As we shall see, public space in the West is an example of a social reality that although overtly neutral and universal in regard to gender – open to all people, all sexes – is in fact implicitly gendered; for the sorts of bodies that are assumed and acceptable in these spaces are those of men, or of women in so far as they can conform to the male model.

Public space

Public space has been the subject of a large and sophisticated literature encompassing work in geography, urban sociology, cultural studies and political theory. A complex and cross cutting category, it can be analysed at the number of levels: concrete, discursive, symbolic, cultural, political and economic. It addresses the literal space of the physical and social world – the concrete reality of city streets or public parks – as well as the discourses and practices within which such space is constituted: codes of manners, legal rules, economic and political structures. It is the product of the intellectual discourses that have analysed it, and that have privileged certain principles in its construction. It also exists in the idealised, abstract version of political theory: the space of universalistic debate and contention. To significant degree it is understood in term of its opposite – private space. This is the space of domesticity, women, family, intimacy, emotional and sexual life – a space constructed around particularity and connectedness, in contrast to the universalistic principles that govern public life. As we noted in Chapter 2, public/private can be located within a series of gendered oppositions in which the private is positioned on the unmarked side of the equation, together with nature, family, women and the body, as opposed to the marked side of culture, public life, men and mind.

The division of public/private was particularly clearly entrenched through the work of social contract theorists of the seventeenth and eighteenth century (Pateman 1989, Rose 1993). Though there had always been accounts that presented a distinct sphere of the family separate from public life and that asserted that women belonged naturally only in the first, these ideas achieved new articulation in the classic period of English liberalism. Pateman (1989) argues that the rise of individualism required new means whereby the collective could be expressed; and this was achieved through the concept of the social contract. This contract was, however, not neutral as to gender; it was a fraternal social contact:

> In the story of the creation of civil society through an original agreement, women are brought into the new social order as inhabitants of a private sphere that is part of civil society and yet is separated from the public world of freedom, equality, rights, contract, interest and citizenship. (Pateman 1989, p. 4)

The fraternal social contact created a new, modern patriarchal order that rested on the doctrine of the two spheres. The first was that of civil society, the universal space of freedom, equality, individualism, reason, contract and impartial law, and the realm of men or of 'individuals'; and the second was the private world of particularity, natural subjection, ties of blood, emotion, love and sexual passion – the world of women, but in which men also rule (Rose 1993). This division had a bodily dimension for in the context of these writings, women's bodies came to 'symbolise everything opposed to political order' (Pateman 1989, p. 4).

The emergence of public space as a political and cultural category is also linked historically to the rise of the city as it developed in the eighteenth and nineteenth centuries in response to the forces of industrialisation and urbanisation. As production moved from the household to the factory, home and paid work were separated. Gender relations were increasingly regulated by the ideology of separate spheres. From the nineteenth century, modern cities came to represent this in built form, divided into zones of production and reproduction. This was epitomised by the development of the suburbs, built around the idea of a commuting husband and domestic wife (Rose 1993).

The urban landscape as it emerged in the nineteenth century was an implicitly gendered one. To this day, women do not occupy public space in the easy ways that men can. For men, one of the meanings of the city and of public space is freedom to move around, to observe and to be observed. The nineteenth century, as Benjamin (1973) argued, saw the emergence of a new social type, the flâneur, or urban stroller, who wandered the streets and arcades, voyeuristically immersing himself in the sensations of the city and the crowd, free to look and to pursue opportunities for pleasure, often of a sexual character. For Benjamin, the flâneur represented the type of modernity. But as Wolff (1985) argues in her article on the Invisible Flâneuse, no such female equivalent existed, or could exist. Women's engagement with public space was fundamentally different in character, constrained both in terms of the areas of space that could be occupied, and the manner in which this could be done.

The changes in women's circumstances that have occurred since the nineteenth century, with the mass movement of women into education and paid employment, and the consequent opening up of social and employment opportunities, have been immense. And yet, there is still some constraint on women's free occupation of public space (Rose 1993). Harassment in the streets in the form of suggestive comments, wolf whistles, appraising stares, touching up, that used to be commonplace in Britain, still occasionally occur, and such behaviour is a common feature of societies where women have yet to establish a secure presence in public space. Harassment acts to destabilise women in the public sphere, sending messages about their implicit sexual subordination as objects of a male gaze that controls, polices and limits them. Harassment at work similarly undermines the legitimacy of women's actions, making them subject to an implicit sexual subordination, reminding them that their presence in the world of work is conditional on their subordination as a gender to men who dominate and control this space.

The fear of violence also acts to police women's presence in public space (Rose 1993). Such feelings are not limited to women; and other vulnerable or marginal social groups are also fearful of public places, particularly at night. In reality the majority of crimes of violence are perpetrated on men, particularly young men, or take place in domestic settings. The fear of violence, however, particularly sexual violence, remains written into the responses of many women to public space. Even if not actively fearful, women tend to be more watchful in such settings, avoiding certain places and situations. Marches to reclaim the night that were a feature of feminism in the 1970s and 1980s were a direct attempt to challenge the gendered assumptions on which public space rests, asserting that women had as full a right to be present in the city at night as men, and attacking the implicit assumption that the responsibility lay with women to protect themselves by avoiding dangerous situations. Place also affects judgements about women's sexuality. Women in public space traditionally run the risk of being perceived as 'public' women; and they learn to be circumspect in their behaviour and appearance in order to emphasise that this is not so.

We now turn to the implications of these ideas concerning public space for two concrete areas of public policy: the provision of public toilets and the social regulation of breastfeeding in public. Both raise questions of the interaction between public spaces and private bodies; and both reveal the implicitly gendered character of these spatial relations.

Public toilets

Public toilets do not feature large in accounts of public policy. At best they are seen as minor matters for local consideration; at worst a slightly squalid subject. But as we shall see, their provision in fact encapsulates a number of larger themes. Public toilets present issues of citizenship, equality and inclusion, having implications, for example, for the capacity of women and other groups to move about urban space. They also illustrate changes in the nature of the public sphere, with the gradual erosion of collectivist values and their replacement by privatised forms of provision and of space. Lastly they raise questions of the meaning of bodily difference, and the implication of this for questions of equity.

As Penner (2001) argues a toilet is not simply a technological response to a physical need, but a cultural product shaped by complex and often competing discourses of sexuality, morality and hygiene. Public toilets like other everyday spaces do not merely reflect existing social relations and identities, but are actively involved in producing and reproducing them (Rose 1993). Daily encounters with the built environment continually position people in relation to dominant power structures, enforcing and reinforcing difference, subtly creating the boundaries that shape experience, including gendered experience. Far from being neutral or self-evident, the planning of conveniences is informed by historically and culturally specific sets of ideas, as the history of the development of public provision, particularly for women, demonstrates.

Prior to the modern industrial period, toilets were frequently communal and mixed. It was only in the nineteenth century with increasingly strict prohibitions of bodily display and the emergence of a more rigid ideology of gender that visual privacy and spatial segregation of the sexes came to be seen as desirable (Penner 2001). Though lavatories for both sexes were among the pioneering facilities at the Great Exhibition of 1851, public provision was in general limited to men, who used street urinals or facilities attached to the side of public houses. This lack of public provision for women acted as a direct impediment on their free movement through urban space. Middle-class women living in the new residential districts served by omnibuses or trains had to limit the duration of their visits to the city to only a few hours. As one women commented 'Either ladies didn't go out, or ladies didn't "go" ' (Rappaport 2000). Another remarked: 'a morning's shopping was all we could manage' (Penner 2001, p. 38). The problem was not just one for bourgeois women, but arose also as women increasingly began to be employed in office and retail jobs and needed to travel to and from these settings and sustain themselves over a long working day.

Public lavatories for women were thus one of series of developments in the late nineteenth century that afforded material comfort to women in the city and that allowed them to move through, and to some extent occupy, urban space. Tea rooms and chains of modest unlicensed eating places like ABCs where women could eat alone also developed from the 1880s (Thorne 1980). Department stores acted similarly for middle-class women, providing new settings for female-oriented forms of display and leisure built around consumption (Rappaport 2000). Entrepreneurs like Whiteley in his store in Westbourne Grove pioneered the provision of restaurants and lavish rest rooms for ladies. In doing so Whitley was subject to a barrage of criticism from conservative moralists anxious about the new freedoms or 'temptations' that such shops offered middle-class women. The enticement to spend, and the free association afforded by restaurants where women could eat unescorted by husbands or fathers, threatened patriarchal control, and endowed women with a toehold in the city. Department stores became and remain female-oriented spaces in cities, and ones that continue to provide a variety of facilities, including toilets, in their attempt to secure the presence of women shoppers.

The significance of public toilets as a means of overcoming limitations on women's lives was recognised by feminists in the nineteenth century, who saw them as part of the wider project of creating a female public space through the development of settings like women's clubs and educational institutions that could parallel and challenge those of men (Rappaport 2000). The Ladies Sanitary Association, a broadly based reform group that promoted health and social causes, was active from the 1870s, pressing local vestries to provide public conveniences for women. The issue achieved some notoriety in the account by George Bernard Shaw in 1909 of the struggles in the St Pancras Vestry over the erection of a female convenience at Park Street, Camden Town (Penner 2001). A woman's lavatory had been sited at the traffic intersection and had become the focus of boisterous attacks by omnibus and other drivers. Opposition was about more than traffic congestion. The location and visibility of the convenience raised questions of gender and class politics. As the Vestrymen, who opposed provision and orchestrated the street opposition, knew 'the presence or absence of a female lavatory on Park Street sent local women a powerful message about their right to occupy and move through the streets of Camden Town' (Penner 2001, p. 37). Its construction contested prevailing cultural notions of privacy, decency and femininity, pushing the boundaries of existing social conceptions of these. Reports in the local papers of the vestry meetings, with their interpolations of laughter and applause, provide hints of 'the highly sexist subtext and innuendo that swirled about the women's convenience debates' (Penner 2001, p. 40). The lavatory's intimate association with the female body, the container of its natural functions – urinating, defecating, menstruating – mean that it raised the spectre of female corporeality and sexuality in a very direct way. Some who opposed public lavatories did so on the basis that they would attract prostitutes, reinforcing the connections that were recurringly made between women who were in public spaces, their bodies and 'public women'. Feelings of exposure and unease were internalised by women themselves. Reports of provision in the nineteenth century and beyond repeatedly refer to an 'excess of modesty' that prevented many women from using prominently sited toilets. As a result there was pressure on them to be hidden in obscure spots or behind dense planting.

Charges were also an issue. While men in the nineteenth century – and today – used urinals free, women had to pay. As Shaw noted, a penny – the standard fee established at the Great Exhibition – was a prohibitive charge for poor women. Concerns were also strongly based in class. Most of the users of public conveniences, such as the one at Camden were working women, and provision for them signalled their presence in more select residential areas. Public lavatories could be read as an erosion of privacy and gentility, symbolising the public quality of the streets in which all classes and sexes intermixed and might encounter one another (Rappaport 2000, Penner 2001).

The Public Health Act 1936, which still governs provision today, gave local authorities powers to provide public conveniences, but did not require them to do so. As a result provision developed in a fairly arbitrary way in the post-war era. Public toilets were, however, still seen as part of civic responsibility, at some level at least. In the last 20 years, however, there has been a steady erosion of provision in Britain. Many of the old underground facilities have been closed. Key sites have been sold off; and peripheral facilities closed. Since there is no formal requirement to provide, there is little systematic data, and letting for tender and privatisation has compounded this. Cavanagh and Ware (1990) in their study for the Women's Design Service found they were faced by a maze of local contractors unwilling to provide information about the numbers, opening hours or frequency of cleansing. Many bodies like public libraries, parks and stations no longer provide toilets. Greed and Daniels (2002) estimate that since 1997 over half of public toilets have been closed.

The issue is still a gendered one. In general, women have greater need, but poorer provision. Women take longer than men to use the toilet due to a combination of physiology, clothing and socially endorsed ideas of modesty. Menstruation and pregnancy can also mean that women need to use these facilities more frequently. Women also often have responsibility for babies and young children who can have urgent needs. Despite this, provision is still biased towards men. There is a long historical imbalance in relation to gender. In an LCC survey of 1928 there were 233 public conveniences for men and 184 for women. Men's provision contained 1260 cubicles for men and 2610 stalls compared with just 876 cubicles for women. There were in addition a further 6891 urinals for men associated with pubs but with direct street access (Cavanagh and Ware 1990). This pattern of provision persists today. Up until its revision in 1996, the British Standard Institute note (currently BS6465) that sets national guidelines for building gave men about a third more provision than women; and the recent revision under pressure from campaigners has only marginally altered this (Greed and Daniels 2002). Even where, as now, it is customary to provide the same floor space, provision is not equal, since men's lavatories have both urinals and cubicles. It is this unequal pattern of need and provision that causes the commonly observed queues that snake outside the Ladies even in newly built theatres and public spaces. Men are also generally accommodated free, perhaps reflecting a reality that unless they are accomodated, they will urinate in the streets. And indeed the growing disinhibition of, particularly young, men has become a problem in city centres at night.

For Edwards and McKie (1997) this unequal provision raises questions of citizenship. The failure to address women's distinct needs reflects a wider failure to value them as full citizens, revealing once again the ways in which concepts of citizenship rest on assumptions that privilege the bodies of men. In their view, the queues are an insult, a denial of women's public value and a systematic waste of their time. Public toilet provision also provides an example of how equality in the literal sense of equal provision of space is an inadequate response in a context where needs are genuinely different. As we noted earlier, feminism has been chary of arguments that emphasise women's physiological difference, seeing them as tending to underwrite oppressive forms of essentialism. But there are areas of bodily life where needs are genuinely different, and where equity means more than sameness.

Public toilets are not only an issue for women, other groups also suffer from poor provision. Older people, for example, often need to go more frequently, and they are also more likely to be on foot, or using public transport, and less likely to have a base in the town centre like an office, or a car that they can drive to other facilities. Parks, which older people and children frequently use, have often had their toilets closed because of vandalism. Women travelling with children at night experience considerable difficult in finding suitable toilets that are open. Those with young children, pushchairs, luggage, sticks or zimmer frames can all find accessing public conveniences difficult. Many are down steps or underground (the first facilities were subterranean because local authorities were given permission to use the space under the highroad). Turnstiles are increasingly common in stations and other semi-public but increasingly privatised places (Greed and Daniels

2002). Increasingly provision is in the form of Automatic Public Toilets (APTs) though these are widely disliked, provoking fears of being trapped or exposed, and regarded as a tokenist gesture by the local authority (Cavanagh and Ware 1990).

Part of the reason why provision is poor concerns the way in which the issue is treated within public policy. Legislation has always been permissive not mandatory; and toilets like other marginal provision are vulnerable to cutbacks. They are not high-profile. Few local authorities have a policy on public toilets. Provision is typically managed within the cleansing department which tends to take a technical, engineering approach to the issue rather than one based on wider considerations of health, leisure or social inclusion. Those who provide and manage toilets are mostly men and the area, Greed (2002) argues, is dominated by their perceptions. To a considerable degree the issue is framed in terms of the agenda of public nuisance, dominated by 'what goes on in the Gents': drugs, cottaging and vandalism. This produces a fortress approach, with destruction-proof facilities and attempts to restrict and discourage use through limited hours, entrance barriers and narrow cubicles. In the view of many councillors and officers the only good toilet is a closed toilet (Greed 2002).

The neglect of the issue also reflects the nature of town planning as a profession and a discipline. Greed (1994) argues that planning embodies a masculinist vision, that has a profound distrust of natural processes. It is an ideology informed by Enlightenment values that promote order over chaos, mind over body. Planning draws on the language of science, is large-scale, future-oriented, impersonal, abstract and quantitative. It is the world seen from the viewpoint of the planner looking down on the city in its abstract form. The female world is blotted out from these pictures, and with it the more ordinary day-to-day needs of the body, particularly the bodies of women. Both the neglect of public toilets and the trivialisation of the topic are part of this.

The failure to deal with the issue adequately is compounded by wider attitudes to the body and excretory functions. Public toilets are often subjects of embarrassment, and even within the trade, hidden in a 'cloud of vulgar humour' (Cavanagh and Ware 1990). Partly this derives from a general reticence about excretion, but it gains greater force from the sexualisation, mainly by men, of excretory functions, their own and women's. Edwards and McKie (1997) point to the careful etiquette of men around the use of urinals that they see as linked to both homophobia and fears of heterosexual judgement. Public toilets for men are potential sites of sex and disorder, and as a result regarded as edgy and at times threatening places. For men, women's toilets offer a focus for prurient curiosity. This fundamentally different gender experience underlies some of the conflicts around public provision; for most of the providers and managers are men, and most of those pressing for better provision are women.

Attempts have been made to mobilise public pressure on the subject. All Mod Cons, a woman's campaign for equal and adequate provision, was started in Cardiff in the 1985, provoked by the announcement that the new public library would have no toilet provision. Though they lost that cause, they continued to press government for better provision, particularly for women and children; in 1991 lobbying successfully to get a woman – for the first time – sitting on the committee discussing the British Standards specification for building. They did get support from the Continence Foundation, but that was help on the basis of incontinence needs, rather than what was for them the central issue, the civil rights of women. The group later merged to form the British Toilet Association which actively presses for better provision, publishes guides and promotes conferences. The Women's Institute and Townswomen's Guide in the UK have also taken up the cause. As Greed found (2002) many women regard public toilets as an important social benefit, something that is paid for by their taxes and valued by them.

Public toilets have never been the only form of provision. There have always been other places that people use: restaurants, pubs, department stores, places of work, museums and meeting rooms. Many pass through urban space without ever using a public toilet. Recently under pressure of resources and in an attempt to locate provision in less vulnerable sites, local authorities have tried to pass responsibility to the private sector, deploying arguments around planning gain. Some London authorities, for example, have required fast food outlets to provide toilets for the general public. Such bargaining, however, can only take place where local officers are willing to interpret the planning and public health regulations in pursuit of such goals (Greed and Daniels 2002, Greed 2003).

The erosion of provision needs also to be seen in terms of changes in the nature of the state. Public toilets were once objects of municipal pride. Like public baths, parks, street lighting and libraries, they were part of the collective amenities of an authority that met local needs and gave dignity to the town. And like them, they have been in steep decline over the past two decades, in parallel with the decline of the post-war welfare state, that itself had roots in inter-war municipalism. The shift to individual consumption, buoyed up by greater affluence, has eroded the ideal of collective provision; and the 1980s and 1990s saw a concerted attack on these values from the perspective of neo-liberalism. The decline of public toilets is thus part of the wider decline of the public, municipal city that Watson (2002) contrasts with the increasingly dominant capitalist city of the private sector. Public space is being replaced by privatised versions of it, in the form of gated communities; shopping malls with security staff that are closed after hours; atriums that only admit those on business; green spaces that are locked. Open collective space is increasingly left to the disadvantaged and the poor. The growing use of private cars and the retreat by some sections of society from all public transport mean that the bodily mixing and mingling that is one of the bases for a sense of the shared nature of society is weakened. The bodily has a profound part to play in our sense of connection with others. It underwrites the sense of fellow feeling and community. Without such linkages and minglings, we retreat into individualism and privatisation. In this context more and more people feel that they have little stake in public provision. Their aim, or aspiration, is to avoid it, across a range of goods and services. Public toilets are but one. As a result, there is only a limited and declining constituency for public provision. As societies get richer, particularly those informed by neo-liberal values and the ethic of individualism, they appear to be less willing to expend resources on the collectivity and upon public space. To this degree, public toilets illustrate very well Galbraith's paradox of private affluence and public squalor.

Public breastfeeding

We will now move on to the second example of issues concerning the management of the body in public space. This concerns breastfeeding. Breastfeeding is now promoted as the preferred method for feeding babies, conferring a range of health benefits on both mothers and children (Galtry 2003). Encouraging women to breastfeed is the aim of public health programmes across the Western world. For example, in the UK, the Department of Health has organised an annual Breastfeeding Awareness Week since 1993; and increasing the rate of breastfeeding by 2 per cent per year is one of the current national targets (Department of Health, 2004). Comparable policies exist in other countries (Galtry 2003). Though the message that 'breast is best' has achieved wide currency, breastfeeding is far from universal. In the UK well over a quarter of babies are not breast fed, and this rate is considerably higher among poorer social groups. Many women who institute breastfeeding, do not continue for the recommended six months. A range of factors underlie this, but among them are questions concerning the management of the body in public space, in particular the acceptability of breastfeeding in public.

In England and Wales the current rate for instituting breastfeeding is 71 per cent (Department of Health 2004). Exclusive breastfeeding rates are lower; and prolonged rates lower still. At two weeks, only 54 per cent are still breastfeeding, dropping to 22 per cent at six months (Department of Health 2004). Breastfeeding is unevenly distributed socially. It is strongly associated with education and social class. In the UK in 2000, breastfeeding was instituted by 88 per cent of mothers who left full-time education at 18 or over, but only 54 per cent of those who left at 16 or under (Social

Trends 33 2001). Ninety-one per cent of mothers from social class I initiated breastfeeding, contrasted with 57 per cent of social class V. White women in Britain are less likely to breastfeed than those from black and ethnic minority groups (Forste *et al*. 2001, Hamlyn *et al*. 2002). Younger mothers, especially teenagers, are also less likely to breastfeed (Department of Health 2004). A similar pattern exists in America, except that 'race' operates in a reverse fashion, with 23 per cent of Black mothers breastfeeding at birth, compared with 59 per cent of White (Blum 1993, Wolf 2001).

Attempts to encourage breastfeeding from the health point of view tend to operate at a rational level, stressing the health benefits, and attempting to resolve individual difficulties by information, or encouragement from health professionals. This sort of approach, however, frames the topic narrowly in medical or nutritional terms. Breastfeeding, as Maher (1995) notes in her anthropological review of the practice, is embedded in complex sets of ideas. Like sexuality and childbirth, it is subject to considerable cultural elaboration, reflecting a range of social and symbolic relations. In the sections that follow, I will explore some of these social and cultural factors and their role in shaping the current pattern.

It is important to recognise that attitudes to breastfeeding in the West have varied historically and geographically. It is wrong to assume that breastfeeding has always been the norm. There have been societies such as Bavaria in the early modern period and Iceland in seventeenth and eighteenth centuries where babies were weaned at birth, with a marked impact on infant survival (Hastrup 1992). In Europe until the twentieth century among the better-off, there was widespread employment of wet nurses. Though they were used where a mother's milk was insufficient, or she was ill, their employment also reflected ideas about social and marital relations. In the early modern period and beyond it was held that sex could not be engaged in while breastfeeding continued, and it was common for the wealthy to send their infants to wet nurses, so that conjugal relations could resume. Fashions in behaviour among the elite have also ebbed and flowed historically, changing in line with wider currents of thought: for example, during the late eighteenth and early nineteenth centuries, it became fashionable to breastfeed under the impact of Romanticist and Rousseauistic ideas of the body that stressed simplicity and nature, rather than artifice and social manners.

By the late nineteenth and early twentieth century, however, the overall trend was away from breastfeeding. As we shall see, this gathered strength in the interwar years, and only began to be reversed from the 1970s. The trend was already established in urban America by the 1890s (Wolf 2001). Women were breastfeeding for shorter periods, and more were reporting difficulties with their supply of milk. By the 1890s in urban America, women were weaning their babies by the third month. This contrasted with the predominant pattern of the past, when the norm in the seventeenth century was to breastfeed until the baby's second summer, and in the eighteenth, for at least a year. By the 1930s in the US, the majority of mothers did not institute breastfeeding at all, but relied solely on the bottle and on the new infant formula foods (Wolf 2001). A comparable, but later pattern, occurred in the UK.

The trend away from breastfeeding was compounded in the early twentieth century by the ideology of scientific motherhood. Promoted by doctors and experts in child care, this echoed other social trends that attempted to colonise domestic life with scientific regulation and control. The discovery and promotion of infant formula milk was part of this. Blessed by science, it fitted well with the wider culture of rationality and hygiene. Increasingly mothers were enjoined to impose scientifically monitored and timed feeding schedules. Up until the late nineteenth century advice had been to feed at will, and to stop and start as frequently as the baby wished. From the early twentieth century, however, four-hourly schedules were instituted in the US (Wolf 2001). Ironically these compounded the problems of lack of milk that women were reporting, since in breastfeeding, supply equals demand, and if mothers do not feed frequently, the milk dries up. 'Scientific' schedules thus inhibited supply, and resulted in a cycle of problems that only infant formula food could 'resolve'.

From the perspective of the mothers, feeding schedules were attractive, because they offered the possibility of predicable time alone, giving some autonomy to middle-class women, who by this period no longer used wet nurses. An alliance developed between the physicians and the formula milk manufacturers in the interwar years, in which formula was increasingly promoting as the nutritional ideal particularly in America (Apple 1987). Hospitals and nursing homes made little attempt to support mothers in breastfeeding, and their own regimes were based around the bottle. In the post-war period, infant food continued to be heavily promoted, and mothers in both the US and the UK were sent home with free supplies provided by manufacturers, sending a clear message about what was best, or at least most practical.

It was not until the 1970s that the pattern of decline began to be reversed. In 1972, 22 per cent of newborns in the US were breastfed; by 1982, it was 62 per cent (Wolf 2001). Medical opinion began to shift, as evidence in favour of breastfeeding accumulated. In 1979 the American Pediatric Association changed its policy to the strongly pro-breast stance that it now takes. These medical shifts were not the only influence. The 1970s saw the upsurge of a broad range of social and cultural movements associated with feminism, ecology, the counter culture and ideas that stressed the natural. These represent the recurring return of Romanticist ideas in Western culture (Campbell 1987, Heelas 1996), and we noted how this had earlier endorsed the virtues of breastfeeding. Breastfeeding reflected the looser, more natural approach to the body of the period, one that favoured flowing hair and fluid shapes; and it fitted with maternalist, women-centred forms of feminism.

Attitudes to breastfeeding also need to be set in the context of a range of social and cultural factors in relation to sexuality, marriage, work and the body – as well as to public space and the expression of the body within it. Despite the strong advocacy of doctors and health experts, there is still unease in the West at public breastfeeding. Many women feel, and are made to feel, discomfit in doing it. Difficulties partly arises from the changed meaning of breasts in modern culture, which have come to be increasingly sexualised. This is not to say that women's breasts were not the focus of erotic interest in the past, but that they were less exclusively perceived so. Public statues and paintings depicted naked breasts, but typically in heroic or maternal contexts, representing nationhood or other abstract virtues (Warner 1985). Their directly erotic presentation was more circumscribed. In the late twentieth century, however, the focus has shifted, and pictures of naked, sexualised breasts abound in the media (Yalom 1998). Breastfeeding images are, however, more rare. Even adverts for baby products tend to avoid them. Breasts have come to mean sex not motherhood.

The sexualisation of breasts also has significance in relation to changes in the nature of marriage. The rise of companionate, romantic marriage with its emphasis on the emotional and sexual bond of the couple changed the way in which women's bodies were seen (Wolf 2001). As couples began to restrict their fertility in the late nineteenth and early twentieth century, the link between sex and procreation weakened, and sex in marriage shifted from being primarily focussed on procreation, to assume a more central role in the relationship. Jeffries (1985) has charted the interwar rise of sexology, with its promotion of the marital sexual bond. This was popularised in the post-war era in advice columns, marriage guidance and family planning services. 'Breasts acquired meaning beyond feeding a new born. A woman's breasts now "belonged" to her husband at least as much if not more, than to her infant. Men and women alike began to define the breast less in physiological terms and more in sexual ones' (Wolf 2001, p. 24). Advice on breastfeeding reflects this tension, enjoining new mothers not to forget that they are their husband's mistress as well as their baby's mother. As a result Blum (1993) suggests women began to experience unease at the dual meaning of their breasts, and this reinforced a reluctance to breastfeed.

The intense bond created by motherhood and the exclusive closeness of breastfeeding can also mean that the baby at the breast is perceived by the father as an intruder and rival. Part of the pleasure of breastfeeding is erotic, and men can find this disturbing, fuelling the sense of jealousy and anger at the loss of the woman's exclusive attention. Breastfeeding can thus intensify difficult feelings around sexuality and motherhood. The use of a bottle by contrast allows the father to be directly involved in the care of the child, undercutting some of the emotional exclusion and permitting a more equal division of labour that is in tune with modern companionate relationships. It should be noted, however, that feeding is one of the more enjoyable aspects of babycare, and men's involvement in it reflects a common pattern in relation to the domestic division of labour whereby men, by and large, take on those household activities that they like.

Breastfeeding also presents images and situations that are at odds with the individualistic nature of modern culture (Longhurst 2001). As we noted earlier in relation to the unbounded body of the hospice or old age, modern society rests on a concept of the individual as separate and clearly defined. It assumes bounded bodies that do not leak or flow, where there is a clearly defined space around each individual. Breastfeeding disturbs this, presenting the image of an intimate physiological bond in which the mother and the baby are not individuals but in some sense one, and where the infant literally feeds on the body of the mother and the mother turns in on the baby. This is not how individuals are seen or present themselves within modern, public culture, where the expectation is that the person should be face outwards, offering a distinct, clearly individuated character.

Although the decline in breastfeeding had set in before women entered the paid labour force in large numbers, the nature of modern employment reinforced the trend. The shift from household-based to factory or office work made combining breastfeeding and working problematic. This was compounded by the ways in which urban space developed, and by the increasing physical distance between home and places of work. This makes it hard for women to combine paid work with family-based responsibilities for care across a range of relationships and tasks, many of which relate to bodily needs of a direct kind.

As we have noted, public space is collective and productive, private space is individual and reproductive. Women who cross the boundary into the public realm are expected to leave behind the attributes of that sphere; and to large extent this means the attributes of femaleness – or at least those that are deemed to belong to the private world of the family. The modern workplace rests on assumptions about workers and their bodily comportment; it assumes that workers possess clearly defined bodies, that are autonomous, separate and fully under their control (Blum 1993). In reality this does not describe any human being, but it does more nearly approach the experiences and bodily performance of men. This abstract 'worker' thus implicitly inhabits a male body. 'He' is unencumbered by biological reproduction or family care. Those tasks are accomplished in the family and predominantly by women. As Acker (1990) argues, activities associated directly with women's bodies – childbearing, lactation and aspects of sexuality – are ruled 'out of order' in the workplace.

For a woman to breastfeed at work is thus a violation of cultural categories, bringing directly into view bodily matters that are deemed to belong in private and at home. For a woman at work, particularly a professional women, it brings together that which has been radically separated: her existence as a professional, operating in the world of men, and as a nurturant women. It brings direct attention to her body and its femaleness, in a context where the presence of this has consciously been suppressed in the aim of conforming to the gendered world of work. This is not to say that women in professional contexts are expected to present themselves or dress in a wholly asexual way, but that their femininity has to be presented in an acceptable, muted and controlled form (Entwhistle 1997, 2000, McDowell 1997). These are female bodies under discipline. Professional women have to walk a tightrope between being condemned as too masculine and threatening, or too feminine and weak. Women who display overt femininity either in the sense of sexuality (low cut blouses, heavy scent) or maternity (mumsy dresses) are discounted in the world of professional work.

This is why the prospect of a female MP breastfeeding her baby in the British Houses of Parliament provoked such disquiet in 2000. (Julia Drown, a Labour MP, attempted to breastfeed her baby in a Select Committee of the House but was told that it was forbidden under the rule that refreshments were not allowed. The Speaker, Betty Boothroyd, later ruled that breastfeeeding was also forbidden in the chamber of the House.) The Houses of Parliament in Britain are the symbolic centre of the democratic process, the essence of what is understood as public space in the sense of the descendant of the agora, the space of open political contention and debate, that stands in opposition of the particularity of the home and family. To breastfeed in this setting is to challenge directly the separation on which such spaces rest. Furthermore women who enter Parliament do so very much on male terms. In general, women MPs have found it difficult to challenge or change the masculine dominance of the place. From the style of debate, to the club-like atmosphere of the bars, to the facilities that include a shooting gallery but not a creche, Parliament remains a deeply masculinist place, structured around the interests and concerns of male MPs. Women have often been subject to sexual harassment in the chamber, their bodies the subject of jokes and lewd comment as they speak. But the prospect of women breast-feeding introduced another and more disturbing form of female body – one that could not be objectified in a directly lewd or sexual way – but that was all the more disturbing for this reason.

Women increasingly face competing demands: that they nurse their babies and that they compete with men for jobs, without regard to sexual difference. For successful professional women, this presents a deeply problematic tension: how to combine two aspects of their lives that are valued, but which the radical separation of public and private has placed in opposition. Liberal feminism struggles to assert equality through attempting to extend liberties and rights to the whole population without distinction of gender. But as Pateman (1989) argues, it cannot address the deeper problem of how women can take an equal place in what is a patriarchal social order. There is an opposition between equality made after a male image and the real social position of women as *women*. Women in civil society are required to 'disavow our bodies and act as part of the brotherhood – but since we are never regarded as other than women, we must simultaneously continue to affirm the patriarchal conception of femininity or patriarchal subjection' (p. 52).

The tensions between breastfeeding, employment and women's lives are borne out in comparative data on rates of breastfeeding. These suggest a complex interplay between the labour market and the welfare state policy (Galtry 2003). Sweden with its famously 'woman friendly' welfare state has very high rates: 97 per cent of mothers initiate breastfeeding, and 73 per cent are still breastfeeding at six months. This is in contrast to America where the comparable figures are 64 per cent at birth and 29 per cent at 6 months. There is a clear evidence of the relationship between the resumption of employment and the cessation of breastfeeding (Galtry 2003). Though Sweden has high levels of labour market participation by women, this is combined with very generous maternity leave and childcare, which means that, although officially still in the labour market, very few mothers are actually at work in the first year after birth. Sweden thus resolves the tension between working and breastfeeding by enabling women to remain at home; thereby also endorsing an ideal of home-based care for very young children. In America, by contrast, there is very little in the way of state-funded support for maternity leave, and what there is varies greatly between the states (Galtry 2003). America, by and large, does not provide public support for women with babies to remain at home. This does not mean that such care is not approved of, it is just that its provision is seen as a private responsibility. The marked class and income differentials reflect this. Breastfeeding, with all the advantages it bestows, is a luxury that only better-off and supported women can afford. In so far as America does attempt to encourage breastfeeding by public interventions, it largely does so by work-based strategies, such as tax breaks for employers to provide lactation rooms or other such facilities in the work place. There has also been legislation endorsing the rights of women to breastfeed in public, a policy intervention that again chimes with liberal values (Wolf 2001, Galtry 2003).

These contrasts bring out the differences between welfare state regimes. Sweden with its social democratic 'institutional' welfare state aims actively to support the work–family balance and to encourage an ideal of child development, at the same time as pursuing gender equity. This is in contrast to the US, with its neo-liberal, residual welfare state, where government is minimally involved in work–family matters, and where issues of equity are seen as questions of legally based civil-rights claims, rather than as state-enabled, benefit-based interventions. Evidence from Ireland, however, suggests that welfare state polices are not the only issue. Ireland has very low rates of breastfeeding: only 38 per cent initiate breast-feeding, and this drops after only one month to 26 per cent. This is despite relatively low levels of labour market participation, and the existence of maternity benefits that, while not as generous as in Sweden, are consider-ately better than the US. Such differences, Galtry (2003) suggests, point to the continuing significance of cultural factors underpinning low levels.

Conclusion

In this chapter, I have explored some of the intersections between public space, the body and public policy. Both the examples I have chosen raise questions about the implicitly gendered nature of public space and its links to the body and the ways in which it is managed. Both also intersect with questions of health, well-being and public policy. This is particularly clearly so in the case of breastfeeding, which presents the policy conundrum of a practice that is heavily endorsed at the level of rational policy, and yet is in many ways at odds with how the public world that produces policy is itself structured.

Chapter 10

Conclusion

The burden of the argument of this book is, I hope, clear: that the new cultural approaches to the body have an important contribution to make to the policy-related fields of health and social care. Bodies, embodiment, bodywork and bodycare are central to these areas; and focussing our analyses more directly on these can bring considerable gains. The body, however, has a protean quality as a subject, and there is no aspect of life or policy that is not relevant, at some level. As a result it is impossible to cover all its dimensions so that, even within the relatively confined areas of health and social care, I have concentrated on only certain, selected areas. Partly these have been chosen to reflect my interests in an inner core of subjects: age, disability, health and care; but partly also to display the central themes of the book in relation to topics such as space, gender, identity, consumption, and their interaction with questions of the body and of public policy. Other analysts might have chosen different subjects; the potential range of these is great. The point, however, remains that the body is a subject of central importance to public policy and one that deserves greater emphasis.

As we have seen, the new literature on the body encompasses an array of theoretical positions and perspectives. There is no single view as to how the body should be theorised or understood. Much of the work in these areas has been influenced by the Cultural Turn and by the impact of postmodern/poststructuralist theorising. These approaches, though not without their own limitations and problems as we noted at the start of the book, have brought considerable intellectual gains, opening our eyes to dimensions of health and social care previously overlooked, allowing new theoretical perspectives on old policy issues, and presenting new ways in which to analyse the discourses that structure the field. For example, in relation to old age or disability, cultural analyses have helped destabilise and challenge common-sense narratives of ageing or disability, problematising the relationship between these accounts and the features of the body that are thought to determine them. Popular accounts of ageing present it as the product of bodily change and decline; but, as we have seen, postmodern/poststructuralist accounts suggest ways in which the body in age, as in earlier stages, is socially constituted. Negative meanings are read on to the aged body, which is then seen as the source of these meanings, and used as a rationale for exclusionary and ageist practices. By these means the old are

170

constituted as a separate category of being, set apart from mainstream culture by virtue of their bodily difference, and discriminated against on this basis. We have seen how similar processes are at work in relation to disability, in which socio-cultural processes ascribe certain meanings to disabled bodies, with damaging consequences for the lives and identities of disabled people. Social exclusion is thus not just a question of access or of socio-economic factors that limit people's lives, but has cultural and visual dimensions. The body and its interpretation are central to these.

Postmodern/poststructuralist approaches also offer the capacity to destabilise and problematise policy frameworks, exposing the normalising processes and legitimations than can underpin them. Social and public policy constructs welfare subjects in particular ways – the 'welfare mother', the 'alcoholic', the 'family known to social services'; and Foucauldian parallels can be helpful here in showing how such classificatory and dividing practices have operated in the past. Exploring the discourses within which subjects are currently constituted can help us present a more sophisticated challenge to these constructions.

Encompassing the wider cultural context may also allow us to question the centrality of policy discourses in the constitution of other categories, for example, the aged. Cultural approaches point us to a wider range of sources that provide the texts and form the practices that shape the lives of older people than simply the narrative of decline that dominates policy-oriented accounts. Among these, as we have seen, are the forces of consumption; and age cannot be understood in modern society without reference to these. Once again the body is a key site for this. Focussing on the body and the themes of age resistance and age denial also enable us to link the Third Age with earlier stages in life in which such practices are also operative, helping to undermine the constitution of old age as separate and different. Focussing on the cultural constitution of the Third Age thus helps to challenge the dominance of social welfare discourse. But, as we have seen, such cultural approaches are rarely extended into the territory of deep old age. There is no reason, however, why they should not be; and the Fourth Age is no more bereft of such influences than earlier stages. Extending such accounts into this territory is an important task for future research. Widening the scope of analysis to include cultural dimensions also enables us to explore the emergence of the politics of appearance, in which bodily attributes like obesity or bad teeth become exemplars of social position, pointing to the possibilities of symbolic and cultural dimensions in stratification and exclusion.

Cultural analyses have also acted to foreground issues in relation to identity. Postmodern theory suggests that the nature of identity has shifted, becoming more fluid and disembedded, so that aspects of culture and lifestyle assume new significance in its negotiation. This has important implications for the analysis of policy which has traditionally focussed on structural factors such as class, gender and 'race' in determining the location of individuals and the impact of policy on them. Postmodern accounts with their decentring narratives suggest the need for more plural and fluid approaches to such questions, and ones that emphasise diversity and difference. The rise of identity-based politics has challenged the unitary, homogenising discourses of both social science and public policy. The post-war welfare state was, to significant degree, predicated on a set of universal assumptions about citizenship and the nature of people's lives that are no longer either accurate or socially acceptable. In particular, challenges have been raised to the implicit assumptions about not only gender and sexuality, but also to some degree 'race', particularly from the postcolonial perspective. The discourse of rights has been extended to encompass new groups – gays, disabled people – and once again this has implications, both for the way in which policy is analysed and for how it is formulated and implemented. In relation to health and social care, it raises a range of questions concerning the ways in which services are provided, how they are allocated, their content, the assumptions that underpin them, as well as the pattern of staff employed within them.

Focussing on the body also enables us to see more clearly some of the things that are central to health and social care. This has perhaps always been easier in relation to health and health policy – the body, after all, dominates the topic of medicine. But in some ways it is so ubiquitous that it becomes difficult to see, so wholly does it occupy the space. But as we noted earlier, medicine constructs the body in a particular way that is objective, neutral, fragmented into its functioning parts, reduced to the cellular level. It is the object body of science. This is not the only way in which the body is understood in medicine. But it is the predominant way, and the one that carries prestige and authority. We saw some of the difficulties, however, presented by this model: difficulties in relation to the meanings of illness, suffering, old age and death; around subjective experiences of embodiment, and the clash between the lived body of the patient and the object body of medicine; in relation to body parts and the potential commodification of these; and around bodily aspects of 'care'. We saw how both nursing and alternative therapies contain elements of a different account of the body and embodiment, though one that in the case of nursing is poorly articulated, and to some degree owned, within the health care sector where the medical account remains dominant. Health care does not just present embodied topics but also embodied practitioners, and we saw the implications of this for how different health professions are represented in culture and how their own embodiment interacts with and shapes their practice. Gender plays a particularly important part in this.

The body is also central to many of the activities of social care. We saw how the sector has not traditionally been conceptualised in these terms, and how the dominant discourses that constitute it either, as in the case of managerialism, are notably non-bodily or, as in the case of social work, regard the body as marking the limits of their remit. Focussing on the body brings key aspects of the territory into view. It also allows us to address bodily matters previously seen as off-limits in relation to, for example, disability, and also old age. It also enables us to grasp the nature of care-work more clearly, recognising its central character as bodywork. This allows us to relate it to other forms of bodywork, exploring the commonalties and differences within this wider occupational category, helping us to understand important features of it, such as its ambivalent status, its character as low-level, demeaned work, its dirty work designation and the ways in which it is naturalised in the lives and bodies of women. Focussing on the body also enables us to explore some of the complexities of 'care' as a category of activity, helping to get behind the aetherialising tendencies that arise from the emphasis on love, emotion and interpersonal subjectivity that derives for the word 'care'. Emphasising the bodily aspects can help to tie the work down to its concrete realities.

Finally, focussing on the body brings benefits because it helps to make the rationalistic world of policy making more concrete, more earthy, more rooted in the realities with which it aims to deal. The world of policy making is a disembodied one, where problems and issues are presented in abstract, neutral terms. It presents a leached out, abstract, dry account that takes little cognisance of the messy, swampy, emotional world of the body and its feelings. This means that there is a central disjunction between the way in which policy making constructs the field of health and social care, and the everyday realities that obtain in that world. Refocussing on the body helps us to refocus our analysis more clearly on that world and, with it, on the front line of care. It promises to bring the world of policy into much closer and direct engagement with its central subjects.

References

Acker, J. (1990) 'Hierarchies, jobs and bodies: A theory of gendered organisation', *Gender and Society*, 4, 2, 139–58.

Adam, B. (1995) *Timewatch: The Social Analysis of Time*, Cambridge: Polity.

Ahmad, W.I.U. (1993) 'Making black people sick: "Race", ideology and health research', in W.I.U. Ahmad (ed.) *'Race' and Health in Contemporary Britain*, Buckingham: Open University.

Ahmad, W.I.U. and Atkin, K. (1996) *'Race' and Community Care*, Buckingham: Open University.

Ahmed, S. (2002) 'Racialized bodies', in M. Evans and E. Lee (eds) *Real Bodies: A Sociological Introduction*, Basingstoke: Palgrave.

Alder Hey (2001) Report of the Royal Liverpool Children's Inquiry: Ordered by the House of Commons, HC 12 I-II, London: Stationary Office.

Allan, G. and Crow, G. (eds) (1989) 'Introduction', *Home and Family: Creating the Domestic Sphere*, London: Macmillan.

American Obesity Association (2002) www.obesity.org, 2002.

Anderson, B. (2000) *Doing the Dirty Work: The Global Politics of Domestic Labour*, London: Zed Books.

Andersson, L. (ed.) (2002) *Cultural Gerontology*, Westport, Conn: Auburn House.

Andrews, M. (1999) 'The seductiveness of agelessness', *Ageing and Society*, 19, 301–18.

Angus, J.E., Kontos, P., Dyck, I., McKeever, P. and Poland, B. (2005) 'The physical significance of home: Habitus and the experience of receiving long term home care', *Sociology of Health and Medicine*, 27, 2, 161–87.

Anthias, F. (2001) 'The concept of "social division" and theorising social stratification: Looking at ethnicity and class', *Sociology*, 35, 4, 835–54.

Apple, R. (1987) *Mothers and Medicine: A Social History of Infant Feeding, 1890–1950*, Madison: University of Wisconsin Press.

Arber, S. and Ginn, J. (1991) *Gender and Later Life: A Sociological Analysis of Resources and Constraints*, London: Sage.

Arber, S. and Ginn, J. (eds) (1995) *Connecting Gender and Ageing: A Sociological Approach*, Buckingham: Open University.

Armstrong, D. (1983) *Political Anatomy of the Body: Medical Knowledge in Britain in the Twentieth Century*, Cambridge: Cambridge University Press.

Armstrong, D. (1995) 'The rise of surveillance medicine', *Sociology of Health and Illness*, 17, 3, 393–404.

Ashton, J. and Seymour, H. (1988) *The New Public Health*, Buckingham: Open University Press.

Atkins, P. and Bowler, I. (2001) *Food in Society: Economy, Culture, Geography*, London: Arnold.

BAAPS (2005) British Association of Plastic Surgeons, website www.baaps.org.uk.

Backett-Milburn, K. and McKie, L. (eds) (2001) *Constructing Gendered Bodies*, London: Routledge.

Baggott, R. (2000) *Public Health: Policy and Politics*, Basingstoke: Palgrave.

Bailey, R. (1996) 'Prenatal testing and the prevention of impairment: A woman's right to choose?', in J. Morris (ed.) *Encounters with Strangers: Feminism and Disability*, London: Women's Press.

Balbo, L. (1987) 'Crazy quilts: Rethinking the welfare state debate from a woman's point of view', in A. Showstack Sassoon (ed.) *Women and the State: The Shifting Boundaries of Public and Private*, London: Hutchinson.

Barling, D., Lang, T. and Caraher, M. (2002) 'Joined up food policy? The trials of governance, public policy and the food system', *Social Policy and Administration*, 36, 6, 556–74.

Barnes, C. and Mercer, G. (2003) *Disability*, Cambridge: Polity.

Barrett, M. and McIntosh, M. (1982) *The Anti-Social Family*, London: Verso.

Bartky, S.L. (1999) 'Unplanned obsolescence: Some reflections in aging' pp. 61–74, in M.U. Walker (ed.) *Mother Time: Women, Ageing and Ethics*, Boulder: Rowman & Littlefield.

Bashford, A. (1998) *Purity and Pollution: Gender, Embodiment and Victorian Medicine*, Basingstoke: Macmillan.

Bates, I. (1993) 'A job which is "right for me"?: Social class, gender and individualisation', in I. Bates and G. Riseborough (eds) *Youth and Inequality*, Buckingham: Open University Press.

Bauman, Z. (1993) *Postmodern Ethics*, Oxford: Blackwell.

Bell, R.M. (1985) *Holy Anorexia*, Chicago: Chicago University Press.

Bendelow, G. (1993) 'Pain perceptions, gender and emotion', *Sociology of Health and Illness*, 15, 3, 273–94.

Benjamin, W. (1973) *Charles Baudelaire: A Lyric Poet in the Era of High Capitalism*, London: Verso.

Benson, S. (1997) 'The body, health and eating disorders', in K. Woodward (ed.) *Identity and Difference*, London: Sage and Open University.

Berger, P.L. (1969) *The Social Reality of Religion*, Harmondsworth: Penguin.

Biggs, S., Phillipson, C. and Kingston, P. (1995) *Elder Abuse in Perspective*, Buckingham: Open University Press.

Black, P. (2002) ' "Ordinary people come through here": Locating the beauty salon in women's lives', *Feminist Review*, 71, 2–17.

Black, P. (2004) *The Beauty Industry: Gender, Culture, Pleasure*, London: Routledge.

Black, P. and Sharma, U. (2001) 'Men are real, women are "made up": Beauty therapy and the construction of femininity', *Sociological Review*, 49, 1, 100–16.

Blaxter, M. (1990) *Health and Lifestyles*, London: Tavistock.

Blum, L.M. (1993) 'Mothers, babies and breastfeeding in late capitalist America: The shifting contexts of feminist theory', *Feminist Studies*, 19, 2, 290–314.

BMA (2004) *Organ Donation in the Twenty-first Century: Time for a Consolidated Approach*, www.bma.org.uk.

Bordo, S. (1993) *Unbearable Weight: Feminism, Western Culture and the Body*, Berkley: University of California Press.

Bourdieu, P. (1984) *Distinction: A Social Critique of the Judgement of Taste*, London: Routledge.

Bovey, S. (1994) *The Forbidden Body: Why Being Fat is Not a Sin*, London: Pandora.

Bray, A. (2004) *Hélène Cixous*, Basingstoke: Palgrave.

Brewer, R.M. (1993) 'Theorizing race, class and gender: The new scholarship of Black feminist intellectuals and Black women's labor', in S.M. James and A.P.A. Busia (eds) *Theorizing Black Feminisms: The Visionary Pragmatism of Black Women*, London: Routledge.

Brook, B. (1999) *Feminist Perspectives on the Body*, London: Longman.

Bruch, H. (1973) *Eating Disorders: Obesity, Anorexia Nervosa and the Person Within*, London: Routledge.

Bundred, P., Kitchiner, D. and Buchan, I. (2001) 'Prevalence of overweight and obese children between 1989 and 1998: Population based series of cross sectional studies', *British Medical Journal*, 322, 10 February, pp. 326–8.

Burleigh, M. (1994) *Death and Deliverance: 'Euthanasia' in Germany 1900–1945*, Cambridge: Cambridge University Press.

Burnett, J. (1974) *Useful Toil: Autobiographies of Working People from the 1820s–1920s*, London: Allen Lane.

Burnett, J. (1979) *Plenty and Want: A Social History of Diet in England from 1815 to the Present Day*, London: Scolar.

Bury, M. (1982) 'Chronic illness as biographical disruption', *Sociology of Health and Illness*, 4, 2, 167–82.

Bury, M. (1991) 'The sociology of chronic illness: A review of research and prospects', *Sociology of Health and Illness*, 13, 4, 451–68.

Bury, M. (1995) 'The body in question' *Medical Sociology News*, 21, 1, 36–48.

Bury, M. (1997) *Health and Illness in a Changing Society*, London: Routledge.

Butler, J.P. (1990) *Gender Trouble: Feminism and the Subversion of Identity*, London: Routledge.

Butler, J.P. (1993) *Bodies that Matter: On the Discursive Limits of 'Sex'*, London, Routledge.

Bynum, C.W. (1987) *Holy Feast, Holy Fast: The Religious Significance of Food to Medieval Women*, Berkeley: University of California Press.

Bytheway, B. (1995) *Ageism*, Buckingham: Open University Press.

Calnan, M. (1984) 'The politics of health: The case of smoking control', *Journal of Social Policy*, 13, 3, 279–96.

Cambridge, P. and Carnaby, S. (2000) 'A personal touch: Managing the risks of abuse during intimate and personal care', *The Journal of Adult Protection*, 2, 4, 4–16.

Campbell, C. (1987) *The Romantic Ethic and the Spirit of Modern Consumerism*, Oxford: Blackwell.

Campbell, J. and Oliver, M. (1996) *Disability Politics: Understanding Our Past, Changing Our Future*, London: Routledge.

Cant, S. and Sharma, U. (1999) *A New Medical Pluralism? Alternative Medicine, Doctors and Patients and the State*, London: UCL Press.

Carabine, J. (1996) 'Heterosexuality and social policy' in D. Richardson (ed.) *Theorising Heterosexuality*, Buckingham: Open University.

Carabine, J. (1998) 'New horizons? New insights? Postmodernising social policy and the case of sexuality', in J. Carter (ed.) *Postmodernity and the Fragmentation of Welfare*, London: Routledge.

Carter, J. (1998) 'Studying social policy after modernity', in J. Carter (ed.) *Postmodernity and the Fragmentation of Welfare*, London: Routledge.

Carter, V. (1992) 'Abseil makes the heart grow fonder: Lesbian and gay campaigning tactics and Section 28', in K. Plummer (ed.) *Modern Homosexualities: Fragments of Lesbian and Gay Experience*, London: Routledge.

Cavanagh, S. and Ware, V. (1990) *At Women's Convenience: A Handbook on the Design of Women's Public Toilets*, London: Women's Design Service.

Charles, N. and Kerr, M. (1988) *Women, Food and Families*, Manchester: Manchester University Press.

Chernin, K. (1981) *Womansize: The Tyranny of Slenderness*, London: Women's Press.

Clarke, J. (1999) 'Coming to terms with culture', in H. Dean and R. Woods (eds) *Social Policy Review 11*, London: Social Policy Association.

Cohen, L. (2001) 'The other kidney: Biopolitics beyond recognition', *Body and Society*, 7, 2–3, 9–29.

Cole, T.C. (1992) *The Journey of Life: A Cultural History of Aging in America*, Cambridge: Cambridge University Press.

Collingham, E.M. (2001) *Imperial Bodies*, Cambridge: Polity.

Connell, R.W. (1995) *Masculinities*, Cambridge: Polity.

Connell, R.W. (2000) *The Men and the Boys*, Cambridge: Polity.

Cooter, R. (1988) 'Alternative medicine, alternative cosmology', in R. Cooter (ed.) *Studies in the History of Alternative Medicine*, Basingstoke: Macmillan.

Coward, R. (1989) *The Whole Truth: The Myth of Alternative Medicine*, London: Faber.

Crossley, N. (2003) 'Prozac nation and the biochemical self', in S.J. Williams, L. Birke and G.A. Bendelow (eds) *Debating Biology: Sociological Reflections on Health, Medicine and Society*, London: Routledge.

Crotty, P. (1999) 'Food and class', in J. Germov and L. Williams (eds) *A Sociology of Food and Nutrition*, Oxford: OUP.

Cummings, D. (1996) *Pretty Ribbons*, Zurich: Stemmle.

Cummings, J.H. and Bingham, A. (1998) 'Diet and the prevention of cancer', *British Medical Journal*, 317, 1636–40.

Curtis, L.P. (1997) *Apes and Angels: The Irishman in Victorian Caricature*, Washington: Smithsonian.

Daatland, S. (1990) 'What are families for?: On family solidarity and preference for help', *Ageing and Society*, 10, 1–15.

Daly, M. (1979) *Gyn/Ecology: The Metaethics of Radical Feminism*, London: Women's Press.

Davidhizar, R. and Giger, J.N. (1997) 'When touch is *not* the best approach', *Journal of Clinical Nursing*, 6, 203–6.

Davidoff, L. and Hall, C. (1987) *Family Fortunes: Men and Women of the English Middle Class 1780–1850*, London: Hutchinson.

Davie, G. (1994) *Religion in Britain Since 1945: Believing Without Belonging*, Oxford: Blackwell.

Davies, C. (1995) *Gender and the Professional Predicament in Nursing*, Buckingham: Open University Press.

Davies, C. (1998) 'Caregiving, carework and professional care', in A. Brechin, J. Walmsley, J. Katz and S. Peace (eds) *Care Matters: Concepts, Practice and Research in Health and Social Care*, London: Sage.

Davis, K. (1995) *Reshaping the Female Body: The Dilemma of Cosmetic Surgery*, London: Routledge.

Davis, K. (ed.) (1997) *Embodied Practices: Feminist Perspectives on the Body*, London, Sage.

Dean, H. (2000) 'Introduction: Towards an embodied account of welfare', in K. Ellis and H. Dean (eds) *Social Policy and the Body: Transitions in Corporeal Discourse*, Basingstoke: Macmillan.

Deaton, A. (2003) 'Health, inequality and economic development', *Journal of Economic Literature*, XLI, 113–58.

Delamothe, T. (1991) 'Social inequalities in health', *British Journal of Medicine*, 303, 1046–50.

Department of Health (2001) *National Service Framework for Older People*, www.doh.gov.uk, accessed 2004.

Department of Health (2004) www.doh.gov.uk, accessed 2004.

Diamond, T. (1992) *Making Gray Gold: Narratives of Nursing Home Care*, Chicago: University of Chicago Press.

Dobson, B. (1994) *Diet, Choice and Poverty: Social, Cultural and Nutritional Aspects of Food Consumption Among Low Income Families*, London: Family Policy Studies Centre.

Doll, R. and Peto, R. (1981) 'The causes of cancer: Quantitative estimates of avoidable risks of cancer in the United States today', *Journal of the National Cancer Institute*, 66, 6, 1193–1308.

Dominelli, L. (1989) 'An uncaring profession? An examination of racism in social work', *New Community*, 15, 3, 391–403.

Donovan, C., Heaphy, B. and Weeks, J. (1999) 'Citizenship and same sex relationships', *Journal of Social Policy*, 28, 4, 689–709.

Donovan, R. (1987) 'Home care work: A legacy of slavery in US health care', *Affilia*, Fall, 33–44.

Donovan, R. (1989) ' "We care for the most important people in your life": Home care workers in New York city', *Women's Studies Quarterly*, 1 & 2, 56–65.

Douglas, M. (1966) *Purity and Danger: An Analysis of the Concepts of Pollution and Taboo*, London: RKP.

Douglas, M. (1970) *Natural Symbols*, Harmondsworth: Penguin.

Dowler, B. and Calvert, C. (1995) *Nutrition and Diet in Lone Parent Families*, London: Family Policy Studies Centre.

Dowler, E. (2002) 'Food and poverty in Britain: Rights and responsibilities', *Social Policy and Administration*, 36, 6, 698–717.

Dowler, E., Tuner, S. and Dobson, B. (2001) *Poverty Bites: Food, Health and Poor Families*, London: CPAG.

Duff, J. (1999) 'Setting the menu: Dietary guidelines, corporate interests and nutritional policy', in J. Germov and L. Williams (eds) *A Sociology of Food and Nutrition*, Oxford: OUP.

Duncan, N. (1996) 'Renegotiating gender and sexuality in public and private spaces', in N. Duncan (ed.) *Body Space*, London: Routledge, pp. 127–45.

Dunlop, M. (1986) 'Is a science of caring possible?', *Journal of Advanced Nursing*, 11, 661–70.

Eade, J. and Mele, C. (2002) *Understanding the City: Contemporary and Future Perspectives*, Oxford: Blackwell.

EDA (2005) Eating Disorders Association, www.edauk.com accessed 2005.

Edwards, J. and McKie, L. (1997) 'Women's public toilets: A serious issue for the body politic', in K. Davis (ed.) *Embodied Practices*, London: Sage.

Eisenberg, D.M., Davis, R.B., Ettner, S.L., Appel, S., Wilkey, S., van Rompay, M. and Kessler, R.C. (1998) 'Trends in alternative medicine use in the United States, 1990–1997', *JAMA*, 280, 18, 1569–75.

Elias, N. (1978) *The Civilizing Process: The History of Manners*, Oxford: Blackwell.

Emerson, R.M. and Pollner, M. (1976) 'Dirty work designations: Their features and consequences in a psychiatric setting', *Social Problems*, 23, 243–54.

Entwhistle, J. (1997) ' "Power dressing" and the construction of the career woman', in M. Nava, A. Blake, I. MacRury and B. Richards (eds) *Buy This Book: Studies in Advertising and Consumption*, London: Routledge.

Entwhistle, J. (2000) *The Fashioned Body: Fashion, Dress and Modern Social Theory*, Cambridge: Polity.

Estes, C. (1979) *The Ageing Enterprise*, San Francisco: Jossey Bass.

Estes, Carroll L. and Binney, Elizabeth A. (1989) 'The biomedicalization of aging', *The Gerontologist*, 29, 5, 587–96.

Evans, M. and Lee, E. (eds) (2002) *Real Bodies: A Sociological Introduction*, Basingstoke: Palgrave.

Fausto-Sterling, A. (2000) 'Gender, race and nation: The comparative anatomy of "Hottentot" women in Europe', in L. Schiebinger (ed.) *Feminism and the Body*, Oxford: OUP.

Featherstone, M. (1991) 'The body in consumer culture', in M. Featherstone, M. Hepworth and B.S.Turner (eds) *The Body: Social Process and Cultural Theory*. London: Sage.

Featherstone, M. and Hepworth, M. (1991) 'The mask of ageing and the postmodern life course', in M. Featherstone, M. Hepworth and B.S. Turner (eds) *The Body: Social Process and Cultural Theory*, London: Sage.

Featherstone, M. and Wernick, A. (eds) (1995) *Images of Aging: Cultural Representations of Later Life*, London: Routledge.

Feldman, P.H., Sapienza, A.M. and Kane, N.M. (1990) *Who Cares for Them? Workers in the Home Care Industry*, New York: Greenwood Press.

Ferlie, E., Ashburner, L., Fitzgerald, L. and Pettigrew, A. (1996) *The New Public Management in Action*, Oxford: OUP.

Fernando, S. (2002) *Mental Health, Race and Culture*, Basingstoke: Palgrave.

Finch, J. and Groves, D. (eds) (1983) *A Labour of Love: Women, Work and Caring*, London: Routledge.

Fine, B., Heasman, M. and Wright, J. (1996) *Consumption in the Age of Affluence: The World of Food*, London: Routledge.

Fineman, S. (ed.) (1993) 'Organisations as emotional arenas', *Emotion in Organisations*, London: Sage.

Finkelstein, V. (1996) 'The disability movement has run out of steam', *Disability Now*, 11 February.

Fischler, C. (1980) 'Food habits, social change and the nature/culture dilemma', *Social Science Information*, 19, 6, 937–53.

Forste, R., Weiss, J. and Lippincott, E. (2001) 'The decision to breastfeed in the US: Does race matter?', *Pediatrics*, 108, 2, 291–6.

Foucault, M. (1971) *Madness and Civilisation: A History of Insanity in the Age of Reason*, London: Tavistock.

Foucault, M. (1973) *The Birth of the Clinic: An Archaeology of Medical Perception*, London: Tavistock.

Foucault, M. (1977) *Discipline and Punish: The Birth of the Prison*, Harmondsworth, Allen Lane.

Foucault, M. (1979) *The History of Sexuality: Introduction, Volume I*, Harmondsworth: Penguin.

Foucault, M. (1987) *The Uses of Pleasure: The History of Sexuality, Volume II*, Harmondsworth: Penguin.

Foucault, M. (1988) *The Care of the Self: The History of Sexuality, Volume III*, Harmondsworth: Penguin.

Fox, R.C. (1996) 'Afterthoughts: Continuing reflections on organ replacement', in S.J. Youngner, R.C. Fox and L.J. O'Connell (eds) *Organ Transplantation: Meanings and Realities*, Madison: University of Wisconsin.

Fox, R.C. (2003) 'Through the lenses of biology and sociology: Organ replacement', in S.J. Williams, L. Birke and G.A. Bendelow (eds) *Debating Biology: Sociological Reflections on Health, Medicine and Society*, London: Routledge.

Frank, A.W. (1995) *The Wounded Storyteller: Body, Illness and Ethics*, Chicago: University of Chicago Press.

Frankenberg, R. (1988) ' "Your time or mine": An anthropological view of the tragic temporal contradictions of biomedical practice', *International Journal of Health Services*, 18, 1.

Friedan, B. (1993) *The Fountain of Age*, London: Vintage.

Freidson, E. (1970) *The Profession of Medicine: A Study of Sociology of Applied Knowledge*, New York: Harper and Row.

Frost, L. (2001) *Young Women and the Body: A Feminist Sociology*, Basingstoke: Palgrave.

Furman, F.K. (1997) *Facing the Mirror: Older Women and Beauty Shop Culture*, New York: Routledge.

Furman, F.K. (1999) 'There are no old Venuses: Older women's responses to their aging bodies', in M.U. Walker (ed.) *Mother Time: Women, Aging and Ethics*, Boulder: Rowman & Littlefield.

Galtry, J. (2003) 'The impact on breastfeeding of labour market policy and practice in Ireland, Sweden and the USA', *Social Science and Medicine*, 57, 167–77.

Gardner, B. (1996) *European Agriculture: Policies, Production and Trade*, London: Routledge.

Gevitz, N. (1988) *Other Healers: Unorthodox Medicine in America*, Baltimore: John Hopkins University Press.

Gibbins, J.R. (1998) 'Postmodernism, poststructuralism and social policy', in J. Carter (ed.) *Postmodernity and the Fragmentation of Welfare*, London: Routledge.

Giddens, A. (1991) *Modernity and Self-Identity*, Cambridge: Polity.

Gilleard, C. (2002) 'Women, ageing and bodytalk', in L. Andersson (ed.) *Cultural Gerontology*, Westport, Conn: Auburn House.

Gilleard, C. and Higgs, P. (2000) *Culture of Ageing: Self, Citizen and the Body*, London: Prentice Hall.

Gillespie-Sells, K., Hill, M. and Robbins, B. (1998) *She Dances to Different Drums*, London: King's Fund.

Gilligan, C. (1982) *In a Different Voice: Psychological Theory and Women's Development*, Cambridge: Harvard University Press.

Gilman, S. (1991) *The Jew's Body*, London: Routledge.

Ginn, J. and Arber, S. (1995) ' "Only connect": Gender relations and ageing', in S.Arber and J. Ginn (eds) (1995) *Connecting Gender and Ageing: A Sociological Approach*, Buckingham: Open University.

Glendinning, F. (1997) 'The mistreatment and neglect of elderly people in residential centres: research outcomes', in P. Decalmer and F. Glendinning (eds) *The Mistreatment of Elderly People*, London: Sage.

Glenn, E.N. (1996) 'From servitude to service work: Historical continuities in the racial division of paid reproductive labour', in C.L. Macdonald and C. Sirianni (eds) *Working in the Service Society*, Philadelphia: Temple University Press.

Goffman, E. (1961) *Asylums: Essays in the Social Situations of Mental Patients and Other Inmates*, New York: Anchor.

Goffman, E. (1968) *Stigma: Notes on the Management of Spoilt Identity*, Harmondsworth: Penguin.

Goffman, E. (1969) *The Presentation of Self in Everyday Life*, Harmondsworth: Penguin.

Graham, H. (1991) 'The concept of caring in feminist research: The case of domestic service', *Sociology*, 25, 1, 61–78.

Greed, C.H. (1994) *Women and Planning: Creating Gendered Realities*, London: Routledge.

Greed, C. (2002) 'Why UK is going down the pan', *Times Higher Education Supplement*, 26 July, 21.

Greed, C. (2003) *Inclusive Urban Design: Public Toilets*, Oxford: Architectural Press.

Greed, C. and Daniels, I. (2002) User and provider perspectives on public toilet provision: Occasional paper 13, Bristol: University of the West of England, Faculty of the Built Environment.

Greer, G. (1991) *The Change: Women, Ageing and the Menopause*, London: Hamish.

Gregson, N. and Lowe, M. (1994) *Serving the Middle Classes: Class, Gender and Waged Domestic Labour in Contemporary Britain*, London: Routledge.

Gubrium, J.F. and Holstein, J.A. (1999) 'The nursing home as a discursive anchor for the ageing body', *Ageing and Society*, 19, 519–38.

Gullette, M.M. (1997) *Declining to Decline: Cultural Combat and the Politics of Midlife*, Charlottesville: University Press of Virginia.

Gunaratnam, Y. and Lewis, G. (2001) 'Racialising emotional labour and emotionalising racialised labour: Anger, fear and shame in social welfare', *Journal of Social Work Practice*, 15, 2, 131–48.

Gurney, C.M. (2000) 'Accommodating bodies: The organization of corporeal dirt in the embodied home', in L. McKie and N. Watson (eds) *Organizing Bodies: Policy, Institutions and Work*, Basingstoke: Macmillan.

Gurney, C.M. and Means, R. (1993) 'The meaning of home in later life', in S. Arber and M. Evandriou (eds) *Ageing, Independence and the Life Course*, London: Jessica Kingsley.

Gustafsson, U. (2002) 'School meals policy: The problem with governing children', *Social Policy and Administration*, 36, 6, 685–97.

Guy, A., Green, E. and Banim, M. (eds) (2001) *Through the Wardrobe: Women's Relationships with Their Clothes*, Oxford: Berg.

Hague, G. and Malos, E. (1998) *Domestic Violence: Action for Change*, Cheltenham: New Clarion Press.

Hall, C. (1992) *White, Male and Middle Class: Explorations in Feminism and History*, Cambridge: Polity.

Hamilton, R.F. (1996) *The Social Misconstruction of Reality: Validity and Verification in the Scholarly Community*, New Haven: Yale University Press.

Hamlyn, B., Brooker, S., Oleinikova, K. and Wands, S. (2002) *Infant Feeding 2000*, London: Stationary Office.

Hanmer, J. and Itzen, C. (eds) (2000) *Home Truths About Domestic Violence: Feminist Influences on Policy and Practice*, London: Routledge.

Harris, B. (1994) 'Health, height, and history: An overview of recent developments in anthropometric history', *Social History of Medicine*, 7, 297–320.

Harrison, B. (1971) *Drink and the Victorians: The Temperance Movement in England, 1815–1870*, London: Faber.

Hastrup, K. (1992) 'A question of reason: Breast-feeding patterns in seventeenth- and eighteenth-century Iceland', in V. Maher (ed.) *The Anthropology of Breast-Feeding: Natural Law or Social Construct*, London: Berg, pp. 91–108.

Heelas, P. (1996) *The New Age Movement*, Oxford: Blackwell.

Hen Co-Op (1993) *Growing Old Disgracefully*, London: Piatkus.

Henley, N.M. (1973) 'The politics of touch', in P. Brown (ed.) *Radical Psychology*, London: Tavistock.

Hepworth, J. (1999) *The Social Construction of Anorexia Nervosa*, London: Sage.

Herzlich, C. (1973) *Health and Illness: A Social Psychological Analysis*, London: Academic Press.

Hevey, D. (1992) *The Creatures Time Forgot: Photography and Disability Imagery*, London: Routledge.

Hinze, S.W. (1999) 'Gender and the body of medicine: Or at least some body parts: (Re) constructing the prestige hierarchy of medical specialities', *Sociological Quarterly*, 40, 2, 217–39.

Hochschild, A. (1983) *The Managed Heart: The Commercialisation of Human Feelings*, Berkley, CA: University of California.

Hockey, J. and James, A. (2003) *Social Identities Across the Life Course*, Basingstoke: Palgrave.

Hoek, H.W. (1991) 'The incidence and prevalence of anorexia nervosa and bulimia nervosa in primary care', *Psychological Medicine*, 21, 455–60.

Hoggett, P. (2000) 'Social policy and the emotions', in G. Lewis, S. Gewirtz and J. Clarke (eds) *Rethinking Social Policy*, London: Sage.

Hogle, L.F. (1999) *Recovering the Nation's Body: Cultural Memory, Medicine and the Politics of Redemption*, New Bruswick: Rutgers University Press.

Holland, S. (2004) *Alternative Femininities: Body, Age and Identity*, Oxford: Berg.

hooks, b. (1984) *Feminist Theory: From the Margin to Centre*, Boston: South End Press.

hooks, b. (1992) 'Selling hot pussy', in b. hooks (ed.) *Black Looks: Race and Representation*, London: Turnaround.

hooks, b. (1994) *Outlaw Culture: Resisting Representation*, London: Routledge.

Home of Commons Health Committee (2004) *Obesity: Third Report 2003–04*, www.publications.parliament.uk.

Howlett, M., McClelland, L. and Crisp, A.H. (1995) 'The cost of the illness that defies', *Postgraduate Medical Journal*, 71, 705–6.

Hughes, B. (1999) 'The constitution of impairment: Modernity and the aesthetic of oppression', *Disability and Society*, 14, 2, 155–72.

Hughes, B. (2000) 'Medicine and the aesthetic invalidation of disabled people', *Disability and Society*, 15, 4, 555–68.

Hughes, B. and Paterson, K. (1997) 'The social model of disability and the disappearing body: Towards a sociology of impairment', *Disability and Society*, 12, 3, 325–40.

Hussey, S. (2001) ' "An inheritance of fear": Older women in the twentieth century countryside', in L. Botelho and P. Thane (eds) *Women and Ageing in British Society since 1500*, Harlow: Longman.

Irwin, S. (1999) 'Later life, inequality and sociological theory', *Ageing and Society*, 19, 6, 691–715.

Jagger, E. (2000) 'Consumer bodies', in P. Hancock *et al.* (eds) *The Body, Culture and Society: An Introduction*, Buckingham: Open University Press.

James, N. (1989) 'Emotional labour: Skill and work in the social regulation of feelings', *Sociological Review*, 1, 15–42.

James, N. (1992) 'Care=organisation and physical labour and emotional labour', *Sociology of Health and Illness*, 14, 4, 488–509.

Jeffries, S. (1985) *The Spinster and Her Enemies: Feminism and Sexuality, 1880–1930*, London: Pandora.

Jewell, K.S. (1993) *From Mammy to Miss America and Beyond: Cultural Images and the Shaping of US Social Policy*, London: Routledge.

Jewson, N.D. (1976) 'The disappearance of the Sick Man from medical cosmology 1770–1870', *Sociology*, 10, 225–44.

Jordanova, L. (1989) *Sexual Visions: Images of Gender in Science and Medicine between the Eighteenth and Twentieth Centuries*, Hemel Hempstead: Harvester Wheatsheaf.

Jourard, S.M. (1966) 'An exploratory study of body accessibility', *British Journal of Social and Clinical Psychology*, 5, 221–31.

Jourard, S.M. and Rubin, J.E. (1968) 'Self disclosure and touching: A study of two modes of interpersonal encounter and their inter-relation', *Journal of Humanistic Psychology*, 8, 1, 39–48.

Jupp, P. (1997) 'Why was England the first country to popularise cremation?', in K. Charmaz, G. Howarth and A. Kelleher (eds) *The Unknown Country: Death in Australia, Britain and the USA*, Basingstoke: Macmillan.

Katz, S. (1996) *Disciplining Old Age: The Formation of Gerontological Knowledge*, Charlottesville: University Press of Virginia.

Kearns, R.A. and Gesler, W.M. (eds) (1998) *Putting Health into Place: Landscape, Identity and Well Being*, Syracuse: University of Syracuse Press.

Kelleher, D. and Hillier, S. (1996) *Researching Cultural Differences in Health*, London: Routledge.

Kelly, M.P. (1992) *Colitis*, London: Routledge.

Kelves, D.J. (1986) *In the Name of Eugenics: Genetics and the Uses of Human Fertility*, Harmondsworth: Penguin.

Key, T.J., Allen, N.E., Spencer, E.A. and Travis, R.C. (2002) 'The effect of diet on the risk of cancer', *The Lancet*, 360, 861–8.

King, M.B. (1986) 'Eating disorders in general practice', *British Medical Journal*, 293, 29 November, 1412–14.

Kitwood, T. (1997) *Dementia Reconsidered: The Person Comes First*, Buckingham: Open University Press.

Kleinman, A. (1988) *The Illness Narratives: Suffering, Healing and the Human Condition*, New York: Basic Books.

Kontos, P.C. (1999) 'Local biology: Bodies of difference in ageing studies', *Ageing and Society*, 19, 6, 677–90.

Kriegel, L. (1987) 'The cripple in literature', in A. Gartner and T. Joe (eds) *Images of the Disabled, Disabling Images*, New York: Praeger.

Laqueur, T. (1990) *Making Sex: Body and Gender from the Greeks to Freud*, Cambridge: Harvard University Press.

Larabee, M.J. (ed.) (1993) *An Ethic of Care: Feminist and Interdisciplinary Perspectives*, London: Routledge.

Law, I. (1996) *Racism, Ethnicity and Social Policy*, London: Prentice Hall.

Lawler, J. (1991) *Behind the Screens: Nursing, Somology and the Problem of the Body*, Melbourne: Churchill Livingstone.

Lawler, J. (1997) 'Knowing the body and embodiment: Methodologies, discourses and nursing', in J. Lawler (ed.) *The Body in Nursing*, Melbourne: Churchill Livingstone.

Lawrence, C. (1998) 'Medical minds and surgical bodies: Corporeality and the doctors', in C. Lawrence and S. Shapin (eds) *Science Incarnate: Historical Embodiments of Natural Knowledge*, Chicago: University of Chicago Press.

Lawrence, R.J. (1987) *Housing, Dwellings and Homes: Design Theory, Research and Practice*, Chichester: Wiley.

Laws, G. (1995) 'Understanding ageism: Lessons from feminism and postmodernism', *Gerontologist*, 35, 1, 112–18.

Lawton, J. (1998) 'Contemporary hospice care: The sequestration of the unbounded body and "dirty dying" ', *Sociology of Health and Illness*, 20, 2, 121–43.

Lawton, J. (2000) *The Dying Process: Patients' Experiences of Palliative Care*, London: Routledge.

Leather, S. (1996) *The Making of Modern Malnutrition: An Overview of Food Poverty in the UK*, London: Caroline Walker Trust.

Leder, D. (1990) *The Absent Body*, Chicago: University of Chicago Press.

Lee-Treweek, G. (1994) 'Bedroom abuse: The hidden work in a nursing home', *Generations Review*, 4, 1, 2–4.

Lee-Treweek, G. (1996) 'Emotion work, order and emotional power in care assistant work', in V. James and J. Gabe (eds) *Health and the Sociology of the Emotions*, Oxford: Blackwell.

Lee-Treweek, G. (1998) 'Women, resistance and care: An ethnographic study of nursing auxitiary work', *Work, Employment and Society*, 11, 1, 47–63.

Lefebvre, H. (1991) *The Production of Space*, trans. D. Nicholson-Smith, Oxford: Blackwell.

Lewis, G. (2000) 'Introduction: Expanding the social policy imaginary', in G. Lewis, S. Gewirtz and J. Clarke (eds) *Rethinking Social Policy*, London: Sage.

Lewis, G., Hughes, G. and Saraga, E. (2000) 'The body of social policy: Social policy and the body', in L. McKie and N. Watson (eds) *Organizing Bodies: Institutions, Policy and Work*, Basingstoke: Macmillan.

Lewis, J. and Meredith, B. (1988) *Daughters who Care: Daughters Caring for Mothers at Home*, London: Routledge.

Lister, R. (1997) *Citizenship: Feminist Perspectives*, Basingstoke: Macmillan.

Lister, R. (2001) 'Towards a citizens' welfare state: The 3+2 "r"s of welfare reform', *Theory, Culture and Society*, 18, 2–3, 91–111.

Lloyd, M. (1996) 'Feminism, aerobics and the politics of the body', *Body & Society*, 2, 2, 79–98.

Longhurst, R. (2001) *Bodies: Exploring Fluid Boundaries*, Routledge: London.

Longmore, P.K. (1987) 'Screening stereotypes: Images of disabled people in television and motion pictures', in A. Gartner and T. Joe (eds) *Images of the Disabled, Disabling Images*, New York: Praeger.

Lonsdale, S. (1990) *Women and Disability: The Experience of Physical Disability*, Basingstoke: Macmillan.

Lovenduski, J. and Randall, V. (1993) *Contemporary Feminist Politics: Women and Power in Britain*, Oxford: Oxford University Press.

Lupton, D. (1994) *Medicine as Culture: Illness, Disease and the Body in Western Societies*, London: Sage.

McClintock, A. (1995) *Imperial Leather: Race, Gender and Sexuality in the Colonial Contest*, London: Routledge.

Macdonald, C.L. and Sirianni C. (1996) 'The service society and the changing experience of work', in C.L. Macdonald and C. Sirianni (eds) *Working in the Service Society*, Philadelphia: Temple University Press.

McDowell, L. (1983) 'Towards an understanding of the gender division of urban space', *Environment and Planning: D*, 1, 59–72.

McDowell, L. (1997) *Capital Culture: Gender at Work in the City*, Oxford: Blackwell.

MacSween, M. (1993) *Anorexic Bodies: A Feminist and Sociological Perspective on Anorexia Nervosa*, London: Routledge.

Madjar, I. (1997) 'The body in health, illness and pain', in J. Lawler (ed.) *The Body in Nursing*, South Melbourne: Churchill Livingstone.

Maher, V. (1995) 'Breastfeeding in cross cultural perspective: Paradoxes and proposals', in V. Maher (ed.) *The Anthropology of Breast Feeding: Natural Law or Social Construct*, London: Berg.

Mama, A. (1992) 'Black women and the British state', in P. Braham, A. Rattansi and R. Skellington (eds) *Racism and Antiracism: Inequalities, Opportunities and Policies*, Buckingham: Open University.

Mamo, L. and Tishman, J. (2001) 'Potency in all the right places: Viagra as a technology of the gendered body', *Body & Society*, 7, 4, 13–35.

Mann, J.I. (2002) 'Diet and risk of coronary heart disease and type 2 diabetes', *The Lancet*, 360, 783–9.

Markus, T.A. (1993) *Buildings and Power: Freedom and Control in the Origin of Modern Building Types*, London: Routledge.

Marmot, M.G. and Shipley, M.J. (1996) 'Do socio-economic differences in mortality persist after retirement?', *British Journal of Medicine*, 313, 1177–80.

Marsden, T., Flynn, A. and Harrison, M. (2000) *Consuming Interests: The Social Provision of Foods*, London: UCL Press.

Marshall, B.L. and Katz, S. (2003) 'Forever functional: Sexual fitness and the ageing male body', *Body & Society*, 8, 4, 43–70.

Martin, D. (1978) *A General Theory of Secularisation*, Oxford: Blackwell.

Mason, D. (2000) *Race and Ethnicity in Modern Britain*, Oxford: OUP.

Massey, D. (1994) *Space, Place and Gender*, Cambridge: Polity.

Mauss, M. (1973, 1934) 'Techniques of the body', *Economy and Society*, 2, 70–88.

Maynard, M. (1994) ' "Race", gender and the concept of "difference" in feminist thought', in H. Afshar and M. Maynard (eds) *The Dynamics of 'Race' and Gender: Some Feminist Interventions*, London: Taylor and Francis.

Means, R. Morbey, H. and Smith, R. (2002) *From Community Care to Market Care? The Development of Welfare Services for Older People*, Bristol: Policy Press.

Merleau-Ponty, M. (1962) *Phenomenology of Perception*, trans. C. Smith, London: Routledge Kegan Paul.

Miller, W.I. (1997) *The Anatomy of Disgust*, Cambridge: Harvard University Press.

Montagu, A. (1986) *Touching: The Human Significance of Skin*, 3rd edn, New York: Harper & Row.

Mooney, J. (2000) *Gender, Violence and the Social Order*, Basingstoke: Palgrave.

Morgan, D. (1993) 'You too can have a body like mine: Reflections on the male body and masculinities', in S. Scott and D. Morgan (eds) *Body Matters: Essays on the Sociology of the Body*, London: Falmer.

Morris, J. (1991) *Pride Against Prejudice: Transforming Attitudes to Disability*, London: Women's Press.

Morris, J. (1992) 'Personal and political: A feminist perspective on researching physical disability', *Disability and Society*, 7, 2, 157–67.

Morris, J. (1993) *Independent Lives: Community Care and Disabled People*, Basingstoke: Macmillan.

Morris, J. (ed.) (1996) *Encounters with Strangers: Feminism and Disability*, London: Women's Press.

Morris, L. (1996) 'Researching living standards: Some problems and some findings', *Journal of Social Policy*, 25, 4.

Mullender, A. (1996) *Rethinking Domestic Violence: The Social Work and Probation Response*, London: Whiting & Birch.

Mullender, A. and Morley, R. (eds) (1994) *Children Living with Domestic Violence: Putting Men's Abuse of Women on the Child Care Agenda*, London: Whiting & Birch.

Munro, M. and Madigan, R. (1993) 'Privacy in the private sphere', *Housing Studies*, 8, 1, 29–45.

Murcott, A. (1982) 'On the social significance of the "cooked dinner" in South Wales', *Social Science Information*, 21, 4/5, 677–96.

Murray, T.H. (1996) 'Organ vendors, families and the gift of life', in S.J. Youngner, R.C. Fox and L.J. O'Connell (eds) *Organ Transplantation: Meanings and Realities*, Madison: University of Wisconsin.

NAO (2001) *Tackling Obesity in England*, National Audit Office, HC 220, London: Stationary Office.

National Association to Advance Fat Acceptance (2005) www.naafa.com.

Nazroo, J.Y. (2001) *Ethnicity, Class and Health*, London: PSI.

Negrin, L. (2002) 'Cosmetic surgery and the eclipse of identity', *Body & Society*, 8, 4, 21–42.

Nelson, M. (1993) 'Social class trends in British diet, 1860–1980', in C. Geissler and D. Oddy (eds) *Food, Diet and Economic Change: Past and Present*, London: Leicester University Press.

Nelson, M. (1999) 'Nutrition and health inequalities', in D. Gordon, M. Shaw, D. Dorling and G.D. Smith (eds) *Inequalities in Health*, Bristol: Policy Press.

Nelson, M. (2002) 'Food budget standards and dietary adequacy in low-income families', *Proceedings of the Nutrition Society*, 61, 569–77.

Nestle, M. (2002) *Food Politics: How the Food Industry Influences Nutrition and Health*, Berkley: University of California Press.

Nettleton, S. and Watson, J. (eds) (1998) *The Body in Everyday Life*, London: Routledge.

Newman, S. (1997) 'Masculinities, men's bodies and nursing', in J. Lawler (ed.) *The Body in Nursing*, South Melbourne: Churchill Livingstone.

Neysmith, S.M. and Aronson, J. (1997) 'Working conditions in home care: Negotiating race and class boundaries in gendered work', *International Journal of Health Services*, 27, 3, 479–99.

Nielsen, S.J. and Popkin, B.M. (2003) 'Patterns and trends in food portion size, 1977–1998', *Journal of American Medical Association*, 289, 4.

Öberg, P. (1996) 'The absent body – a social gerontological paradox', *Ageing and Society*, 16, 6, 701–19.

Offer, A. (2001) 'Body weight and self control in the United States and Britain since the 1950s', *Social History of Medicine*, 14, 1, 79–106.

Offer, A. (2006) *The Challenge of Affluence: Self Control and Well Being in the US and Britain Since 1945*, Oxford: Oxford University Press.

Oliver, K. (1993) *Reading Kristeva: Unravelling the Double-bind*, Bloomingdale: Indiana University Press.

Oliver, M. (1990) *The Politics of Disablement*, Basingstoke: Macmillan.

Orbach, S. (1986) *Hunger Strike: The Anorectic's Struggle as a Metaphor for Our Age*, London: Faber.

Orbach, S. and Eichenbaum, L. (1983) *Understanding Women*, Harmondsworth: Penguin.

Pahl, J., Hasanbegovic, C. and Yu, M-K (2004) 'Globalisation and family violence', in V. George and R. Page (eds) *Global Social Problems*, Cambridge: Polity.

Parker, G. (1993) *With This Body: Caring and Disability in Marriage*, Buckingham: Open University.

Parsons, T. (1954) 'The professions and social structure', in T. Parsons (ed.) *Essays in Sociological Theory*, Glencoe: Free Press.

Pateman, C. (1989) *The Disorder of Women: Democracy, Feminism and Political Theory*, Cambridge: Polity.

Paterson, K. and Hughes, B. (1999) 'Disability studies and phenomenology: The carnal politics of everyday life', *Disability and Society*, 14, 5, 597–610.

Pearson, M.P. and Richards, C. (1994) 'Ordering the world: Perceptions of architecture, space and time', in M.P. Pearson and C. Richards (eds) *Architecture and Order: Approaches to Social Space*, London: Routledge.

Peiffer, J. (1999) 'Assessing neuropathological research carried out on victims of the "euthanasia" programme', *Medizin Historisches Journal*, 34, 339–56.

Penna, S. and O'Brien, M. (1996) 'Postmodernism and social policy: A small leap forwards?', *Journal of Social Policy*, 25, 1, 39–62.

Penner, B. (2001) 'A world of unmentionable suffering: Women's public conveniences in Victorian London', *Journal of Design History*, 14, 1, 35–51.

Petersen, A. and de Bere, S. Regan (2005) 'Dissecting masculinity: Gender in the discourses and practices of medical anatomy', in D. Rosenfeld, and C. Faircloth (eds) *Medicalized Masculinities*, Temple University Press.

Phillipson, C. (1998) *Reconstructing Old Age: New Agendas in Social Theory and Practice*, London: Sage.

Phillipson, C. and Walker, A. (eds) (1986) *Ageing and Social Policy: A Critical Assessment*, Aldershot: Gower.

Piachaud, D. and Webb, J. (1996) *The Price of Food: Missing Out on Mass Consumption*, London: STICERD, LSE.

Plummer, K. (ed) (1992) *Modern Homosexualities: Fragments of Lesbian and Gay Experience*, London: Routledge.

Porter, R. (1997) *The Greatest Benefit to Mankind: A Medical History of Humanity*, London: Harper Collins.

Porter, S. (1992) 'Women in a women's job: The gendered experience of nurses', *Sociology of Health and Illness*, 14, 4, 510–27.

Pringle, K. (1995) *Men, Masculinities and Social Welfare*, London: UCL Press.

Pringle, R. (1989) *Secretaries Talk: Sexuality, Power and Work*, London: Verso.

Pringle, R. and Collings, S. (1993) 'Women and butchery: Some cultural taboos', *Australian Feminist Studies*, 17, 29–45.

Rabinow, P. (ed.) (1984) *The Foucault Reader: An Introduction to Foucault's Thought*, Harmondsworth: Penguin.

Rappaport, E.D. (2000) *Shopping for Pleasure: Women in the Making of London's West End*, Princeton: Princeton University Press.

Reverby, S.M. (1987) *Ordered to Care: The Dilemma of American Nursing, 1850–1945*, Cambridge: Cambridge University Press.

Rich, A. (1986) 'Compulsory heterosexuality and lesbian existence', *Blood, Bread and Poetry: Selected Prose 1979–1985*, London: Virago.

Richardson, D. (1992) 'Constructing lesbian sexualities', in K. Plummer (ed.) *Modern Homosexualities: Fragments of Lesbian and Gay Experience*, London: Routledge.

Richardson, D. (1996) 'Heterosexuality and social theory', in D. Richardson (ed.) *Theorising Heterosexuality: Telling It Straight*, Buckingham: Open University Press, pp. 1–20.

Richardson, R. (1987) *Death, Dissection and the Destitute*, London: Routledge.

Richardson, R. (1996) 'Fearful symmetry: Corpses for anatomy, organs for transplantation?', in S.J. Youngner, R.C. Fox and J. O'Connell (eds) *Organ Transplantation: Meanings and Realities*, Madison: University of Wisconsin Press.

Robertson, M. (1992) *Starving in the Silences: An Exploration of Anorexia Nervosa*, Sidney: Allen & Unwin.

Rodaway, P. (1994) *Sensuous Geographies: Body, Sense and Place*, London: Routledge.

Room, R., Babor, T. and Rehm, J. (2005) 'Alcohol and public health', *The Lancet*, 365, 519–30.

Rose, G. (1993) *Feminism and Geography: The Limits of Geographical Knowledge*, Cambridge: Polity.

Rose, R. and Falconer, P. (1992) 'Individual taste or collective decision? Public policy on school meals', *Journal of Social Policy*, 21, 3, 349.

Routasalo, P. and Isola, A. (1996) 'The right to be touch and be touched', *Nursing Ethics*, 3, 2, 165–76.

Royal College of Physicians (2004) *Storing Up Problems: The Medical Case for a Slimmer Nation*, London: Royal College of Physicians, Royal College of Paediatrics and Child Health, Faculty of Public Health.

Rozak, T. (1971) *The Making of a Counter Culture: Reflections in the Technocratic Society and Its Youthful Opposition*, London: Faber.

Rubinstein, R.L. (1989) 'The home environments of older people: A description of the psychosocial processes linking person to place'. *Journal of Gerontology*, 44, 2, S45–53.

Rubinstein, R.L. and Parmelee, P.A. (1992) 'Attachment to place and the representation of the life course by the elderly', in I. Altman and S.M. Low (eds) *Place Attachment*, New York: Plenum Press.

Sabo, D. and Gordon, D.F. (eds) (1995) *Men's Health and Illness: Gender, Power and Illness*, London: Sage.

Sacks, O. (1984) *A Leg to Stand On*, London: Duckworth.

Saks, M. (ed.) (1992) *Alternative Medicine in Britain*, Oxford: Clarendon Press.

Saks, M. (1994) 'The alternatives to medicine', in J. Gabe, D. Kelleher and G. Williams (eds) *Challenging Medicine*, London: Routledge.

Saraga, E. (1998) 'Abnormal, unnatural and immoral? The social construction of sexualities', in E. Saraga (ed.) *Embodying the Social: Constructions of Difference*, London: Routledge.

Savage, J. (1995) *Nursing Intimacy: An Ethnographic Approach to Nurse–Patient Interaction*, London: Scutari Press.

Scambler, G. (1988) *Epilepsy*, London: Routledge.

Scheper-Hughes, N. (2000) 'The global traffic in human organs', *Current Anthropology*, 41, 2.

Scheper-Hughes, N. (2001a) 'Bodies for sale – whole or in parts', *Body & Society*, 7, 2–3, 1–8.

Scheper-Hughes, N. (2001b) 'Commodity fetishism in organs trafficking', *Body & Society*, 7, 2–3, 31–62.

Schmidt, U. (2002) *Medical Films, Ethics and Euthanasia in Nazi Germany*, Husum: Matthiesen Verlag.

Scott, S. and Morgan, D. (eds) (1993) *Body Matters: Essays on the Sociology of the Body*, London: Falmer Press.

Sedgwick, E.K. (1990) *Epistemology of the Closet*, Berkley: University of California Press.

Segal, L. (1997) 'Sexualities', in K. Woodward (ed.) *Identity and Difference*, London: Sage, pp. 182–238.

Sellers, S. (ed.) (1994) *The Hélène Cixous Reader*, London: Routledge.

Seymour, W. (1998) *Remaking the Body: Rehabilitation and Change*, London: Routledge.

Shakespeare, T. (1994) 'Cultural representations of disabled people: Dustbins for disavowal?', *Disability and Society*, 9, 3, 283–99.

Shakespeare, T. (1998) 'Choices and rights: Eugenics, genetics and disability equality', *Disability and Society*, 13, 5, 665–81.

Shakespeare, T, Gillespie-Sells, K. and Davies, D. (1996) *The Sexual Politics of Disability: Untold Desires*, London: Cassell.

Sharma, U. (1992) *Complementary Medicine Today*, London: Routledge.

Sharma, U. (1996) 'Using complementary therapies: A challenge to orthodox medicine?', in J. Gabe, D. Kelleher and G. Williams (eds) *Challenging Medicine*, London: Routledge.

Shaw, M., Dorling, D., Gordon, D. and Smith, G.D. (1999) *The Widening Gap: Health Inequalities and Policy in Britain*, Bristol: Policy Press.

Sheldon, S. (2002) 'The masculine body', in M. Evans and E. Lee (eds) *Real Bodies*, Basingstoke: Palgrave.

Shilling, C. (1993) *The Body and Social Theory*, London: Sage.

Showalter, E. (1987) *The Female Malady: Women, Madness and English Culture, 1830–1980*, London: Virago.

Sibley, D. (1995) *Geographies of Exclusion*, London: Routledge.

Sixsmith, A. (1990) 'The meaning and experience of "home" in later life', in B. Bytheway and J. Johnson (eds) *Welfare and the Ageing Experience*, Aldershot: Avebury.

Skeggs, B. (1997) *Formations of Class and Gender: Becoming Respectable*, London: Sage.

Smith, A.M. (1992) 'Resisting the erasure of lesbian sexuality: A challenge for queer activism', in K. Plummer (ed.) *Modern Homosexualities: Fragments of Lesbian and Gay Experience*, London: Routledge.

Smith, D.F. (1999) 'Nutrition science and the two world wars', in D.F. Smith (ed.) *Nutrition in Britain: Science, Scientists and Politics in the Twentieth Century*, London: Routledge.

Smith, M.J. (1989) 'Changing agendas and policy communities: Agricultural issues in the 1930s and the 1980s', *Public Administration*, 67, 150–65.

Social Trends 33 (2001) London: HMSO.

Solomos, J. and Back, L. (1996) *Racism and Society*, London: Palgrave.

Song, M. (2003) *Choosing Ethnic Identity*, Cambridge: Polity.

Sontag, S. (1979) 'The double standard of ageing', in V. Carver and P. Liddiard (eds) *An Ageing Population*, New York: Touchstone.

Sterns, P.N. (1997) *Fat History: Bodies and Beauty in the Modern West*, New York: New York University.

Strong, P.M. (1979) *The Ceremonial Order of the Clinic: Parents, Doctors and Medical Bureaucracies*, London: Routledge and Kegan Paul.

Sutherland, A.T. (1981) *Disabled We Stand*, London: Condor.

Synnott, A. (1993) *The Body Social: Symbolism, Self and Society*, London: Routledge.

Taylor, P. (1984) *Smoke Ring: The Politics of Tobacco*, London: Bodley Head.

Taylor-Gooby, P. (1994) 'Postmodernism and social policy: A great leap backwards', *Journal of Social Policy*, 23, 3, 385–404.

Teather, E.K. (1999) 'Geographies of personal discovery', in E.K. Teather (ed.) *Embodied Geographies*, London: Routledge.

Thomas, C. (1993) 'De-constructing concepts of care', *Sociology*, 27, 4, 649–69.

Thomas, C. (1999) *Female Forms: Experiencing and Understanding Disability*, Buckingham: Open University Press.

Thomson, R.G. (1996) *Freakery: Cultural Spectacles of the Extraordinary Body*, New York: New York University Press.

Thomson, R.G. (1997) *Extraordinary Bodies: Figuring Physical Disability in American Culture and Literature*, New York: Columbia University Press.

Thorne, R. (1980) 'Places of refreshment in the nineteenth century city', in A.D. King (ed.) *Buildings and Society: Essays on the Social Development of the Built Environment*, London: RKP.

Tomlinson, M. (2003) 'Lifestyle and social class', *European Sociological Review*, 19, 1, 97–111.

Townsend, P., Davidson, N. and Whitehead, M. (1992) *Inequalities in Health*, Harmondsworth: Penguin.

Tronto, J.C. (1993) *Moral Boundaries: A Political Argument for an Ethic of Care*, London: Routledge.

Tseelon, E. (1995) *The Masque of Femininity*, London: Sage.

Tulle-Winton, E. (1999) 'Growing old and resistance: The new cultural economy of old age?', *Ageing and Society*, 19, 281–99.

Tulle-Winton, E. (2000) 'Old bodies', in P. Hancock, B. Hughes, E. Jagger, K. Paterson, R. Russell, E. Tulle-Winton and M. Tyler (eds) *The Body, Culture and Society*, Buckingham: Open University.

Turner, B.S. (1984) *The Body and Society: Explorations in Social Theory*, Oxford: Blackwell.

Turner, B.S. (1991) 'Recent developments in the theory of the body', in M. Featherstone, M. Hepworth and B.S. Turner (eds) *The Body: Social Process and Cultural Theory*, London: Sage.

Twigg, J. (1983) 'Vegetarianism and the meaning of meat', in A. Murcott (ed.) *The Sociology of Food and Eating: Essays in the Sociological Significance of Food*, Aldershot: Gower.

Twigg, J. (2000a) *Bathing – The Body and Community Care*, London: Routledge.

Twigg, J. (2000b) 'Social policy and the body', in G. Lewis, S. Gewirtz and J. Clarke (eds) *Rethinking Social Policy*, London: Sage.

Twigg, J. (2003) 'The body, gender and age: Feminist insights in social gerontology', *Journal of Aging Studies*, 18, 59–73.

Twigg, J. and Atkin, K. (1994) *Carers Perceived: Policy and Practice in Informal Care*, Buckingham: Open University.

Ungerson, C. (1983) 'Women and caring: Skills, tasks and taboos', in E. Gamarnikow, D. Morgan, J. Purvis and D. Taylorson (eds) *The Public and the Private*, London: Heinemann.

Ungerson, C. (1987) *Policy Is Personal: Sex, Gender and Informal Care*, London: Tavistock.

Ungerson, C. (1993) 'Payment for caring: mapping a territory', in N. Deakin and R. Page (eds) *The Costs of Welfare*, Aldershot: Avebury.

Ungerson, C. (1999) 'Hybred forms of work and care: The case of personal assistants and disabled people', *Work, Employment and Society*, 13, 4, 583–600.

UPIAS (1976) *Fundamental Principles of Disability*, London: Union of the Physically Impaired Against Segregation.

Urry, J. (1996) 'Sociology of time and space', in B.S. Turner (ed.) *The Blackwell Companion to Social Theory*, Oxford: Blackwell.

Ussher, J. (1991) *Women's Madness: Misogyny or Mental Illness?* Hemel Hempstead: Harvester.

Valentine, G. (1996) ' "Re"negotiating the "heterosexual street": Lesbian productions of space', in N. Duncan (ed.) *Body Space*, London: Routledge.

Valentine, G. (2001) *Social Geographies: Space and Society*, Harlow: Prentice Hall.

van der Riet, P. (1997) 'The body, the person, technologies and nursing', in J. Lawler (ed.) *The Body in Nursing*, Melbourne: Churchill Livingstone.

Vincent, J. (1999) 'Consumers, identity and old age', *Education and Ageing*, 14, 2, 141–58.

Vincent, J. (2003) *Old Age*, London: Routledge.

Viscusi, W.K. (1992) *Smoking: Making the Risky Decision*, New York: Oxford University Press.

Waerness, K. (1987) 'On the rationality of caring', in A. Showstack Sassoon (ed.) *Women and the State: The Shifting Boundaries of Public and Private*, London: Hutchinson.

Walby, S. (1990) *Theorizing Patriarchy*, Oxford: Blackwell.

Walker, M.U. (ed.) (1999) *Mother Time: Women, Aging and Ethics*, Boulder: Rowman & Littlefield.

Wanless, D. (2004) *Securing Good Health in the Whole Population: Final Report*, Norwich: HMSO.

Ward, C.R. and Duquin, M.E. (1998) 'Effects of intergenerational massage on future caregivers' attitudes towards ageing, the elderly and caring for the elderly', *Educational Gerontology*, 24, 35–46.

Ward, L. (1993) 'Race, equality and employment in the NHS', in W.I.U. Ahmad (ed.) *'Race' and Health in Contemporary Britain*, Buckingham: Open University Press.

Warde, A. (1997) *Consumption, Food and Taste*, London: Sage.

Warner, M. (1985) *Monuments and Maidens: The Allegory of the Female Form*, London: Weidenfeld.

Warren, K.J. (ed.) (1994) *Ecological Feminism*, London: Routledge.

Watson, J. (2000) *Male Bodies: Health, Culture and Identity*, Buckingham: Open University.

Watson, S. (2000) 'Foucault and the study of social policy', in G. Lewis, S. Gewirtz and J. Clarke (eds) *Rethinking Social Policy*, London: Sage.

Watson, S. (2002) 'The public city', in J. Eade and C. Mele (eds) *Understanding the City: Contemporary and Future Perspectives*, Oxford: Blackwell.

Webster, C. (1997) 'Government policy on school meals and welfare foods, 1939–70', in D.F. Smith (ed.) *Nutrition in Britain: Science, Scientists and Politics in the Twentieth Century*, London: Routledge.

Weeks, J. (1985) *Sexuality and Its Discontents: Meaning, Myths and Modern Sexualities*, London: RKP.

Whitcher, J.S. and Fisher, J.D. (1979) 'Multidimensional reaction to therapeutic touch in a hospital setting', *Journal of Personality and Social Psychology*, 37, 1, 87–96.

WHO (2000) *Obesity: Preventing and Managing the Global Epidemic*, WHO Technical Report Series 894, Geneva: World Health Organisation.

Whitford, M. (ed.) (1991) *The Irigaray Reader*, Oxford: Blackwell.

Wilkinson, R. (1992) 'Income distribution and life expectation', *British Medical Journal*, 304, 165–8.

Wilkinson, R. (1996) *Unhealthy Societies: The Afflictions of Inequality*, London: Routledge.

Williams, A.S. (1999) 'Relief and research: The nutrition work of the National Birthday Trust Fund, 1935–9', in D.F. Smith (ed.) *Nutrition in Britain: Science, Scientists and Politics in the Twentieth Century*, London: Routledge.

Williams, C.L. (1989) *Gender Differences at Work: Women and Men in Non Traditional Occupations*, Berkeley: University of California Press.

Williams, F. (1989) *Social Policy: A Critical Introduction, Issues of Race, Gender and Class*, Cambridge: Polity.

Williams, F. (1995) 'Race/ethnicity, gender, and class in welfare states: A framework for comparative analysis', *Social Politics*, 2, 2, 127–59.

Williams, S. (1996) 'Representing disability: Some questions of phenomenology and politics', in C. Barnes and G. Mercer (eds) *Exploring the Divide: Illness and Disability*, Leeds: Disability Press.

Williams, S.J. (1999) 'Is anybody there? Critical realism, chronic illness and the disability debate', *Sociology of Health and Illness*, 21, 6, 797–819.

Williams, S.J. (2001) 'Sociological imperialism and the profession of medicine revisited: Where are we now?', *Sociology of Health and Illness*, 23, 2, 135–58.

Williams, S.J. and Bendelow, G. (1998) *The Lived Body: Sociological Themes, Embodied Issues*, London: Routledge.

Willis, D. and Williams, C. (2002) *The Black Female Body: A Photographic History*, Philadelphia: Temple University Press.

Wilson, B. (1982) *Religion in Sociological Perspective*, Oxford: Oxford University Press.

Wilson, E. (1977) *Women and the Welfare State*, London: Tavistock.

Wilson, E. (1985) *Adorned in Dreams: Fashion and Modernity*, London: Virago.

Wilton, T. (2000) *Sexualities in Health and Social Care*, Buckingham: Open University Press.

Wolf, J.H. (2001) *Don't Kill Your Baby: Public Health and the Decline of Breastfeeding in the Nineteenth and Twentieth Century*, Columbus: Ohio State University Press.

Wolf, N. (1990) *The Beauty Myth*, London: Vintage.

Wolf, Z.R. (1988) *Nurses' Work, the Sacred and the Profane*, Philadelphia: University of Pennsylvania Press.

Wolff, J. (1985) 'The invisible flâneuse: Women and the literature of modernity', *Theory, Culture and Society*, 2, 3, 37–46.

Wolkowitz, C. (2002) 'The social relations of bodywork', *Work, Employment and Society*, 16, 3, 497–510.

Woodward, K. (1991) *Aging and Its Discontents: Freud and Other Fictions*, Bloomington: Indiana University Press.

Woodward, K. (ed.) (1999) *Figuring Age: Women, Bodies, Generations*, Bloomington: Indiana.

Wrigley, N. and Lowe, M. (eds) (1996) *Retailing, Consumption and Capital*, Harlow: Longmans.

Yalom, M. (1998) *A History of the Breast*, London: Pandora.

Young, I.M. (1990) *Throwing Like a Girl and Other Essays in Feminist Philosophy*, Bloomingdale: Indiana University Press.

Zweiniger-Bargielowska, I. (2000) *Austerity in Britain: Rationing, Controls and Consumption, 1939–1955*, Oxford: Oxford University Press.

Index

abjection 17
abortion in relation to disability 63–4
abuse 16, 44, 151
Acker, J. 89
age and ageing 27, 40–54, 170
    and consumer culture 46–8
    cultural approaches to 42–4, 48–50
    and gender 43, 47, 48
    see also fourth age; third age
ageism 44–6, 170
Ahmed, S. 32, 34
alcohol, public policy and 115
Alder Hey hospital enquiry 76–8
alternative medicine 92–8
anatomy 72, 92
Anatomy Act 1832 75
Anderson, B. 143, 145, 147
Angus et al 127
anorexia see eating disorders
Anthias, F. 26, 27

Bashford, A. 89, 91, 92, 149
bathing 123, 124, 126, 128
beauty culture 43, 135, 138
Benjamin, W. 155
Berkeley Organ Watch 80
body
    and age 40–54
    in alternative medicine 92–8
    and consumption 48, 106
    debates about the body 13–39
    and denigration 11, 121
    and difference 29–30
    and disability 55–70
    gendered bodies 43, 48, 102–5,
        148–9
    and home care 119–33, 137–42,
        148–52
    ideals 102, 108
    in medicine and health care 1–2,
        71–98

neo-Platonic tradition 9, 105
    in nursing 86–9
    perfectionism 102
    in political theory 14, 154
    and public space 153–69
    'real' bodies 24–5
    in social care 119–52, 173
    and subordination 11, 130
    transcendence of 15, 105, 121
bodyparts 33, 73–83
bodywork 71, 85–9, 133–52
    gender and 148–51
Bordo, S. 102
Bourdieu, P. 31, 127
breastfeeding 162–9
British Medical Association 79
bulimia see eating disorders
Butler, J. 19
Butler, R. 44
Bynum, C.W. 101

care, debate on 147
carework 136–52
careworkers 45, 152
Cartesian dualism 15, 49, 51, 84
charity fundraising 60–1
Chernin, K. 103
citizenship 5, 54
class see social class
classificatory practices 20–1
Cohen, L. 80–1
Cole, T. 51–2
complementary medicine see
    alternative medicine
Connell, R.W. 69
consumer culture 22–3, 41, 54,
    106
consumption 22–3, 106
cosmetic surgery 46
Coward, R. 94
cremation 76

cultural analyses   2–6, 42–4, 57, 70, 106, 170–2
cultural turn   1, 3, 170

death   49, 51
diet, body and   99–118
difference   18, 26–38
dirty dying   84
dirty work   88, 135, 136–7, 145, 150
disability   55–70
    and eugenics   61–4
    and gender   67–9
    and selective abortion   63–4
    and sexuality   64–7, 69
    social model, critiques of   56–7
    and visual culture   58–61
Disability Discrimination Act 1995   61
discourse   4, 49
dissection   73–6, 91–2
diversity   5
    see *also* difference
dividing practices   20
domestic labour   28, 143–6
Douglas, M.   10, 17

eating disorders   100–7
economics   9
Edwards, J. and McKie, L.   159, 160
Elias, N.   10, 44
embodied practitioners   89–92
embodiment, patient's experiences of   83–5
emotion   7, 135, 138, 146
    in organisations   7
emotional labour   34, 146–7, 150
Enlightenment   13
ethnicity   32
    see *also* 'race'
eugenics   61–4
euthanasia   61–3, 78

fashion   24
fast food   110, 116
Featherstone, M. and Hepworth, M.   43, 49

feminism   14–20, 24, 26, 41, 43, 102, 103–5, 147
Fineman, S.   7
Finkelstein, V.   56, 57
food and body   99–118
food industry   109–10, 112–13, 116
Foucault, M.   4–5, 11–12, 17, 20–2, 36, 58, 90, 117, 124, 135, 140
fourth age   50–1
Fox, R.C.   82
freak shows   60
Furman, F.   43

gender   11, 14–20, 26, 28, 30, 43, 48, 88–9, 91, 101–5, 135–6, 139–40, 142–5, 148–51, 158–60, 166–8
    and bodywork   148–52
    and disability   67–9
    and public space   153–68
Giddens, A.   5, 51
Gilleard, C. and Higgs, P.   44, 45, 48, 50
Goffman, E.   19, 42, 85, 130
Greed, C.   160
Gullette, M.   42, 48, 50
Gunaratnam and Lewis   7, 34

habitus   31
health care   1–2, 85–9
heterosexuality   19, 36
Hinze, S.W.   90–1
Hochschild, A.   146
Hockey, J. and James, A.   49
Hoggett, P.   7
home   124–7
    and identity   125
    and power   129–30
    spatio-temporal ordering of   124–8
home care   119–32, 144
homosexuality   35–8, 69, 140
hooks, b.   33
'Hottentot Venus'   33, 78
Hughes, B. and Paterson, K.   56, 58
Human Tissue Act 2004   78

identity   5, 23, 53, 70, 131
ingestion, politics of   114–18

intersectionality 27
Irigaray, L. 18

Jordanova, L. 91

Katz, S. 51–2
Kleinman, A. 83, 84
Kontos, P. 49
Kristeva, J. 17

Laqueur, T. 16
Lawler, J. 86, 137
Lawrence, C. 90
Lawton, J. 84, 122
Lee-Treweek, G. 141–2,
    146, 147
Longhurst, R. 11, 17

McDowell, L. 68
MacSween, M. 104
managerialism 87, 121
masculinity 19, 67, 68, 106, 142,
    150, 160
mask of ageing 43, 49
Maynard, M. 26
medicine 37, 59, 71–3, 77, 83–4,
    85–6, 90–2, 93–7, 120, 172
Merleau-Ponty, M. 25
Morris, J. 56–7

nakedness 123, 134, 141
neo-liberalism 8, 81–2, 117–18
new age ideas 94
Nietzsche 13, 20
normalising processes/practices 4–5,
    21
nursing 1, 8, 84, 86–90, 97, 137,
    149, 150

obesity 106–13
Offer, A. 109
old age *see* age and ageing
Olympic movement 59
Orbach, S. 104
organ donation 77–83
organs, trade in 80–3

pain 84
Pateman, C. 14, 154
patient's experience of embodiment
    83–5
Penner, B. 156
Personal Assistants (PA) 141
personal care 121–4, 127
policy world 9, 10, 26, 121, 173
Political Economy of ageing 41, 54
politics of the body/political theory
    14, 154
Porter, S. 89
postmodernism 3–5, 8–9, 18, 171
poststructuralism 3–5, 8–9, 20–2, 171
power 3–4, 14, 16, 20, 149
    bio-power 124, 135, 140–1
    and home 129–30
    and knowledge 4, 21
private space 125
public health 21, 99, 116–17
public/private divide 7, 16, 153
public space 153–69
public toilets 156–62

queer theory 36

'race' 11, 15, 28–9, 32–5, 142,
    144–6, 149
    and health care 34–5
    and social care 35
religion 23, 27, 95
Richardson, D. 74–6

Savage, J. 86
Scheper-Hughes, N. 81, 83
school meals 100, 113
secularisation 76, 95
service sector 142–3
sexuality 4, 19, 29, 35–8, 47, 134,
    139, 141, 150, 165
    and ageing 47
    and disability 64–7, 69
    and public space 38
Seymour, W. 57, 68–9
Shakespeare, T. 61, 63, 64, 65, 66, 69
Shaw, G.B. 157

smoking   114
social care   2, 119–22
social class   6, 15, 28, 29, 30–2, 116,
    144, 146
social model of disability, critiques of
    56–7
social policy   2, 4–5, 20, 48
social work   2, 7, 120–1
Sontag, S.   43, 47, 59
space   6, 124–9
sport   59, 68
subordinated groups   15
subordination   11

Taylor-Gooby, P.   8, 118
technologies of the self   17, 22, 23, 46
teeth   6
third age   50
Thomas, C.   57, 147
Thomson, R.G.   60
time   6, 126, 128–30

toilets *see* public toilets
touch   122–3, 134, 138
Tulle-Winton, E.   47
Turner, B.S.   13, 14, 105

Ungerson, C.   141, 147, 149

vegetarianism   94, 105
Vincent, J.   51
visual, the and visual culture   6, 47,
    58–61

welfare state   6, 37, 54, 100,
    168–9, 172
Williams, F.   27
Williams, S.J. and Bendelow, G.   25,
    56, 84
Wolff, J.   155
Woodward, K.   42, 43

Young, I.M.   16